Therapist's Guide to Positive Psychological Interventions

Therapist's Guide to Positive Psychological Interventions

Jeana L. Magyar-Moe, Ph.D.
University of Wisconsin – Stevens Point

AMSTERDAM • BOSTON • HEIDELBERG • LONDON
NEW YORK • OXFORD • PARIS • SAN DIEGO
SAN FRANCISCO • SINGAPORE • SYDNEY • TOKYO

Academic Press is an imprint of Elsevier

Academic Press is an imprint of Elsevier
30 Corporate Drive, Suite 400, Burlington, MA 01803, USA
525 B Street, Suite 1900, San Diego, CA 92101-4495, USA
32 Jamestown Road, London, NW1 7BY, UK
360 Park Avenue South, New York, NY 10010-1710, USA

First edition 2009

Library of Congress Cataloging-in-Publication Data
A catalog record for this book is available from the Library of Congress

British Library Cataloguing in Publication Data
A catalogue record for this book is available from the British Library

ISBN: 978-0-12-374517-0

For information on all Academic Press publications
visit our website at elsevierdirect.com

Typeset by Macmillan Publishing Solutions
(www.macmillansolutions.com)

Printed and bound in the United States of America

09 10 11 12 13   9 8 7 6 5 4 3 2 1

Working together to grow
libraries in developing countries

www.elsevier.com | www.bookaid.org | www.sabre.org

ELSEVIER   BOOK AID International   Sabre Foundation

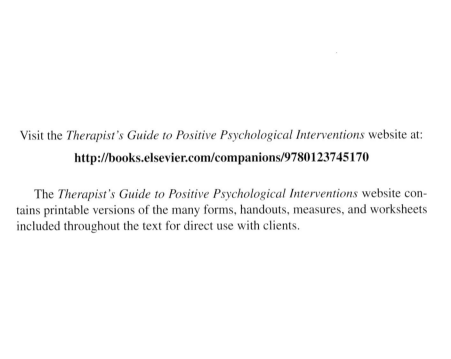

Visit the *Therapist's Guide to Positive Psychological Interventions* website at:

http://books.elsevier.com/companions/9780123745170

The *Therapist's Guide to Positive Psychological Interventions* website contains printable versions of the many forms, handouts, measures, and worksheets included throughout the text for direct use with clients.

Contents

I became a positive psychologist in April 1998. With my coursework behind me, I was wrapping up my last few months of clinical training at the Eisenhower VA Medical Center. The staff psychiatrist popped into my office. He had a case for the soon-to-be psychologist. Dr McNutt (real name… you couldn't make that up) threw me several softballs during my time in the clinic. The case of John Marcus (pseudonym to protect client confidentiality) was not what I expected.

John was a full-bodied 63-year old veteran who had spent his life in the farm fields of Kansas. He was a pragmatist, from his work boots to his flat-top to his no-nonsense approach to life. In shock from a diagnosis of kidney failure he had only one fix – suicide. See, John had never heard of a farmer running a farm while on dialysis, so that treatment option did not make sense. Not getting treated would leave him too sick to work the fields. Get treatment, lose the farm. Don't get treatment, lose the farm. Lose the farm, lose all sense of meaning. Paul wanted to avoid losing the farm, by any means necessary.

Though few of my clinical techniques worked with Paul that first day, he did get to the point where he was no longer a danger to himself. With the help of his family and friends, we made sure that John had a safe home to return to and plenty of support.

The next day, he came back to the clinic and started with a question, "What's my story?" After fumbling a bit, I was able to grasp the full meaning of what he was asking. John wanted to know how to talk about being ill, going to treatment, and getting better or getting worse. He hated the question, "How are you doing?" and wanted to have a go-to answer. We spent the next two hours talking about hope as an active process that requires constant attention. At the beginning of the next session, he told me, "I got it. 'I am working on it.' When people ask me how I am doing, I tell them, 'I am working on it.'"

That spring I learned that we all need a hopeful story about the future. Over the last 11 years, I have come to realize that story can be crafted by knowing our strengths, managing our weaknesses, and practicing love, gratitude, and kindness.

In *Therapist's Guide to Positive Psychological Interventions*, Jeana L. Magyar-Moe does a masterful job of creating multiple paths to a hopeful story with our clients. She reframes progress and mental health and gives us the tools we need to spark and sustain change.

I wish John and I had this book in 1998. I am glad you have it now.

Shane J. Lopez
Omaha, Nebraska

I will never forget the first client that I met during my first counseling practicum experience as a graduate student, nor how helpless I felt as his therapist. After several sessions of listening empathically to all of his various struggles in life, I had no idea how to be of assistance. Although this was partially due to the fact that I was a beginning helper, I quickly discovered that it was also partially due to the fact that I was equating my client to his problems only. A wise mentor asked me what the strengths of this client were and I was not really able to answer this question, for I had not attended to strengths in the midst of all the problems that he was reporting. I was amazed to discover how many strengths my client possessed, when I simply took the time to attend to, look for, and ask about his strengths and resources. I was relieved and uplifted to learn this information (as was my client!) and to utilize it in my treatment planning. I felt as if I could actually be of some assistance to this client and many others whom I worked with from that point forward.

Several months later, I encountered another client for whom I could not identify any major problems or diagnosable conditions. I recall wondering how I could be of assistance to someone who was not really experiencing any substantial problems. Again, the same wise mentor pointed out that just because a person is not experiencing symptoms of mental illness does not necessarily mean that he or she is happy and satisfied with life. Again, this was a powerful lesson for a beginning helper who envisioned therapy as a place where only serious problems would be addressed.

Although the field of positive psychology was in its infancy at the time of my first therapeutic encounters, the basic foundations of this perspective on psychology had been established and came to play a vital role in my work as a clinician, teacher, and scholar. I am excited to share the lessons I have learned over the past decade related to utilizing positive psychology in the practice of counseling and therapy with other clinicians, some of whom may be beginning helpers while others may have many years of clinical experience under their belts. Indeed, my goal in writing this text is to provide a wealth of scholarly based, practical resources to busy practitioners and practitioners in training who are interested in applying positive psychology in their work, but lacking the time to sort through all of the scholarship from this field and figure out for themselves how to apply it with their own clients. While this text provides the necessary theoretical background and scholarly foundations to support the interventions offered, the primary focus is on the various ways therapists can apply positive psychological principles and theories with their clients.

I hope that the readers of this text will find this information useful and highly applicable to their therapeutic endeavors. I hope that the clients who are exposed to these positive psychological interventions will benefit from them as well. Finally, many of the exercises and activities provided in this text can and perhaps should be completed by clinicians themselves, in order to deepen their understanding of these positive psychological interventions while also reaping the benefits that these exercises have to offer.

Acknowledgements

This book would not have been possible without the wonderful mentorship I received as a graduate student at the University of Kansas from Shane J. Lopez. Thank you, Shane, for introducing me to the field of positive psychology and helping me to discover my strengths, many of which I utilized or called upon in the process of writing this text.

I would also like to thank Dennis Elsenrath, my mentor as an undergraduate student at the University of Wisconsin–Stevens Point (UWSP) and later, my valued colleague at UWSP as well. Thank you, Dennis, for supporting my interests in positive psychology both in the classroom and therapy room settings.

I would like to thank my husband, David, who has supported all of my career endeavors, including the long hours dedicated to writing this text. Thank you, Dave, for being understanding and encouraging of me throughout the writing process. I would also like to thank our beautiful four-year-old daughter, Tahlia, for being patient with me when I worked on this text from the home office and for providing so much love, joy, and zest in my life. Although I have not formally met him yet, I would also like to thank my son, Jace. We are expecting his birth in about two weeks and I know he will fill my life with even more joy, happiness, and love.

Chapter 1

What is Positive Psychology and Why is it Important?

Positive psychology is the scientific study of optimal human functioning, the goals of which are to better understand and apply those factors that help individuals and communities to thrive and flourish. Perusal of the literature on positive psychology reveals many potential applications of the emerging research for a diversity of people within a wide variety of settings (Linley and Joseph, 2004; Snyder and Lopez, 2002, 2007). There seems to be no better fit, however, for positive psychology than within the therapy room. Indeed, research to date supports the notion that client conceptualizations and the incorporation of exercises informed by positive psychology can provide lasting positive outcomes for therapy clients (Duckworth et al., 2005; Seligman et al., 2005, 2006). In this text, strategies and exercises that therapists can use to begin incorporating positive psychology into their work with clients are provided.

1.1 THE HISTORY OF POSITIVE PSYCHOLOGY

In his 1998 presidential address to members of the American Psychological Association, Martin Seligman put a call out to applied psychologists to return to their roots and focus on not only curing mental illness, but also on making the lives of people more productive and fulfilling, and identifying and nurturing talent (Seligman and Csikszentmihalyi, 2000). Indeed, these were the main foci of applied psychologists prior to World War II. After the war, however, the emphasis shifted to curing mental illness with the other two aims almost completely forgotten. Such a change in focus is understandable, given the number of soldiers coming back from war with psychological problems and the resulting issues they and their loved ones faced as they tried to reorient themselves to civilian life. Following these societal changes, the development of Veterans Administration Hospitals proliferated, as did the availability of research funding by the National Institute of Mental Health for those researching cures for mental illness (Seligman and Csikszentmihalyi, 2000). Hence, psychologists realized that jobs and research funding were readily available to those who focused on mental illness. The same could not be said for those focusing on the other two aims of applied psychology.

As a result of the almost exclusive shift in focus to curing mental illness, therapists adopted a disease model of client functioning which almost completely overlooked individual strengths, virtues, and areas of well-being, focusing instead upon pathology, weaknesses, and deficits. Since Seligman's declaration in 1998, however, a large group of scholars has looked to abandon this negative focus in psychology and to replace or at least augment it with a focus on positive emotions, positive traits, strengths, and talents, as well as positive institutions (Seligman, 2002). According to Seligman and Csikszentmihalyi (2000), the time is right for the study of positive mental health since psychologists' understanding of mental illness and of human survival under conditions of adversity is thorough, whereas our knowledge of what makes life meaningful and how people flourish under more benign conditions is lacking.

In the past decade, research in positive psychology has proliferated. Indeed, in 2008 the first issue of the *Journal of Positive Psychology* was published to accommodate much of the research being done on positive emotions, traits, strengths, and well-being. A variety of books devoted exclusively to positive psychology and even textbooks for use in the college classroom are available as well. Positive psychology is now being taught at over 100 colleges and universities in the USA and Britain and several schools even offer a master's degree in applied positive psychology. Furthermore, there are several professional organizations (i.e., the International Positive Psychology Association and the Positive Psychology Section of the Society of Counseling Psychology within the American Psychological Association) and conventions (i.e., The Gallup Global Well-Being Forum, the International Positive Psychology Summit, the European Conference on Positive Psychology, and the World Congress on Positive Psychology) devoted to the study of positive psychology.

Although there is still much to be done to fully understand and implement what positive psychology has to offer, the available literature suggests that positive psychology can play a prominent role in counseling and psychotherapy. The rest of this chapter is devoted to addressing some of the core theories and concepts from positive psychology that serve as a foundation for many of the activities and client exercises that will be presented in later chapters.

1.2 CORE POSITIVE PSYCHOLOGY THEORIES AND CONCEPTS

1.2.1 Strengths Theory

> Enter every activity without giving mental recognition to the possibility of defeat. Concentrate on your strength, instead of your weaknesses… on your powers, instead of your problems.
>
> Paul J. Meyer

Those who study and practice positive psychology subscribe to strengths theory or the idea that it is vital to understand and build from one's strengths while managing (rather than focusing on or repairing) weaknesses (Clifton and Nelson, 1996). This perspective is not a common one. According to Clifton and Nelson (1996), many employers, teachers, parents, and leaders work off the following unwritten rule: "Let's fix what's wrong and let the strengths take care of themselves" (p. 9). (It seems that this is the perspective of many therapists as well *if* they fail to practice from a strengths-based or positive psychology viewpoint, but we will address this in more detail in the following chapter.) Indeed, many managers send their employees off to be trained in areas that they struggle with and when they provide reviews of their work, the focus is on what needs improvement while what they are doing well gets little, if any, attention. Many children bring their report cards home and are afraid to show their parents their grades because they know they got a D+. It doesn't matter that in addition to the D+ were several A's and B's. The parental focus, and therefore the child's focus, is on the area of weakness. Teachers often fall into this same "weakness trap" as well, honing in on what is wrong with a student, rather than what is going right.

Why is this focus on fixing what is wrong while overlooking what is right so prevalent? According to Clifton and Nelson (1996), it is because of several errors in thinking and logic to which most people fall victim. The first error is the idea that fixing or correcting a weakness will result in making a person or organization stronger. This is not true, as eliminating a weakness does not make one great; at best it will only help the individual or organization become normal or average.

The second error is the notion that there is no need to foster strengths, as they will take care of themselves and develop naturally (Clifton and Nelson, 1996). Again, this is faulty because taking one's strengths for granted results in just normal or average outcomes, as those strengths do not mature to their full potential. In order to capitalize upon strengths, they must be nurtured and honed. For example, a child who does well in spelling but struggles with math is often assisted with his math skills while the spelling ability is ignored. While the child's math skills may get a bit better, his spelling will likely only slightly improve as well. Ideally, teachers and parents would work to manage his math weakness while simultaneously honing his spelling skills. With such an approach, they may be able to nurture the next national spelling bee winner.

The third error in thinking is the belief that strengths and weaknesses are opposites (Clifton and Nelson, 1996). Although many people think that if they shore up their weaknesses they can turn them into strengths, this simply is not true. We do not learn about strengths by studying weaknesses. For example, we cannot learn why college students stay in school and make it to graduation by studying those that drop out, nor can we understand how to create secure infant attachments by studying infants with insecure attachment styles. Yet, this is often the approach taken by those trying to improve the lives of individuals and organizations. Unfortunately, the study of weaknesses and deficits provides erroneous information about what to work on to improve performance.

The final error in thinking that keeps people from approaching life from a strengths perspective is the idea that people can do anything they put their minds to (Clifton and Nelson, 1996). This notion suggests that *anyone* can be successful at *anything* if they are willing to work hard. This is not the case, however, as all people have their own unique sets of strengths that will empower them to be successful in certain areas but not others. Clifton and Nelson (1996) state that "the reality is that we can (and should) *try* anything we wish to try, but long-term success will elude us unless we determine early on that we have a basic talent for the endeavor" (p. 16). Indeed, working hard to be successful in an area that fails to capitalize on one's strengths leads to a negative view of oneself and one's abilities. For example, a person who is tone deaf who "puts her mind to" becoming a musical theater star will surely feel bad about herself as she is rejected over and over again at auditions. However, if she focused on her wonderful acting abilities and tried out for plays, rather than musicals, her dream to be on Broadway could become a reality.

Research on strengths theory has been conducted for the past fifty years, largely by researchers at the Gallup Organization who have studied successful managers, executives, teachers, coaches, athletes, doctors, nurses, salespeople, and more. More recently, research on strengths theory has been carried out by researchers in positive psychology. Indeed, a major ingredient in Seligman's (2002) happiness formula is for one to discover his or her character strengths and then to find ways to capitalize upon those strengths on a regular basis. Doing this will lead one to feel engaged with life and therefore to be more satisfied and happy. There are many applications of strengths theory and many measures of strengths that can be utilized in the therapy room. These applications and measures will be further elucidated in the following chapters.

1.2.2 The Broaden and Build Theory of Positive Emotions

The strangest and most fantastic fact about negative emotions is that people actually worship them.

P.D. Ouspensky

The broaden and build theory of positive emotions is another key theory that underpins many of the ideas of positive psychology. This theory provides an explanation of the utility and importance of positive emotions in people's lives. Prior to the development of this theory about a decade ago, little to no research existed on the value of positive emotions. In contrast, negative emotions have been studied for many decades and most people understand that negative emotions are important for a variety of reasons, including survival. For example, if you were to ask the average person if they would like the ability to no longer feel negative emotions such as fear, anger, or sadness, most, if not all, would say "no" to this ability. This is because they realize that these emotions are important for functioning safely in the world. Indeed, without the ability to feel fear, one would not run from danger and without the ability to feel anger, one would not defend oneself when appropriate. However, most people, including those who have researched negative emotions, conclude that positive emotions have little utility beyond signaling that one is free of negative emotions. The broaden and build theory explains that positive emotions do much more than just signal that there are no problems. In fact, this theory posits that positive emotions are just as important to our survival and our ability to flourish in life as negative emotions (Fredrickson, 1998, 2001).

The broaden and build theory is a multifaceted model of positive emotions, consisting of the broaden hypothesis, the build hypothesis, the undoing hypothesis, the resilience hypothesis, and the flourish hypothesis (Fredrickson, 1998, 2001). In the following sections, each of these hypotheses will be defined and examples of research findings that support these ideas will be described as well.

The Broaden Hypothesis

We are wide-eyed in contemplating the possibility that life may exist elsewhere in the universe, but we often wear blinders when contemplating the possibilities of life on earth.

Norman Cousins

According to Fredrickson (1998, 2001), positive emotions broaden momentary thought-action repertoires, resulting in a wider range of thoughts and actions one is likely to pursue. In other words, when someone is feeling positive emotions, they are able to see more possibilities. This broadening effect of positive emotions is essentially the opposite of what happens when people experience negative emotions (see Figure 1.1 for a pictorial representation of the differences between broadened and narrow mindsets).

According to Frijda (1986), Lazarus (1991), and Levinson (1994), negative emotions narrow momentary thought-action repertoires. In other words, when one experiences negative emotions, it is as if they have tunnel vision and the range of possibilities is narrowed. Very specific action tendencies narrow the action-urges that come to mind and at the same time, prepare the body to take that specific action. For example, when a person feels afraid, they have the action-urge to run, and the body prepares for taking flight by increasing blood flow to the appropriate muscles. The narrowed action-urges that come to mind when one experiences negative emotions are thought to be adaptive from an evolutionary perspective. Indeed, such fight-or-flight responses in the face of fear or anger helped to ensure the survival of our ancestors in life-threatening situations (Toobey and Coosmides, 1990).

FIGURE 1.1   The impact of negative and positive emotions on mindsets.

The broadening effect of positive emotions is also adaptive from an evolutionary perspective; however, not in the same way as negative emotions. More specifically, while the narrowing of thought-action repertoires helps to ensure survival in specific life-threatening circumstances, the broadened thought-action repertoires that correspond to the experience of positive emotions are adaptive over the long-term (Fredrickson and Branigan, 2005). This is largely a result of the *building* of personal resources that this broadened mindset brings. The building hypothesis will be explained in the following section; however, first a brief summary of the research that supports the broadening hypothesis is reviewed.

Most of the research that supports the broadening hypothesis has been done utilizing video clips that elicit various emotions in the viewers. For example, to induce joy, Fredrickson and Branigan (2005) showed participants a short

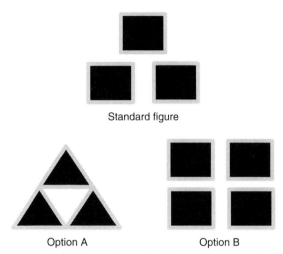

Standard figure

Option A   Option B

FIGURE 1.2   Global-local visual processing task. When experiencing positive emotions, people are more likely to choose the global response (Option A) as being more like the standard figure than the local response (Option B) in global-local visual processing tasks. This is because positive emotions broaden people's mindsets (Fredrickson, 2003).

video of penguins at play; to induce contentment, they saw a video of various nature scenes; a video of a group of men taunting an Amish family was used to elicit anger; a video of a mountain climber who is hanging precariously from the edge of a mountain elicits fear; and a video of a screen-saver consisting of colored sticks piling up on one another was used for the control condition, eliciting virtually no emotion.

Participants viewed one of the five video clips and then completed a series of global-local processing tasks. Essentially, these tasks consisted of viewing a standard figure and then deciding which of two comparison figures was most like the standard figure (see Figure 1.2). Although these tasks do not consist of correct or incorrect answers, the global response consists of choosing the comparison figure that is more similar to the standard figure based on the overall shape (option A in figure 1.2), whereas the local response consists of choosing the comparison figure that is more similar to the standard figure based on the individual shapes that make up the total figure (option B in Figure 1.2). According to Fredrickson and Branigan (2005), the global response option represents more broadened thinking. The results of this study support the broaden hypothesis, as participants in the positive emotion conditions choose the global response options more often in comparison to those in the neutral or negative emotion conditions, suggesting a more broadened pattern of thinking (Fredrickson and Branigan, 2005).

A second study supporting the broaden hypothesis was conducted by Fredrickson and Branigan (2005) using the same video clips but asking participants to then imagine being in a situation in which the most powerful emotion they felt while viewing the film clips was occurring. Given that emotion, they were instructed to list as many things as they felt like doing right at that moment. Each participant was given a handout that had 20 blank lines that began with the statement "I would like to ____." The number of sentences completed was tallied. The more sentences completed represented broader thought-action repertoires. The results of this study confirmed that those who felt positive emotions were able to complete more sentences in comparison to those in the neutral and negative emotion conditions, supporting the broaden hypothesis of positive emotions as well as the narrowing hypothesis associated with negative emotions (Fredrickson and Branigan, 2005).

The Build Hypothesis

> In spite of illness, in spite even of the archenemy sorrow, one can remain alive long past the usual date of disintegration if one is unafraid of change, insatiable in intellectual curiosity, interested in big things, and happy in small ways.

> Edith Wharton

When positive emotions broaden momentary thought-action repertoires, a variety of personal resources are also built up over time (Fredrickson, 1998, 2001). These resources include physical resources (i.e., coordination, cardiovascular health, and muscle strength), social resources (i.e., friendships, social skills and support), intellectual resources (i.e., knowledge and problem-solving), and psychological resources (i.e., creativity, optimism, and resilience). Although the positive emotions that lead to the building of these resources are transient, the personal resources acquired are lasting and can be utilized later when one finds oneself in a potentially life-threatening situation or experiencing hard times.

To better understand how positive emotions build durable physical, social, intellectual, and psychological resources, consider children. Play is the work of childhood. When children are at play, they are typically experiencing positive emotions such as joy, happiness, or contentment. While playing and experiencing positive emotions, the children are also gaining physical strength. As they run at the park and play kick ball, they are building their cardiovascular strength and lung capacity, honing their motor skills, and fine-tuning their coordination. At the same time, they are building social bonds with their playmates and learning the rules of the game and teamwork. These resources are lasting, even after the positive emotional experience is over. Although one hopes this is never the case, should children find themselves in a situation in which their well-being is at stake, for example, being attacked by a bully, they can turn to the reserve of personal resources they have developed to safely navigate through that negative experience. The physical resources they have developed can help them physically fight off their bully, while the friends they made when at play can also come to their aid. Indeed, a few simple photos (see Figure 1.3) illustrate how the very behaviors children engage in while at play are the same behaviors they utilize when under attack. Had the children not learned

FIGURE 1.3　Similarities between the behaviors children engage in when at play (left) and when under attack (right). According to the broaden and build theory of positive emotions, when in positive emotional states, individuals build enduring personal resources, including physical resources such as coordination, cardiovascular and muscular strength (Fredrickson, 2000). The children in the photo on the left who are in a positive emotional state during play are developing the physical resources necessary to defend themselves when under attack as depicted by the children who are fighting in the photo on the right.

these skills under a positive emotional state, they would not have the skills necessary to protect themselves in a fight-or-flight situation. Later in life, these same resources can be called upon to help in other stressful life situations, even if those situations do not involve danger of life or limb (Fredrickson, 2000).

Research that supports the building hypothesis includes studies of securely attached children who are more resourceful, flexible, and perseverant when it comes to problem-solving in comparison to their insecurely attached peers (Arend et al., 1979; Matas et al., 1978). Other studies show that securely attached adults also show superior intellectual resources. More specifically, they are more curious and open to new information (Mikulincer, 1997). In general, research supports the notion that people learn faster and demonstrate improvements in intellectual performance when in a positive emotional state in comparison to neutral or negative emotional states (Bryan and Bryan, 1991; Bryan et al., 1996). Furthermore, research with both humans and animals indicates that social play is positively related to the building of social relationships (Boulton and Smith, 1992; Lee, 1983; Marinueau, 1972). Finally, evidence for the development of physical resources under positive emotional states is available via studies with nonhuman mammals. Indeed, the juvenile play of many mammals has been linked with specific survival maneuvers they utilize later in life to avoid predators and to fight off enemies (Boulton and Smith, 1992; Caro, 1988). Similarly, rats that were deprived of the ability to engage in play as juveniles were slower to learn a complex motor task in comparison to rats that were not play-deprived (Einon et al., 1978).

The Undoing Hypothesis

The way to overcome negative thoughts and destructive emotions is to develop opposing, positive emotions that are stronger and more powerful.

Tenzin Gyatso

In addition to broadening momentary thought-action repertoires and building enduring personal resources, positive emotions have the potential to *undo* lingering negative emotions. Fredrickson labels this idea the undoing hypothesis. More specifically, the idea behind this hypothesis is that thought-action repertoires cannot be narrowed and broadened simultaneously. Hence, inducing positive emotions in the wake of on-going negative emotions may loosen the grip of the negative emotion, as the broadening qualities of positive emotions begin to widen the lens through which one views the world. This undoing effect occurs not only at the cognitive level, but at the physiological level as well (Fredrickson, 2003).

Fredrickson et al. (2000) tested the undoing hypothesis by measuring the baseline heart rates, blood pressure rates, and peripheral vasoconstriction indices of research participants just before inducing the negative emotion of fear or anxiety in them by telling them that they had one minute to develop a speech that they would present in front of a video camera. They were told that the recording of their speeches would then be evaluated by a group of their peers. Given the popular notion that the number one fear of the average American is public speaking, these instructions indeed elicited fear in many of the participants. (Interestingly, the number two fear of the average American is death. According to a comedy routine by Jerry Seinfeld, this is very interesting, as it means that for the average American, at a funeral they would rather be in the coffin than giving the eulogy!) The participants reported an increase in anxiety and their measures of heart rate, blood pressure, and peripheral vasoconstriction were elevated as well. Participants were then randomly assigned to view one of four emotion-inducing film clips. Two of the clips induced the positive emotions of joy and contentment, one was neutral, and the other elicited sadness. The participants' cardiovascular measures were monitored from the time they began viewing the film clips until the point at which their cardiovascular activity had returned to baseline levels. The results of this study support the undoing hypothesis, as those who saw the two positive emotion videos returned to their baseline levels of cardiovascular activity significantly more quickly than those in the neutral and negative emotion conditions, with those in the negative emotion condition taking the longest to return to baseline functioning (Fredrickson et al., 2000).

The undoing hypothesis explains why there is often much laughter at the receptions following funerals or why friends often crack jokes or make light of a situation for a friend in need. Best friends and loved ones often help us find meaning in the difficult experiences we face, which also has the effect of increasing positive emotions. Indeed, it seems that many people intuitively know that positive emotions can have this undoing effect. With this research, however, we can help those who do not have such intuition to understand the utility of eliciting positive emotions when negative emotions are lingering and getting in the way of one's ability to cope and move forward in life.

The Resilience Hypothesis

> Our greatest glory is not in never falling, but in rising every time we fall.
>
> Confucius

The resilience hypothesis of the broaden and build theory of positive emotions states that positive emotions, through their broadening affects, trigger upward spirals of well-being (Fredrickson, 2000). The idea of upward spirals of well-being is the conceptual opposite of the common notion of downward spirals of depression. When people have negative experiences and therefore negative affect, they begin to experience tunnel vision which often leads to negative, pessimistic thinking. This negative thinking leads to more negative affect that can spiral downward very quickly. In contrast, positive emotions take the blinders off, allowing people to see more possibilities and to think more optimistically. Those who experience positive emotions more regularly are likely to experience upward spirals of well-being, which is enjoyable in and of itself. However, perhaps more importantly, upward spirals of well-being also serve to build one's toolbox of coping skills. Hence, those who experience positive emotions more often are better able to cope and are more resilient in the face of adversities in life (Fredrickson, 2000).

Research on the resilience hypothesis includes a study of college students who completed self-report measures of affect and coping on two different occasions, five weeks apart. Results showed that positive affect at time one predicted broad-minded coping at time two and broad-minded coping at time one predicted more positive affect at time two. Furthermore, mediational analyses revealed that broad-minded coping and positive affect serially enhanced each other (Fredrickson and Joiner, 2002). A similar study was conducted in the days following the terrorist attacks of September 11, 2001, with a portion of the participants from the previously reported study (Fredrickson et al., 2003). The participants were asked to report what emotions they were feeling in the wake of the attacks, what they learned from the attacks, and how they felt about the future. Almost all the participants reported feeling sad, angry, and afraid, yet those that had been identified as resilient in the previous study also reported feeling positive emotions in the wake of the tragedy as well. More specifically, they reported positive feelings such as gratitude and optimism, as they could find goodness in people who were helping in the aftermath of the event. Statistical analyses showed that the tendency to feel positive emotions buffered the resilient people against depression.

The Flourish Hypothesis

> Feelings of worth can flourish only in an atmosphere where individual differences are appreciated, mistakes are tolerated, communication is open, and rules are flexible – the kind of atmosphere that is found in a nurturing family.
>
> Virginia Satir

The final hypothesis of the broaden and build theory of positive emotions is the flourish hypothesis. To flourish is to live optimally and to experience the good things in life such as personal growth, generativity, and resilience (Keyes, 2002). The flourish hypothesis states that a key predictor of human flourishing is the ratio of positive to negative affect that one experiences (Fredrickson and Losada, 2005). More specifically, the ratio of positive feelings or sentiments to negative feelings or sentiments over time that one needs in order to flourish has been hypothesized to be 2.9 to 1. In other words, for each negative affective experience, one must experience 3 positive affective experiences over the course of time to keep moving forward in life. As the ratio dips below 2.9 to 1, flourishing becomes less likely and problems may arise. Based on the research of Fredrickson and Losada (2005), this ratio holds true for individuals, marriages, and business teams. Furthermore, positive to negative affect ratios up to 11.6 to 1 will promote flourishing, however, ratios beyond 11.6 to 1 may lead to the disintegration of flourishing (Fredrickson and Losada, 2005).

1.3 A NOTE ON WHAT POSITIVE PSYCHOLOGY IS NOT

Before moving onto the applications of positive psychology in counseling and psychotherapy, it is important to note some common misperceptions of positive psychology. Those who study and practice positive psychology are not people who are naïve or engage in Pollyanna thinking. They do not see the world through rose-colored glasses, ignoring the problems in life and focusing instead only on the positives. In fact, positive psychologists are as concerned with building strengths and the best things life has to offer as in managing weaknesses and repairing the worst things in life. Positive psychologists, especially those who work in applied fashion with clients, are as interested in helping those who experience pathology to overcome it as they are in helping those who are free of pathology to lead the most fulfilling lives possible (Seligman and Csikszentmihalyi, 2000).

Those who subscribe to the theories and principles of positive psychology are seeking a vital balance in the way that people are understood and treated. Indeed, many years ago the famous psychoanalyst, Karl Menninger, noted a need for a vital balance in mental health care when he challenged the standard view of mental illness as progressive and refractory, calling instead for mental health practitioners to view mental illness as amenable to change and improvements (Menninger et al., 1963). Positive psychologists today are calling for a similar vital balance in which all people are understood according to both their weaknesses and strengths (Lopez et al., 2003).

Such a vital balance seems to be lacking in applied psychology at large, given that the focus of applied psychologists has largely been upon the study of what is wrong with people. This may be due to the path that Freud took in studying patients many years ago. A simple way to understand where psychology at large has come from is the story of "watchology" as described by Laura King (2007). King puts forth a question to college students who read the introductory psychology text she has written from a non-pathological perspective. She asks them which of two watches they would choose to study if they were charged with the task of creating the science of "watchology" or the science of how watches work. She tells them that both watches have gone through the worst trauma a watch can go through – the laundry cycle. One watch comes out still working while the other is broken and no longer ticking. Which watch would one choose to work with? Hopefully the obvious answer is the one that is working, as one could not learn much about how a watch works by studying the broken one. She explains, however, that Freud chose to study the one that was not working, so to speak, when he set out to understand human behavior. Based on his work with people who were experiencing pathology, Freud generalized his work to all people. Essentially, he used the exception to explain the rule. Why not use the rule to explain the rule? Although positive psychologists find the study of pathology important and many utilize the research from the study of pathology in their daily work, the need to study and incorporate information about what works for people and what factors buffer people from pathology is just as crucial. Again, it is all about striking a delicate, vital balance.

1.4 APPLICATIONS OF POSITIVE PSYCHOLOGY

In the past decade, research in positive psychology has proliferated. Along with the advancements in research have come many applications of this work. Indeed, research from positive psychology has been applied in education, business, organizational consulting, marriage and interpersonal relationships, parenting, athletics, coaching, and more. As noted in the introduction of this chapter, it seems that there is no better application of positive psychology than in the therapy room. This, of course, is the main focus of this text and the many applications of positive psychology for clients in counseling and therapy will be elucidated in the remaining chapters.

Chapter 2

The Intersection of Positive Psychology and the Practice of Counseling and Psychotherapy

There are many applications of positive psychology within the practice of counseling and psychotherapy. These applications include not only specific client activities and exercises informed by research in positive psychology, but also client conceptualizations and definitions of successful therapeutic outcomes, and the process of psychological assessment. The applications of positive psychology to each of these components of counseling and psychotherapy are explored in the following sections.

2.1 CLIENT CONCEPTUALIZATIONS AND OUTCOME EXPECTATIONS

2.1.1 The Four-Front Approach

To put positive psychology into action in the therapy room, therapists must first begin by taking the stance that *all* clients have both strengths and weaknesses as well as both opportunities and destructive forces in their environments (Wright and Lopez, 2003). Furthermore, they seek information about their clients on all four of these fronts. Typically, therapists attend to client weaknesses and psychosocial and environmental problems because most clients enter therapy with identified problems or concerns in their lives. Strengths and environmental resources, however, are often overlooked, as they are not as salient as the problems with which clients present. Failure to start the therapeutic process with this belief system intact will likely result in the clinician overlooking completely or failing to utilize fully the strengths and resources of the client. For those who take this stance, however, assessment and thereby client conceptualizations according to this four-front approach become possible.

There are a variety of reasons why therapists may overlook strengths and environmental resources in their work, including issues related to the current assessment system set up by the *Diagnostic and Statistical Manual of Mental Disorders* (*DSM*; American Psychiatric Association, 2000, which is utilized by many mental health agencies and required by most insurance companies for reimbursement purposes), biases in human thinking, and lack of instruction about the importance of such an approach in the formal training of clinicians. These issues are explored more fully in the following sections.

2.2 PROBLEMS WITH THE CURRENT *DSM* ASSESSMENT SYSTEM

The current five-axis assessment system of the *Diagnostic and Statistical Manual of Mental Disorders*, fourth edition – text revision (American Psychiatric Association, 2000) encourages practitioners to focus on pathology while failing to hold therapists accountable for finding strengths and resources as well. More specifically, Axes I (clinical syndromes and other conditions that may be a focus of clinical attention) and II (personality disorders and mental retardation) provide ample opportunities for therapists to document the weaknesses of a client, while Axis IV allows for psychosocial and environmental problems to be noted. Even Axis V, the Global Assessment of Functioning Scale, is focused exclusively on pathology. A score of 1 represents extremely severe pathology while the highest score of 100 simply indicates the absence of symptomology (American Psychiatric Association, 2000).

According to Lopez et al. (2003), a few simple changes or additions to the current *DSM* five-axis assessment system would assist clinicians in conceptualizing clients in a more balanced way. More specifically, broadening Axis IV to include not only psychosocial and environmental problems but also psychosocial and environmental resources would surely help therapists to tend to all aspects of a client's environment. Indeed, the developers of the *DSM* note that Axis IV is included because the nine categories of psychosocial and environmental problems that are to be assessed on this axis might contribute to or exacerbate the various disorders listed on Axes I and II. It appeals to common sense, then, that if such problems can exacerbate pathology, then psychosocial and environmental resources might serve as protective factors that could potentially minimize the impact of disorders, and therefore should be assessed as well (Snyder et al., 2003a). To broaden Axis IV, therapists are encouraged to refer to Table 2.1.

Sue et al. (2006) recommend the addition of an axis that focuses therapist attention on the cultural contexts of client's lives. Indeed, failure to attend to the cultural background and context that impacts so much of who our clients are can completely override the utility of all of the other data that is collected. Information on ways to assess the cultural contexts of clientele is provided in Chapter 3.

Broadening Axis V to include two global assessment of functioning scales with one focused on symptoms of mental illness and the other on symptoms

Table 2.1   Broadening Axis IV of the current *DSM-IV-TR* assessment system to include environmental and psychosocial resources (Snyder et al., 2003).

Current problem areas to be assessed by clinicians using the *DSM-IV-TR* assessment system	Resources also to be assessed by clinicians who practice from a positive psychology perspective
1. Problems with primary support group	1. Attachment/love/nurturance with primary support group
2. Problems related to the social environment	2. Connectedness/empathic relationships
3. Educational problems	3. Accessible educational opportunities and support
4. Occupational problems	4. Meaningful work/career satisfaction/self-efficacy
5. Housing problems	5. Safe housing with essential elements that foster healthy development
6. Economic problems	6. Financial resources adequate to meet basic needs and beyond
7. Problems with access to health care services	7. Access to high quality/reliable health care services
8. Problems related to interaction with the legal system – crime	8. Contributions made to society via donation of resources and time
9. Other psychosocial and environmental problems	9. Other psychosocial and environmental resources

Reproduced with permission of the American Psychological Association.

of well-being would also make for a more complete assessment model. To broaden Axis V, therapists can utilize the current global assessment of functioning scale provided in the *DSM*, in which they rate clients on a scale of 1 (severely impaired functioning) to 100 (absence of symptomology) and then complete a second global assessment of positive functioning scale with anchors of 1 representing a complete absence of well-being symptoms and 100 representing optimal functioning. Table 2.2 has been designed to assist practitioners in broadening Axis V.

Finally, adding one more axis, Axis VI, in which the personal strengths and facilitators of client growth are documented is also recommended (Snyder et al., 2003a).

Through these changes and additions to the current *DSM* assessment system, therapists and clients would become more aware of not only the problems or areas of concern, but also of the strengths and resources that could be utilized in sound treatment planning.

Since the revised assessment system is not currently a part of the *DSM*, most mental health agencies and insurance companies do not require this information to be provided; however, that does not mean that therapists should not or could

Table 2.2   Broadening Axis V of the current *DSM-IV-TR* assessment system to include a Global Assessment of Positive Functioning scale.

Current *DSM-IV-TR* Global Assessment of Functioning scale (GAF)		Global Assessment of *Positive* Functioning scale (GAPF) to be used in addition to the GAF	
91–100	Superior functioning in a wide range of activities, life's problems never seem to get out of hand, is sought out by others because of his or her many qualities. No symptoms.	91–100	Optimal functioning in a wide range of activities, very high levels of psychological, social, and emotional well-being, and satisfaction with life. Consistently capitalizes upon strengths and has a strong sense of purpose and meaning in life.
81–90	Absent or minimal symptoms, good functioning in all areas, interested and involved in a wide range of activities, socially effective, generally satisfied with life, no more than everyday problems or concerns.	81–90	High functioning in a wide range of activities, high levels of psychological, social, and emotional well-being, and satisfaction with life. Understands strengths and uses them fairly regularly. Has found some sense of purpose and meaning in life.
71–80	If symptoms are present they are transient and expectable reactions to psychosocial stresses; no more than slight impairment in social, occupational, or school functioning.	71–80	Moderate functioning in a wide range of activities, moderate levels of psychological, social, and emotional well-being, and satisfaction with life. Is learning about and beginning to implement strengths and to develop a sense of purpose and meaning in life.
61–70	Some mild symptoms OR some difficulty in social, occupational, or school functioning, but generally functioning pretty well, has some meaningful interpersonal relationships.	61–70	Moderate functioning in most activities, moderate levels of well-being in at least two of the following areas: psychological, social, or emotional well-being. Somewhat satisfied with life and aspiring to develop an understanding of strengths and a sense of purpose and meaning in life.
51–60	Moderate symptoms OR any moderate difficulty in social, occupational, or school functioning.	51–60	Moderate functioning in some activities, moderate levels of well-being in at least one of the following areas: psychological, social, or emotional well-being. Some dissatisfaction with life, lacking insight into strengths, and confusion about purpose and meaning in life.

(Continued)

Table 2.2 (Continued)

Current *DSM-IV-TR* Global Assessment of Functioning scale (GAF)		Global Assessment of *Positive* Functioning scale (GAPF) to be used in addition to the GAF	
41–50	Serious symptoms OR any serious impairment in social, occupational, or school functioning.	41–50	Low functioning in some activities, low levels of well-being in one of the following areas: psychological, social, or emotional well-being. Dissatisfied in life, uninterested in strengths, and somewhat lacking a sense of purpose and meaning in life.
31–40	Some impairment in reality testing or communication OR major impairment in several areas, such as work or school, family relations, judgment, thinking, or mood.	31–40	Low functioning in most activities, low levels of well-being in two or more of the following areas: psychological, social, or emotional well-being. Very dissatisfied in life, unwilling to explore strengths, and completely lacking a sense of purpose and meaning in life.
21–30	Behavior is considerably influenced by delusions or hallucinations OR serious impairment in communications or judgment OR inability to function in all areas.	21–30	Low functioning in all activities, extremely low levels of psychological, social, and emotional well-being. Extreme dissatisfaction in life, denial of strengths, and denial of purpose or meaning in life.
11–20	Some danger of hurting self or others OR occasionally fails to maintain minimal personal hygiene OR gross impairment in communication.	11–20	Extremely low functioning in all activities, extremely low levels of psychological, social, and emotional well-being. Extremely negative, hopeless, and unwilling/ unable to examine strengths/resources/ purpose/meaning.
1–10	Persistent danger of severely hurting self/others OR persistent inability to maintain minimum personal hygiene OR serious suicidal act with clear expectation of death.	1–10	Complete absence of all psychological, social, and emotional well-being indicators, inability to detect/determine strengths and purpose or meaning in life.

not include this information in their work with clients. There is no harm that can be done by utilizing this system in one's work with clients and the extra time it takes to gather and share this information with clients is well worth it, as it will save time in the end. For example, when clients feel understood as whole people, rather than being equated with their problems only, the working alliance between therapist and client is strengthened and clients also become more motivated to work in therapy. When the treatment plan incorporates building from client strengths, clients have more hope that things really can change. These are just a few examples of how a balanced conceptualization can lead to positive therapeutic outcomes.

In order to begin utilizing this revised assessment system, Worksheets 2.1 and 2.2 may be useful. Please note that it may be important to provide a rationale to some clients for why they are being asked about areas of personal strength and resources in their environment. This may be especially true for clients who have been in therapy in the past with therapists who did not practice from a strengths-based or positive psychology perspective. Indeed, since strengths and resources are so often overlooked, it may strike some clients as odd that they are being asked about these areas of their lives. It is also important to keep a balance and not swing too far in the direction of focusing on strengths and resources, as this could serve to invalidate the client's concerns. Indeed, balance is the key.

Worksheet 2.1 Therapist's Guide to Utilizing the Four-Front Approach to Client Assessment (Wright and Lopez, 2002)

Four-Front Assessment Approach

1. **Areas of client weakness** (i.e., impaired social skills, low intelligence, emotion dysregulation, labile moods, personality problems)

2. **Areas of client strength** (i.e., hopeful, grateful, forgiving, courageous, resilient, high intelligence, mood stability, healthy personality)

3. **Deficits or destructive forces in the client's environment** (i.e., unsafe living conditions/neighborhood, presence of abusive relationships or neglect, exposure to discrimination or victim of prejudice)

4. **Assets or resources in the client's environment** (i.e., secure living conditions/neighborhood, supportive relationships, opportunities for success, stable employment)

Worksheet 2.2 Therapist's Guide to Implementing a Revised Client Assessment System Based on the Principles of Positive Psychology

Seven-Axis System of Positive Psychological Assessment

Axis I: _____

_____

(clinical syndromes and other conditions that may be a focus of clinical attention)

Axis II: _____

_____

(personality disorders and mental retardation)

Axis III: _____

_____

(general medical conditions)

Axis IV (broadened):_____

_____

_____

(psychosocial and environmental problems and resources)

Axis V (broadened): Global Assessment of Functioning scale score: _____
  Global Assessment of *Positive* Functioning scale score: _____

Axis VI: _____

_____

(client strengths)

Axis VII:_____

_____

(client cultural background information)

2.3 BIASES IN HUMAN THINKING

The tendency for practitioners to emphasize only the negative aspects of clients in assessment may be due, in part, to the fact that most clients enter therapy as a result of experiencing problems that they perceive as being negative; thus, inferences about the causes of the problems are also negative (Wright and Lopez, 2002). Indeed, under many conditions people, in general, tend to weigh negative aspects of situations more heavily than positive aspects (Kanhouse and Hanson, 1971). Additionally, practitioners may fall victim to the fundamental negative bias when dealing with behaviors, thoughts, or emotions that are salient, that are negative in valence, and that occur in a vague context (Wright, 1998). Under these circumstances the major factor that guides perception of the behavior, thought, or emotion is its negative quality. For example, when a client comes into therapy reporting feeling very sad, tired, irritable, and hopeless and that these feelings are consistent across time and situation, most practitioners will immediately begin assessing for depression and may overlook or simply fail to ask about any signs or symptoms to the contrary, as they are sucked in by the fundamental negative bias.

Failure to consider the role of the environment is an error to which many practitioners subscribe, partly because it is much harder to assess the environment in comparison to the individual when working with a client for one hour per week in the context of one's therapy office. Indeed, the client commands attention, whereas his or her environment is not as accessible (Lopez et al., 2003). Another reason practitioners may fail to assess the environment may be due to the fundamental attribution error. This bias in human thinking is defined as the tendency of people to explain the behavior of others through attributions to the others' internal characteristics while ignoring external situational or environmental factors (Wright, 1998; Lopez et al., 2003). Interestingly, the opposite is true when one explains his or her own behaviors. For example, when another person trips on the stairs at the movie theater, people often assume that the person who tripped is simply a klutz (i.e., internal behavioral attribution); however, if one were to trip on the stairs oneself, he or she would explain that the reason for tripping was the lack of light in the theater (i.e., external behavioral attributions). Similarly, practitioners who are detached from the client's situation (e.g., outsiders) are also more prone to see negatives in the client's situation in comparison to the client (e.g., insider), who is directly affected by the situation (Goldberg, 1978). Hence, even those who set out to assess the environment may still fail to see the resources within it, in lieu of the more obvious deficits.

Due to these biases in thinking, practitioners must make a conscious effort to assess all four fronts, lest they risk falling victim to these thinking errors. Such errors can be detrimental to the success of therapy and even worse, could potentially lead to declines in client functioning if inappropriate attributions for the sources of client problems are made.

2.4 LACK OF INFORMATION ON THE STRENGTHS PERSPECTIVE IN FORMAL TRAINING

Many people who become therapists do so because they have the desire to help people. When thinking about helping people, we naturally think about helping people to overcome problems. Indeed, it would be absolutely absurd to conduct therapy without asking questions about what is wrong or not going well for clients. Unfortunately, until recently, failing to ask about what is going right for people was not seen as equally absurd. Hence, many mental health practitioners have been well educated in asking questions about problems and detecting symptoms of pathology with little to no formal training in asking about what is going well and detecting symptoms of well-being. Unless therapists stay abreast of the research in positive psychology or take continuing education classes related to this area of psychology, it is unlikely that they even realize the disservice they are doing to themselves and their clients by focusing on pathology only.

2.5 THE COMPLETE STATE MODEL OF MENTAL HEALTH

In addition to the four-front approach to assessing client functioning, another model of conceptualizing mental health that therapists can utilize for creating a balanced perspective of clients is the Complete State Model of Mental Health (Keyes and Lopez, 2002). This new model of client conceptualization defines mental health and mental illness as existing on two separate continuums. Therapists who subscribe to this model are challenged to conceptualize clients and perhaps re-conceptualize treatment outcomes in a unique way. More specifically, from this perspective, the absence of mental illness is not equal to the presence of mental health (Keyes and Lopez, 2002). Rather, clients should be assessed according to the degree of symptoms of mental illness they are experiencing (high to low), as well as the degree of symptoms of well-being they are experiencing (high to low). Combining these continua together, a client can be conceptualized as: (1) completely mentally healthy or flourishing (low symptoms of mental illness and high symptoms of well-being); (2) completely mentally ill or floundering (high symptoms of mental illness and low symptoms of well-being); (3) incompletely mentally healthy or languishing (low symptoms of mental illness and low symptoms of well-being); or (4) incompletely mentally ill or struggling (high symptoms of mental illness and high symptoms of well-being; Keyes and Lopez, 2002).

Based on the Complete State Model, therapists are able to see for themselves, as well as share with their clients, where each client falls and to discuss with the client his or her therapy outcome goals. For example, a client who is floundering may have come to therapy simply hoping to decrease his or her symptoms of mental illness, thereby leading to a label of languishing. However, when he or she is able to see that there is more to life than being free of symptoms of pathology, the client's goal may become two-fold, namely, to not only decrease symptoms of mental illness but to also purposefully increase symptoms of well-being, ultimately leading him or her to the flourishing category.

The connection between the Complete State Model of Mental Health and optimal therapy outcomes is illustrated in Figure 2.1. Whereas many therapists and clients consider therapy to be successful when clients have reached a baseline level of functioning, the Complete State Model reveals that there is more that can be done to help people achieve optimal functioning. Indeed, therapy that results in baseline functioning for those who started below the baseline should be considered successful, as it has lead to improvements in client functioning. However, such therapy stops short, as there is much more to life

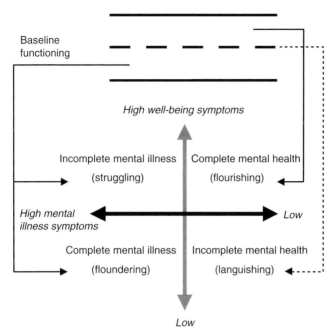

FIGURE 2.1   The connection between the Complete State Model of Mental Health and optimal therapy outcomes. Whereas many therapists and clients consider therapy to be successful when clients have reached a baseline level of functioning, the Complete State Model of Mental Health (Keyes and Lopez, 2002) reveals that there is more that can be done to help people achieve optimal functioning above the baseline.

than just feeling neutral or functioning at the baseline. For many, functioning beyond the baseline can be the marker of therapeutic success. For those with unrelenting mental illness, complete mental health may not be possible, but rather than simply accepting that life will include on-going issues related to pathology, he or she can be assisted to see that despite this, a life full of symptoms of well-being is still possible.

Worksheet 2.3 is designed to help therapists document where clients fit within the Complete State Model of Mental Health. There are a variety of ways to determine symptoms of mental illness and symptoms of well-being. A simple way includes plotting the two global assessment of functioning scale scores based on the broadened version of Axis V as previously described (see Table 2.2) and then connecting those scores together as demonstrated in Figure 2.2. Another option is to have clients complete a measure of symptoms of mental illness and a measure of symptoms of well-being and plotting the scores from these measures on the appropriate continua. Two exemplary measures that therapists may want to use are the Outcome Questionnaire-45.2 (OQ-45.2; Lambert et al., 1996) and the Mental Health Continuum – Long Form (MHC-LF; Keyes, 2002, 2005).

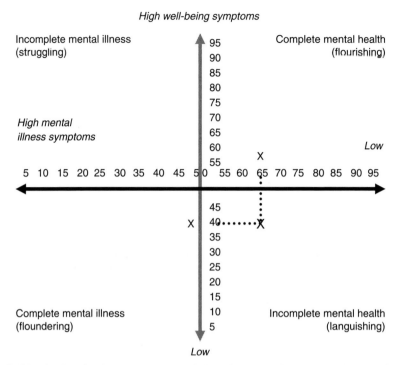

FIGURE 2.2   Sample of a completed plot of client functioning based on the Complete State Model of Mental Health. In this example, the client has been evaluated to have a Global Assessment of Functioning score of 65 and a Global Assessment of Positive Functioning score of 40. By plotting and connecting these two scores, one can see that this client best fits into the incomplete mental health or languishing category. Although the client may have some symptoms of mental illness upon which therapy should focus, this individual also needs assistance with increasing symptoms of well-being in order to experience a complete state of mental health.

The OQ-45.2 (Lambert et al., 1996) was designed to measure common symptoms across a wide range of adult mental disorders and syndromes. More specifically, subjective discomfort, interpersonal relations, and social role performance are measured by the OQ-45.2. The MHC-LF was designed to assess growth and improvement beyond symptom relief. The MHC-LF is a comprehensive self-report measure of subjective well-being, consisting of three major domains, namely, emotional, psychological, and social well-being (Keyes and Magyar-Moe, 2003). Worksheets 2.4 and 2.5 contain the full-item measures for use with clients. Once total scores on these measures are obtained, they can be plotted on Worksheet 2.6 and used to understand which category of the Complete State Model of Mental Health best fits the client. As therapy progresses, clients can be asked to retake these measures and any changes should be documented and shared with the client. Information regarding the psychometric properties of these two exemplary outcome measures follows.

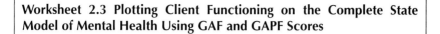

Worksheet 2.3 Plotting Client Functioning on the Complete State Model of Mental Health Using GAF and GAPF Scores

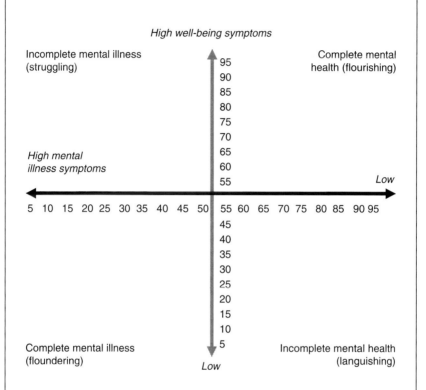

In order to document where a client fits within the Complete State Model of Mental Health (Keyes and Lopez, 2002), determine his or her Global Assessment of Functioning score and plot it on the horizontal axis. Next, determine his or her Global Assessment of Positive Functioning score (see Table 2.2) and plot it on the vertical axis. Then connect the two points to determine which of the four categories best describes the client. In addition, a more objective rating of client functioning can be determined by plotting client scores from completed measures of symptoms of mental illness (i.e., the OQ-45.2) and measures of symptoms of well-being (i.e., the MHC-LF) on the appropriate continua.

Worksheet 2.4 Outcome questionnaire 45.2 (Lambert et al., 1996)

Outcome Questionnaire (OQ®-45.2)

Name: _____

ID# _____

Age: _____ yrs.

Sex

M ☐   F ☐

Instructions: Looking back over the last week, including today, help us understand how you have been feeling. Read each item carefully and mark the box under the category which best describes your current situation. For this questionnaire, work is defined as employment, school, housework, volunteer work, and so forth. Please do not make any marks in the shaded areas.

Session # _____   Date ___/___/___

	Never	Rarely	Sometimes	Frequently	Almost Always
1. I get along well with others.	4	3	2	1	0
2. I tire quickly.	0	1	2	3	4
3. I feel no interest in things.	0	1	2	3	4
4. I feel stressed at work/school.	0	1	2	3	4
5. I blame myself for things.	0	1	2	3	4
6. I feel irritated.	0	1	2	3	4
7. I feel unhappy in my marriage/significant relationship.	0	1	2	3	4
8. I have thoughts of ending my life.	0	1	2	3	4
9. I feel weak.	0	1	2	3	4
10. I feel fearful.	0	1	2	3	4
11. After heavy drinking, I need a drink the next morning to get going. (If you do not drink, mark "never")	0	1	2	3	4
12. I find my work/school satisfying.	4	3	2	1	0
13. I am a happy person.	4	3	2	1	0
14. I work/study too much.	0	1	2	3	4
15. I feel worthless.	0	1	2	3	4
16. I am concerned about family troubles.	0	1	2	3	4
17. I have an unfulfilling sex life.	0	1	2	3	4
18. I feel lonely.	0	1	2	3	4
19. I have frequent arguments.	0	1	2	3	4
20. I feel loved and wanted.	4	3	2	1	0
21. I enjoy my spare time.	4	3	2	1	0
22. I have difficulty concentrating.	0	1	2	3	4
23. I feel hopeless about the future.	0	1	2	3	4
24. I like myself.	4	3	2	1	0
25. Disturbing thoughts come into my mind that I cannot get rid of.	0	1	2	3	4

SD   IR   SR

DO NOT MARK BELOW

		0	1	2	3	4
26.	I feel annoyed by people who criticize my drinking (or drug use). (If not applicable, mark "never")	0	1	2	3	4
27.	I have an upset stomach.	0	1	2	3	4
28.	I am not working/studying as well as I used to.	0	1	2	3	4
29.	My heart pounds too much.	0	1	2	3	4
30.	I have trouble getting along with friends and close acquaintances.	0	1	2	3	4
31.	I am satisfied with my life.	4	3	2	1	0
32.	I have trouble at work/school because of drinking or drug use. (If not applicable, mark "never")	0	1	2	3	4
33.	I feel that something bad is going to happen.	0	1	2	3	4
34.	I have sore muscles.	0	1	2	3	4
35.	I feel afraid of open spaces, of driving, or being on buses, subways, and so forth.	0	1	2	3	4
36.	I feel nervous.	0	1	2	3	4
37.	I feel my love relationships are full and complete.	4	3	2	1	0
38.	I feel that I am not doing well at work/school.	0	1	2	3	4
39.	I have too many disagreements at work/school.	0	1	2	3	4
40.	I feel something is wrong with my mind.	0	1	2	3	4
41.	I have trouble falling asleep or staying asleep.	0	1	2	3	4
42.	I feel blue.	0	1	2	3	4
43.	I am satisfied with my relationships with others.	4	3	2	1	0
44.	I feel angry enough at work/school to do something I might regret.	0	1	2	3	4
45.	I have headaches.	0	1	2	3	4

Total=

Worksheet 2.5   Mental Health Continuum – Long Form ©2008 Corey L. M. Keyes, Ph.D.

EWB1. During the past 30 days, how much of the time did you feel…

	ALL THE TIME	MOST OF THE TIME	SOME OF THE TIME	A LITTLE OF THE TIME	NONE OF THE TIME
a. …cheerful?	1	2	3	4	5
b. …in good spirits?	1	2	3	4	5
c. …extremely happy?	1	2	3	4	5
d. …calm and peaceful?	1	2	3	4	5
e. …satisfied?	1	2	3	4	5
f. …full of life?	1	2	3	4	5

EWB2. Using a scale from 0 to 10 where 0 means "the worst possible life overall" and 10 means "the best possible life overall," how would you rate your life overall these days?

WORST										BEST
0	1	2	3	4	5	6	7	8	9	10

PWB. Please indicate how strongly you agree or disagree with each of the following statements.

	AGREE				DISAGREE		
	STRONGLY	SOME WHAT	A LITTLE	DON'T KNOW	A LITTLE	SOME WHAT	STRONGLY
1. I like most parts of my personality	1	2	3	4	5	6	7
2. When I look at the story of my life, I am pleased with how things have turned out so far	1	2	3	4	5	6	7
3. Some people wander aimlessly through life, but I am not one of them	1	2	3	4	5	6	7

	AGREE			DON'T KNOW	DISAGREE		
	STRONGLY	SOMEWHAT	A LITTLE		A LITTLE	SOMEWHAT	STRONGLY
4. The demands of everyday life often get me down	1	2	3	4	5	6	7
5. In many ways I feel disappointed about my achievements in life	1	2	3	4	5	6	7
6. Maintaining close relationships has been difficult and frustrating for me	1	2	3	4	5	6	7
7. I live life one day at a time and don't really think about the future	1	2	3	4	5	6	7
8. In general, I feel I am in charge of the situation in which I live	1	2	3	4	5	6	7
9. I am good at managing the responsibilities of daily life	1	2	3	4	5	6	7
10. I sometimes feel as if I've done all there is to do in life	1	2	3	4	5	6	7
11. For me, life has been a continuous process of learning, changing, and growth	1	2	3	4	5	6	7
12. I think it is important to have new experiences that challenge how I think about myself and the world	1	2	3	4	5	6	7
13. People would describe me as a giving person, willing to share my time with others	1	2	3	4	5	6	7
14. I gave up trying to make big improvements or changes in my life a long time ago	1	2	3	4	5	6	7
15. I tend to be influenced by people with strong opinions	1	2	3	4	5	6	7

	AGREE				DISAGREE		
	STRONGLY	SOME WHAT	A LITTLE	DON'T KNOW	A LITTLE	SOME WHAT	STRONGLY
16. I have not experienced many warm and trusting relationships with others	1	2	3	4	5	6	7
17. I have confidence in my own opinions, even if they are different from the way most other people think	1	2	3	4	5	6	7
18. I judge myself by what I think is important, not by the values of what others think is important	1	2	3	4	5	6	7

SWB. Please indicate how strongly you agree or disagree with each of the following statements.

	AGREE				DISAGREE		
	STRONGLY	SOME WHAT	A LITTLE	DON'T KNOW	A LITTLE	SOME WHAT	STRONGLY
1. The world is too complex for me	1	2	3	4	5	6	7
2. I don't feel I belong to anything I'd call a community	1	2	3	4	5	6	7
3. People who do a favor expect nothing in return	1	2	3	4	5	6	7
4. I have something valuable to give the world	1	2	3	4	5	6	7
5. The world is becoming a better place for everyone	1	2	3	4	5	6	7

	AGREE			DON'T KNOW	DISAGREE		
	STRONGLY	SOME WHAT	A LITTLE	DON'T KNOW	A LITTLE	SOME WHAT	STRONGLY
6. I feel close to other people in my community	1	2	3	4	5	6	7
7. My daily activities do not create anything worthwhile for my community	1	2	3	4	5	6	7
8. I cannot make sense of what's going on in the world	1	2	3	4	5	6	7
9. Society has stopped making progress	1	2	3	4	5	6	7
10. People do not care about other people's problems	1	2	3	4	5	6	7
11. My community is a source of comfort	1	2	3	4	5	6	7
12. I try to think about and understand what could happen next in our country	1	2	3	4	5	6	7
13. Society isn't improving for people like me	1	2	3	4	5	6	7
14. I believe that people are kind	1	2	3	4	5	6	7
15. I have nothing important to contribute to society	1	2	3	4	5	6	7

Worksheet 2.6 Plotting Client Functioning on the Complete State Model of Mental Health Using OQ-45.2 and MHC-LF scores

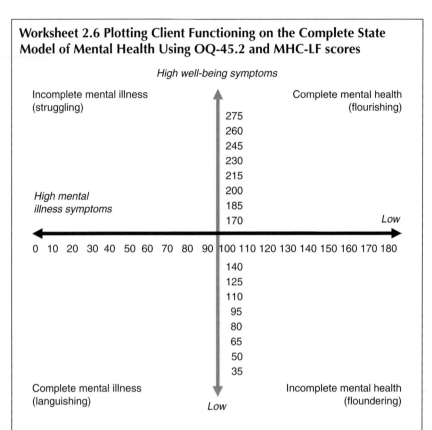

In order to document where a client fits within the Complete State Model of Mental Health (Keyes and Lopez, 2002), determine his or her total score on the OQ-45.2 (see Worksheet 2.4) and plot it on the horizontal axis. Next, determine his or her total score on the MHC-LF (see Worksheet 2.5) and plot it on the vertical axis. Then connect the two points to determine which of the four categories best describes the client. In addition, scores on each of the subscales of both measures can be plotted on the appropriate continua in order to determine individual areas of poor functioning that may need extra attention or areas of strength that can be built upon in treatment planning.

2.6 PSYCHOMETRIC PROPERTIES OF THE OUTCOME QUESTIONNAIRE-45.2

The Outcome Questionnaire-45.2 (OQ-45.2; Lambert et al., 1996) is a 45-item questionnaire designed to measure client progress and outcomes in therapy along three dimensions: (a) subjective discomfort (i.e., how the person feels inside); (b) interpersonal relationships (i.e., how the person is getting along with others); and (c) social role performance (i.e., how the person is doing in important life tasks such as work and school). Items are answered using a 5-point Likert scale with 0 being "almost always" and 4 being "never." The 45 items are summed to produce a total score ranging from 0 to 180 with higher scores indicating more disturbance. The symptom distress subscale consists of 25 items added together to produce scores ranging from 0 to 100, the interpersonal relations subscale is made up of 11 items summed to produce scores ranging from 0 to 44, and the social role subscale consists of 9 items with scores ranging from 0 to 36.

Lambert and colleagues (1996) report that the OQ-45.2 addresses limitations in other current outcome measures. Specifically, it is brief, sensitive to change over short periods of time, and is "designed to assess common symptoms across a wide range of adult mental disorders and syndromes including stress related illness and v. codes" while maintaining high levels of reliability and validity (p. 8). Test–retest reliability estimates range from 0.82 over a two-week period to 0.66 over a ten-week period. Internal consistency reliability ranges from 0.70 to 0.93 for each of the subscale and total scores (Lambert et al., 1996). Concurrent validity is reported as being moderately high with a variety of measures intended to assess similar variables. For example, concurrent validity is estimated at 0.78 between the OQ-45.2 and the General Symptom Index of the Symptom Check List-90-Revised, 0.79 with the Beck Depression Inventory, 0.87 with the Zung Self-Rating Depression Scale, 0.80 with the Zung Self-Rating Anxiety Scale, 0.53 with the Inventory of Interpersonal Problems, 0.64 with the Social Adjustment Scale, and 0.81 with the Friedman Well-Being Scale (Lambert et al., 1996).

2.7 PSYCHOMETRIC PROPERTIES OF THE MENTAL HEALTH CONTINUUM – LONG FORM

The Mental Health Continuum – Long Form (MHC-LF; Keyes, 2002; 2005) measures emotional, psychological, and social well-being. The scale contains 35 items that can be summed together to produce a total well-being score ranging from 39–271 with higher scores indicating higher levels of well-being. The overall emotional well-being subscale ranges from 5–40, the overall psychological well-being subscale ranges from 18–126, and the overall social well-being subscale ranges from 15–105, again with higher scores representing higher well-being levels.

The scales of psychological well-being and social well-being in Worksheet 2.4 are the reduced three-item scales (see Ryff (1989b) for the full 20-item scales of psychological well-being and Keyes (1998) for the full 10-item scales of social well-being) for use in large studies that often include an extensive assessment schedule (Ryff and Keyes, 1995). These reduced-item scales possess moderate internal reliabilities that range from 0.40 to 0.70. When the scales are summed to form scales of overall psychological well-being and overall social well-being, the internal reliabilities are very good at 0.80 or higher (Keyes and Ryff, 1998).

The scales of social well-being correlated approximately -0.30 with a measure of dysphoric symptoms (Keyes, 1998). Keyes and Lopez (2002) also reported an average correlation of the scales of psychological well-being with standard measures of depression (i.e., the Center for Epidemiologic Studies – Depressed Mood Scale (CES-D; Radloff, 1977) and the Zung (1965) Self-Rating Depression Scale) around -0.50, whereas measures of life satisfaction and quality of life correlated, on average, around -0.40 with these depression scales. Confirmatory factor analyses of the CES-D subscales and the psychological well-being scales in the USA (as well as South Korea) have shown that a two-factor model consisting of a mental illness and a mental health latent factor provided the best fit to the data (Keyes et al., submitted). In that same study, the overall CES-D and psychological well-being scales were negatively correlated (-0.68) in the USA.

2.8 THE PROCESS OF POSITIVE PSYCHOLOGICAL ASSESSMENT

The process of positive psychological assessment is similar to "assessment as usual"; however, there are several additional steps to be taken. Many of the key aspects of positive psychological assessment, as defined by Snyder et al. (2003b), have already been provided in the preceding sections. For example, the process of positive psychological assessment begins with therapist awareness of his or her own biases and by taking the stance that all people have strengths and weaknesses as well as environmental deficits and resources that can be identified and utilized in the process of therapy.

Next, therapists observe and interview clients with a focus on understanding both the person as well as the person within his or her environmental context. Gathering data that has a complementary focus on strengths and weaknesses remains key (Snyder et al., 2003b). Most therapists have many resources for detecting weakness, for example, structured interviews, symptom checklists, various personality measures, and tests of symptoms of various psychological disorders. Similar methods can be used for identifying strengths. Indeed, there is a structured interview of character strengths, multiple measures of symptoms of well-being, and various formal tests of strengths and other aspects of positive functioning. Finally, measures of environmental deficits and resources also exist. In addition to formal means of client assessment, therapists often rely on more informal means of gathering information as well. Both the formal and informal strategies that therapists can utilize to assess client strengths and environmental resources are addressed in the following chapter on positive psychological tests and measures.

Based on the complementary data gathered, the next step of positive psychological assessment entails developing hypotheses about the client and testing those hypotheses during subsequent therapy sessions (Snyder et al., 2003b). As hypotheses are supported or refuted, a comprehensive, yet flexible conceptualization of the client is made and a balanced report of the weaknesses, strengths, environmental deficits, and resources is shared. As therapy continues, the assessment process continues as well, with new hypotheses and changes in conceptualization being made as more complementary data is gathered over time (Snyder et al., 2003b).

It is important to note that the process of assessment, be it "assessment as usual" or positive psychological assessment, must always be culturally appropriate. Indeed, one must remember that cultural and societal factors affect how people pursue and experience happiness as well as what traits, strengths, and goals are considered positive within their own contexts (Lopez et al., 2002). In other words, a single definition of happiness, well-being, or what constitutes a character strength cannot be applied to all people in the exact same way since "culture counts as a primary influence on the development and manifestation of human strengths and optimal human functioning" (Lopez et al., 2006, p. 224). Hence, in the following section, detailed information regarding conducting culturally sensitive positive psychological assessment is provided.

2.9 CULTURALLY SENSITIVE POSITIVE PSYCHOLOGICAL ASSESSMENT

> We become not a melting pot but a beautiful mosaic. Different people, different beliefs, different yearnings, different hopes, different dreams.
>
> Jimmy Carter

According to Flores and Obasi (2003), culturally sensitive positive psychological assessment is multidimensional and begins with an understanding of the meaning of positive constructs among people of diverse cultures. Based on this understanding, culturally encompassing information should be gathered utilizing culturally appropriate tests and means of assessment, followed by providing culturally appropriate interpretations of the assessment results.

2.10 CULTURALLY ENCOMPASSING DATA GATHERING

Culturally encompassing data gathering includes an examination of a client's sociocultural context, cultural identity, and worldview (Flores and Obasi, 2003). Constantine and Sue (2006) suggest that optimal human functioning can be appropriately assessed for people of diverse backgrounds by studying the cultural values, beliefs, and practices that moderate racial stress, such as collectivism, racial and ethnic pride, spirituality, religion, holistic health, and family and community importance. In addition, attending to client skills and strengths that have developed through overcoming adversity such as racism, prejudice, or oppression can also lead to important discoveries about culturally sensitive optimal human functioning (Constantine and Sue, 2006).

Sue (2003) has noted that some of the skills or strengths that may develop for clients who overcome racial or cultural adversity include heightened perceptual wisdom (i.e., the ability to correctly perceive underlying motives, intentions, and meanings of others; to see beyond the obvious or to read between the lines), the ability to rely on non-verbal or contextual meanings (i.e., the ability to accurately read communication by attending to non-verbal behavior), and bicultural flexibility (i.e., openness to multiple worldviews, sensitivity to other's viewpoints, and behavioral flexibility). Indeed, Constantine and Sue (2006) point out that since we live in a multicultural world, bicultural flexibility is a major advantage for people of color in the USA that also positively affects them on an individual level. Sue (2003) also notes that such flexibility often leads to a broadened world view, an appreciation of the strengths and weaknesses of all people, comfort with cultural differences and better effectiveness in relating to those of diverse backgrounds, an enhanced sense of self-fulfillment, and a sense of connection and commitment to better citizenship and social responsibility. Several methods for assessing cultural identities are provided in the following sections.

2.11 THE ADDRESSING MODEL OF CULTURAL ASSESSMENT

A useful tool that can be utilized to better ensure that all aspects of a client's cultural identity are considered is the ADDRESSING model by Hayes (1996, 2001). Indeed, this model was designed to help therapists conceptualize individual's identities across multiple dimensions. Worksheet 2.7 defines each letter of the ADDRESSING acronym that therapists can complete with all clients early on in the process of therapy. The ADDRESSING model can be used in a complementary manner in which both strengths and weaknesses associated with each of the ten components of cultural identity are explored. In addition, because the practice of conducting multiculturally competent counseling entails that therapists have a thorough understanding of how their own cultural background affects their belief systems and worldviews, it is recommended that clinicians complete and examine this ADDRESSING worksheet for themselves prior to engaging in cross-cultural work with clients (for more detailed information on becoming a multiculturally competent counselor, see Hayes, 2001 and Sue et al., 1992).

Worksheet 2.7 Using the ADDRESSING Framework (Hayes, 2001) to Facilitate Understanding of Client Cultural Influences

By using the ADDRESSING acronym as a guide, you can become more familiar with the multiple group memberships and cultural identities of your clients. Examination of this information can provide useful information regarding areas of client strength/resources and areas of weakness/deficits. Although you may not ask every client questions about all of the ADDRESSING categories, you are encouraged to at least consider the relevance of each dimension for each client and to follow-up on those influences and identities that appear to be highly valued by your clients (Hayes, 2001).

Definitions of ADDRESSING framework	Client information Client name:
Age and generational influences	
Disability status (developmental disability)	
Disability status (acquired physical/cognitive/psychological disabilities)	
Religion and spiritual orientation	
Ethnicity	
Socioeconomic status	
Sexual orientation	
Indigenous heritage	
National origin	
Gender	

Chart reproduced with permission of the American Psychological Association.

It is important to note that therapists must be cautious when asking questions about client identities, since "the way in which an identity-related question is asked can subtly determine the client's response" (Hayes, 2001, p. 59). Hayes (2001) suggests phrasing questions about the 10 dimensions of the ADDRESSING model as follows: (a) "How would you describe yourself?"; (b) "Would you tell me about your cultural heritage or background? (follow up with questions about ethnicity, racial identification, national origin, indigenous heritage, and primary language, as relevant)"; (c) "What was your religious upbringing? Do you have a religious or spiritual practice now?"; (d) "What was your family's economic situation growing up?"; (e) "Do you have experience with disability, or have you been a caregiver for someone who does?"; (f) "Are there ways in which your disability is a part of [your presenting problem]?"; and (g) "What did it mean to grow up as a girl (boy) in your culture and family?" (p. 60).

Hayes (2001) further suggests that therapists consider the following questions when seeking to better understand client identities: (a) "What are the ADDRESSING influences on this client?"; (b) "What are this client's salient identities related to each of these influences? What are the possible meanings of these identities in the dominant culture, in the client's culture, and from the personal perspective of the client?"; and (c) "How are my salient identities interacting with those of the client? How am I being perceived by this client, based on my visible identity? Am I knowledgeable about those groups with which this client identifies? How might my identity and related experiences, values, and beliefs limit my understanding of this client?" (p. 60).

2.12 THE COMMUNITY GENOGRAM

The community genogram is another useful tool for gathering culturally encompassing client data (Ivey and Ivey, 1999). Indeed, the goal for using such a genogram is to bring cultural issues to the forefront in the assessment process and to focus on the positive resources that come from understanding the multiple components of one's cultural experiences. Ivey and Ivey (1999) explicitly recommend that when helping clients construct community genograms, therapists should focus on stories of strength, rather than on problems. Such a focus often leads to client recollections of useful strategies they had relied upon in the past that can be implemented to help solve current issues.

The process of constructing a community genogram entails two major steps (Ivey and Ivey, 1999). First, clients should be instructed to develop a visual representation of the community in which they were primarily raised and/or the community support network that they are currently residing within. Client representations of such communities will vary from concrete pictures to more abstract or symbolic representations (see Figure 2.3 for an example of a completed community genogram). Once the community is drawn, the next step is to have clients draw themselves or a symbol of themselves within that community,

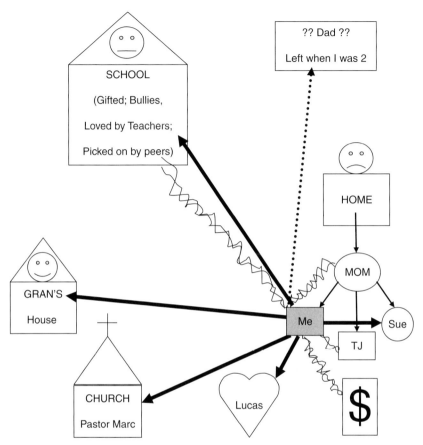

FIGURE 2.3 Example of a completed community genogram. Based on the development and discussion of this community genogram, the strengths and resources identified for this client included his high intelligence level and ability to excel in school, supportive relationships with his teachers, grandmother, sister, boyfriend, pastor and church community. Areas of weakness and destructive forces included his difficulties in relating to his peers, brother, and mother and his complete lack of information related to his estranged birth father. He identified that many of the conflictual relationships in his life centered around issues related to his sexuality and his family's low socioeconomic status, which were issues out of his control. He also identified how resilient he had been and how optimistic he remained about his future.

followed by a representation of their family members' places within that context. Then clients are instructed to place the most important or influential people or groups in their lives onto the community genogram and to connect the various individuals and groups to the client in such a way as to indicate which people are most influential (i.e., bold lines to represent stronger ties, dashed lines to represent more distant associations).

The second major step in the use of genograms includes helping the client to find images and to tell narratives of strengths based on the community representation that he or she previously developed. To find these positive resources, clients should be instructed to choose one community group or the family to focus upon. Once a focus group is chosen, clients are asked to develop and fully experience visual, auditory, or kinesthetic images that represent something positive about their connection to that community group. This step is repeated with at least two more positive images from different community groups. Therapists then engage clients in a discussion of what they learned, thought, and felt via the process of this genogram construction and reflection on positive images.

The process of constructing a community genogram is often very powerful and emotion-laden for clients. For therapists, the process typically provides a window into the unique cultural background of clients. Finally, constructing a community genogram leads to a "reservoir of positive experiences that can be drawn on to help you and the client throughout counseling" (Ivey and Ivey, 1999, p. 240). Indeed, placing the community genogram on the wall at each therapy session will further ensure that clients and therapists call upon the cultural strengths identified and remember to always consider multiple perspectives on any issue (Ivey and Ivey, 1999).

2.13 SELECTION AND INTERPRETATION OF CULTURALLY APPROPRIATE TESTS AND MEASURES

Selection of testing instruments that are culturally appropriate is achieved "when the constructs being assessed are conceptually equivalent across cultures or have the same meaning in the culture the instrument was developed and in the culture of the individual taking the test" (Flores and Obasi, 2003, p. 48). Furthermore, it is suggested that any construct under investigation be discussed with the client to ensure that the meaning of that construct is the same for the client as the definition of the construct as provided by the test developer (Flores and Obasi, 2003). In the following chapter, a variety of key positive psychology tests and measures will be discussed and considerations for using these measures with diverse populations will also be addressed.

Chapter 3

Positive Psychological Tests and Measures

Many self-report measures are available to assist practitioners in the identification of client strengths and symptoms of well-being. Most of the measures are available free of charge, are quick to administer and score, and many are available on-line. The instruments available are related to the measure of character strengths, personal talents, life satisfaction, positive emotions, positive coping, and a host of other positive psychology constructs such as gratitude, forgiveness, empathy, hope, optimism, creativity, and more. Some of the most popular measures in positive psychology are described in this section and where possible, full versions of the scales are provided. For those scales that could not be reproduced, information on where to obtain such measures is provided.

3.1 VALUES IN ACTION INVENTORY OF CHARACTER STRENGTHS

The Values in Action Inventory of Character Strengths (VIA-IS; Peterson and Seligman, 2004) is a very popular strengths measure based off the Values in Action Classification System developed by Peterson and Seligman (2004). The VIA Classification System was created in order to be an adjunct or alternative to the *DSM*. Just as the *DSM* provides useful information about psychological disorders and a common lexicon for therapists to use in describing pathology, the VIA Classification System provides important information and a common lexicon for therapists to use in describing strengths. Perusal of the *VIA Classification Handbook* reveals that in addition to defining the 24 strengths that make up the classification, the handbook also provides therapists with a host of other information such as ways to assess and apply each strength, interventions that foster the strengths, paragons or examples of the strengths, the theoretical and research underpinnings of the strengths, the known correlates and consequences of the strengths, how the strengths develop and manifest across the life span, gender differences, and cross-cultural aspects of the strengths (Peterson and Seligman, 2004).

The VIA-IS (Peterson and Seligman, 2004) can be taken for no fee on-line at www.authentichappiness.org or www.viacharacter.org. The measure takes about 30 40 minutes to complete, as it consists of 240 items that tap 24 different character strengths. (For practitioners who work with children, a youth version of the VIA for children ages 9–17 is also available at the aforementioned web-sites.) Upon completion of this measure, clients are provided with information about their top five strengths, as well as a rank order listing of all 24. Table 3.1 contains a list and definitions of the 24 strengths measured by this survey. On the VIA Institute on Character website (www.viacharacter.org), one can find useful information on the psychometric properties of the VIA measure, results from various studies that have utilized the VIA-IS, as well as tips for help-ing people to capitalize on their strengths. Additionally, the VIA Institute on Character offers an expanded, 16-page results report for a small fee. This report

---

TABLE 3.1 Definitions of the 24 strengths measured by the Values in Action Inventory of Character Strengths.

Strengths of wisdom and knowledge: cognitive strengths that entail the acquisition and use of knowledge

1. **Creativity (originality, ingenuity):** Thinking of novel and productive ways to conceptualize and do things; includes artistic achievement but is not limited to it
2. **Curiosity (interest, novelty-seeking, openness to experience):** Taking an interest in ongoing experience for its own sake; finding subjects and topics fascinating; exploring and discovering
3. **Judgement and Open-mindedness (critical thinking):** Thinking things through and examining them from all sides; not jumping to conclusions; being able to change one's mind in light of evidence; weighing all evidence fairly
4. **Love of learning:** Mastering new skills, topics, and bodies of knowledge, whether on one's own or formally; obviously related to the strength of curiosity but goes beyond it to describe the tendency to add systematically to what one knows
5. **Perspective (wisdom):** Being able to provide wise counsel to others; having ways of looking at the world that make sense to oneself and to other people

Strengths of courage: emotional strengths that involve the exercise of will to accomplish goals in the face of opposition, external or internal

6. **Bravery (valor):** Not shrinking from threat, challenge, difficulty, or pain; speaking up for what is right even if there is opposition; acting on convictions even if unpopular; includes physical bravery but is not limited to it
7. **Perseverance (persistence, industriousness):** Finishing what one starts; persisting in a course of action in spite of obstacles; "getting it out the door"; taking pleasure in completing tasks
8. **Honesty (authenticity, integrity):** Speaking the truth but more broadly presenting oneself in a genuine way and acting in a sincere way; being without pretense; taking responsibility for one's feelings and actions
9. **Zest (vitality, enthusiasm, vigor, energy):** Approaching life with excitement and energy; not doing things halfway or halfheartedly; living life as an adventure; feeling alive and activated

TABLE 3.1   (Continued)

Strengths of humanity: interpersonal strengths that involve "tending and befriending" others

10. **Capacity to Love and Be Loved:** Valuing close relations with others, in particular those in which sharing and caring are reciprocated; being close to people
11. **Kindness (generosity, nurturance, care, compassion, altruistic love, "niceness"):** Doing favors and good deeds for others; helping them; taking care of them
12. **Social intelligence (emotional intelligence, personal intelligence):** Being aware of the motives and feelings of other people and oneself; knowing what to do to fit into different social situations; knowing what makes other people tick

Justice: civic strengths that underlie healthy community life

13. **Teamwork (citizenship, social responsibility, loyalty):** Working well as a member of a group or team; being loyal to the group; doing one's share
14. **Fairness:** Treating all people the same according to notions of fairness and justice; not letting personal feelings bias decisions about others; giving everyone a fair chance
15. **Leadership:** Encouraging a group of which one is a member to get things done and at the same time maintain good relations within the group; organizing group activities and seeing that they happen

Temperance: strengths that protect against excess

16. **Forgiveness and Mercy:** Forgiving those who have done wrong; accepting the shortcomings of others; giving people a second chance; not being vengeful
17. **Modesty and Humility:** Letting one's accomplishments speak for themselves; not regarding oneself as more special than one is
18. **Prudence:** Being careful about one's choices; not taking undue risks; not saying or doing things that might later be regretted
19. **Self-regulation (self-control):** Regulating what one feels and does; being disciplined; controlling one's appetites and emotions

Transcendence: strengths that forge connections to the larger universe and provide meaning

20. **Appreciation of beauty and excellence (awe, wonder, elevation):** Noticing and appreciating beauty, excellence, and/or skilled performance in various domains of life, from nature to art to mathematics to science to everyday experience
21. **Gratitude:** Being aware of and thankful for the good things that happen; taking time to express thanks
22. **Hope (optimism, future-mindedness, future orientation):** Expecting the best in the future and working to achieve it; believing that a good future is something that can be brought about
23. **Humor (playfulness):** Liking to laugh and tease; bringing smiles to other people; seeing the light side; making (not necessarily telling) jokes
24. **Religiousness and Spirituality (faith, purpose):** Having coherent beliefs about the higher purpose and meaning of the universe; knowing where one fits within the larger scheme; having beliefs about the meaning of life that shape conduct and provide comfort

includes detailed descriptions of one's highest strengths, ideas for utilizing one's strengths, and a variety of other graphs and reports to help individuals gain a better sense of their strengths profiles. In the following chapter, ideas for incorporating client strengths in treatment planning and the power of naming and nurturing strengths will be provided.

3.1.1 Cultural Considerations of the VIA-IS

When utilizing the VIA-IS (Peterson and Seligman, 2004) with clients of diverse backgrounds, one must be sure to consider the cultural appropriateness of the survey. Although the developers of this survey report that the 24 character strengths are ubiquitous or recognized and valued by virtually all people and cultures (Peterson and Seligman, 2004), they also note that the strengths are not universal (Seligman et al., 2005). Indeed, research by others suggests that culture and individual differences must always be considered. For example, Chang (1996) has found that in comparison to Caucasians, Asian Americans tend to be more pessimistic and this pessimism serves them well, as it is related to positive problem-solving behaviors within this population and does not contribute to depression. This is important information, as it appears that pessimism, rather than optimism, is a strength in this context. The VIA-IS (Peterson and Seligman, 2004) includes only optimism as a strength, thereby leading one to conclude that pessimism is a weakness. While pessimism may be a weakness for some, it clearly is not the case for all.

Similarly, Norem and Cantor (1986) have researched a type of pessimism, called defensive pessimism, that works very well for some people. More specifically, defensive pessimism occurs when people set their expectations low as they think through possible future outcomes (Norem and Cantor, 1986; Norem and Illingworth, 1993). They set these low expectations in order to prepare themselves for potential failure while at the same time motivating themselves to try to avoid that failure. People who are defensive pessimists initially feel anxious and out of control when faced with future challenges, even though they have previously performed well on such tasks (Norem and Cantor, 1986). Indeed, Norem and Cantor (1986) report that many straight-A students are actually defensive pessimists. They worry that they are going to fail, and then not surprisingly, they get the highest grade in the class. Defensive pessimism is a way for such individuals who feel anxious and out of control to regain control and to find motivation to prepare themselves to possibly avoid failure. It is as if they are thinking that if they are going to fail anyway, then what is there to be so nervous about, which serves to reduce the anxiety, while at the same time working to further reduce their anxiety by finding a strategy to avoid the failure that they perceive as right around the corner. Indeed, according to Norem and Illingworth (1993), "typical thoughts of defensive pessimists include 'thinking about how unprepared I am in order to get myself to work harder,' 'thinking about the exam,' 'thinking about what will happen if I fail,' as well as frequent expressions of anxiety, low expectations, and alternative outcomes" (p. 823).

For defensive pessimists, being optimistic can actually be detrimental (Norem and Cantor 1986a,b). Contrary to logic, the low expectations of defensive pessimists do not become self-fulfilling prophecies and in fact, when guiding defensive pessimists to think more like optimists, their performance declines (Norem and Illingworth, 1993; Rich and Dahlheimer, 1989).

Finally, the results of the VIA-IS (Peterson and Seligman, 2004) must always be considered within the context of the client's life. For example, a client who is struggling in school because he is spending more time making jokes and teasing his classmates than he is paying attention to his teacher may have humor and playfulness come up as a top strength on the VIA-IS. However, in this context, humor and playfulness are not serving him well and therefore not working as a strength for him. Similarly, consider a client who has tons of potential and a strong desire to become a physician but decides not to apply to medical school because she sees it as too risky since there is no guarantee that she will be accepted. This client takes the VIA-IS (Peterson and Seligman, 2004) and caution and prudence comes up as her top strength. In this situation, it appears that this strength is not serving her well.

While the VIA-IS (Peterson and Seligman, 2004) is a useful tool for assessing character strengths, like all psychological assessment measures, it should never be taken at face value. The measure should always be interpreted within the broader context of the lives of the clients who complete the measure.

3.1.2 Psychometric Properties of the VIA-IS

The VIA-IS is reported to have adequate internal consistency reliability, with alphas greater than 0.70 being reported for all scales. Test–retest reliability has been established as evidenced by correlations of 0.70 or higher over four-month testing intervals. Many of the subscales have been found to have convergent validity with similar measures, for example, the strengths of appreciation of beauty, curiosity, and love of learning correlate positively ($r = 0.65$, 0.73, and 0.58, respectively) with the construct of openness as measured by the NEO Personality Inventory (Costa and McCrae, 1982). Likewise, the strength of teamwork correlates positively with agreeableness ($r = 0.42$), and perseverance and self-regulation strengths correlate positively ($r = 0.73$ and 0.55, respectively) with conscientiousness (Peterson and Park, 2004).

3.2 CLIFTON STRENGTHSFINDER

The Clifton StrengthsFinder 2.0 (CSF 2.0; Asplund et al., 2007; Rath, 2007) is a measure of personal talents, originally developed by Donald Clifton of the Gallup Organization. The measure was developed based upon empirically sound, semistructured interviews. Through the interview data, the 34 talent themes found in Table 3.2 were identified. The personal talents identified on the CSF 2.0 (Asplund et al., 2007; Rath, 2007) can be developed and utilized to increase success and

TABLE 3.2 Definitions of the 34 talent themes measured by the Clifton StrengthsFinder 2.0 (CSF 2.0; Asplund et al., 2007; Rath, 2007).

Achiever: People strong in the achiever theme have a great deal of stamina and work hard. They take great satisfaction from being busy and productive.

Activator: People strong in the activator theme can make things happen by turning thoughts into action. They are often impatient.

Adaptability: People strong in the adaptability theme prefer to "go with the flow." They tend to be "now" people who take things as they come and discover the future one day at a time.

Analytical: People strong in the analytical theme search for reasons and causes. They have the ability to think about all the factors that might affect a situation.

Arranger: People strong in the arranger theme can organize, but they also have a flexibility that complements that ability. They like to figure out how all of the pieces and resources can be arranged for maximum productivity.

Belief: People strong in the belief theme have certain core values that are unchanging. Out of those values emerges a defined purpose for their life.

Command: People strong in the command theme have presence. They can take control of a situation and make decisions.

Communication: People strong in the communication theme generally find it easy to put their thoughts into words. They are good conversationalists and presenters.

Competition: People strong in the competition theme measure their progress against the performance of others. They strive to win first place and revel in contests.

Connectedness: People strong in the connectedness theme have faith in links between all things. They believe there are few coincidences and that almost every event has a reason.

Consistency: People strong in the consistency theme are keenly aware of the need to treat people the same. They try to treat everyone in the world with consistency by setting up clear rules and adhering to them.

Context: People strong in the context theme enjoy thinking about the past. They understand the present by researching its history.

Deliberative: People strong in the deliberative theme are best characterized by the serious care they take in making decisions or choices. They anticipate the obstacles.

Developer: People strong in the developer theme recognize and cultivate the potential in others. They spot the signs of each small improvement and derive satisfaction from those improvements.

Discipline: People strong in the discipline theme enjoy routine and structure. Their world is best described by the order they create.

Empathy: People strong in the empathy theme can sense the feelings of other people by imagining themselves in others' lives and in others' situations.

Focus: People strong in the focus theme can take a direction, follow through, and make the corrections necessary to stay on track.

Futuristic: People strong in the futuristic theme are inspired by the future and what could be. They inspire others with their vision of the future.

Harmony: People strong in the harmony theme look for consensus. They don't enjoy conflict; rather, they seek areas of agreement.

TABLE 3.2 (Continued)

Ideation: People strong in the ideation theme are fascinated by ideas. They are able to find connections between seemingly disparate phenomena.

Includer: People strong in the includer theme are accepting of others. They show awareness of those who feel left out and make efforts to include them.

Individualization: People strong in the individualization theme are intrigued with the unique qualities of each person. They have a gift for figuring out how people who are different can work together productively.

Intellection: People strong in the intellection theme are characterized by their intellectual activity. They are introspective and appreciate intellectual discussions.

Input: People strong in the input theme have a craving to know more. Often they like to collect and archive all kinds of information.

Learner: People strong in the learner theme have a great desire to learn and want to improve continuously.

Maximizer: People strong in the maximizer theme focus on strengths as a way to stimulate professional and group excellence. They seek to transform strong into something superb.

Positivity: People strong in the positivity theme have an enthusiasm that is contagious. They are upbeat and can get others excited about what they are going to do.

Relator: People strong in the relator theme enjoy close relationships with others. They find deep satisfaction in working hard with friends to achieve a goal.

Responsibility: People strong in the responsibility theme take psychological ownership of what they say they will do. They are committed to stable values such as honesty and loyalty.

Restorative: People strong in the restorative theme are adept at dealing with problems. They are good at figuring out what is wrong and resolving it.

Self-assurance: People strong in the self-assurance theme feel confident in their ability to manage their own lives. They possess an inner compass that gives them confidence that their decisions are right.

Significance: People strong in the significance theme want to be very important in the eyes of others. They are independent and want to be recognized.

Strategic: People strong in the strategic theme create alternative ways to proceed. Faced with any given scenario, they can quickly spot the relevant patterns and issues.

Woo: Woo stands for "winning others over." People strong in the woo theme love the challenge of meeting new people and winning them over. They derive satisfaction from breaking the ice and making a connection with another person.

satisfaction in a number of life roles, including academia and work (Buckingham and Clifton, 2000; Clifton and Anderson, 2002; Clifton and Nelson, 1992).

The CSF 2.0 (Asplund et al., 2007; Rath, 2007) is available on-line at www. strengthsfinder.com. A code is required to access the measure; such access codes are included in the purchase of StrengthsFinder 2.0 (Rath, 2007), a resource book to accompany the CSF 2.0 measure. This text is highly useful for helping clients to develop ways to implement their talents in their daily lives. The CSF 2.0 (Asplund et al., 2007; Rath, 2007) consists of 178 items, takes about 30 45 minutes to complete, and is appropriate for use with adolescents and adults with reading levels of 10th grade or higher. The measure is also available in 17 languages (Asplund et al., 2007; Rath, 2007). For those who work with children, the StrengthsExplorer measure, appropriate for use with youth ages 10–14, can be found at www.strengthsexplorer.com. The ten talent themes measured by the StrengthsExplorer are defined in Table 3.3. Finally, for those working with college students who are primarily focused upon applying strengths in academia and beyond, the StrengthsQuest measure is recommended and can be found at www.strengthsquest.com.

Upon completion of the CSF 2.0 (Asplund et al., 2007; Rath, 2007), clients receive a report on their top five talent themes, 10 ideas for putting each of their top five talent themes into action, and a "strength-based action plan" for designing and implementing short and long-term goals for utilizing talents and building strengths at home and work. Additionally, a host of other resources related to the CSF 2.0 measure are available on-line to those who complete the measure. Ideas for implementing the results of the CSF 2.0 in treatment planning will be discussed in the next chapter.

TABLE 3.3   The 10 talent themes of the Clifton Youth StrengthsExplorer.

Achieving: Youths especially talented in the achieving theme like to accomplish things and have a great deal of energy.

Caring: Youths especially talented in the caring theme enjoy helping others.

Competing: Youths especially talented in the competing theme enjoy measuring their performance against that of others and have a great desire to win.

Confidence: Youths especially talented in the confidence theme believe in themselves and their ability to be successful in their endeavors.

Dependability: Youths especially talented in the dependability theme keep their promises and show a high level of responsibility.

Discoverer: Youths especially talented in the discoverer theme tend to be very curious and like to ask "Why?" and "How?"

Future thinker: Youths especially talented in the future thinker theme tend to think about what's possible beyond the present time, even beyond their lifetime.

Organizer: Youths especially talented in the organizer theme are good at scheduling, planning, and organizing.

Presence: Youths especially talented in the presence theme like to tell stories and be at the center of attention.

Relating: Youths especially talented in the relating theme are good at establishing meaningful friendships and maintaining them.

3.2.1 Psychometric Properties of the CSF 2.0

Internal consistency reliabilities for the CSF are reported at alphas ranging from 0.50 to 0.76 (Asplund et al., 2007). Test–retest reliabilities of 0.52–0.84 over 8–12 week time intervals have also been reported (Schreiner, 2006).

Concurrent validity has been found between the talent themes measured by the CSF and a variety of similar constructs as measured by various well-validated personality instruments (Schreiner, 2006). For example, the Discipline theme, as measured by the CSF, correlates positively ($r = 0.81$) with the conscientiousness subscale of the NEO – Personality Inventory. Likewise, the Woo theme correlates with extroversion ($r = 0.83$), and the Positivity theme correlates with Agreeableness ($r = 0.58$) as measured by the NEO – Personality Inventory (Asplund et al., 2007).

3.3 POSITIVE AND NEGATIVE AFFECT SCHEDULE

The Positive and Negative Affect Schedule (PANAS; Watson et al., 1988) is a useful tool for therapists who are interested in tracking changes in positive and negative emotions for clients from week to week as they engage in day-to-day life. The PANAS (Watson et al., 1988) can also be used to chart the immediate effects of therapy sessions as well as outcomes associated with positive psychological interventions, exercises, or activities. The measure consists of 20 items (10 which measure positive affect and 10 that measure negative affect) and takes less than 5 minutes to complete. The scale is sensitive to momentary changes in affect when clients are directed to complete the form based on their affect *at the present time* and can also be used as a more global measure of affect when clients are directed to complete the form based on their affect *over the course of the past week*. Worksheet 3.1 contains the 20 items that make up the PANAS inventory as well as scoring instructions. The Positive and Negative Affect Schedule for Children (PANAS-C; Larent et al., 1999) is available for use by therapists who work with school-age children.

Worksheet 3.1   The Positive and Negative Affect Schedule (PANAS; Watson et al., 1988)

PANAS Questionnaire

This scale consists of a number of words that describe different feelings and emotions. Read each item and then list the number from the scale below next to each word. **Indicate to what extent you feel this way right now, that is, at the present moment *OR* indicate the extent you have felt this way over the past week (circle the instructions you followed when taking this measure)**

1	2	3	4	5
Very Slightly or Not at All	A Little	Moderately	Quite a Bit	Extremely

_____ 1. Interested   _____ 11. Irritable

_____ 2. Distressed   _____ 12. Alert

_____ 3. Excited   _____ 13. Ashamed

_____ 4. Upset   _____ 14. Inspired

_____ 5. Strong   _____ 15. Nervous

_____ 6. Guilty   _____ 16. Determined

_____ 7. Scared   _____ 17. Attentive

_____ 8. Hostile   _____ 18. Jittery

_____ 9. Enthusiastic   _____ 19. Active

_____ 10. Proud   _____ 20. Afraid

Scoring Instructions:

Positive Affect Score: Add the scores on items 1, 3, 5, 9, 10, 12, 14, 16, 17, and 19. Scores can range from 10 – 50, with higher scores representing higher levels of positive affect. Mean Scores: Momentary = 29.7 (*SD* = 7.9); Weekly = 33.3 (*SD* = 7.2)

Negative Affect Score: Add the scores on items 2, 4, 6, 7, 8, 11, 13, 15, 18, and 20. Scores can range from 10 – 50, with lower scores representing lower levels of negative affect. Mean Score: Momentary = 14.8 (*SD* = 5.4); Weekly = 17.4 (*SD* = 6.2)

3.3.1 Psychometric Properties of the PANAS

The PANAS has been reported to have very good internal consistency reliability, with alphas ranging from 0.86 to 0.90 for Positive Affect and from 0.84 to 0.87 for Negative Affect. This level of internal consistency reliability is found regardless of the time instructions used when administering the measure. Test–retest reliability is good over an 8-week time period, with correlations of 0.54 for momentary Positive Affect, 0.45 for momentary Negative Affect, 0.47 for Positive Affect over the past week, and 0.47 for Negative Affect over the past week. As expected, test–retest reliability was found to be higher as the rated time frame lengthened, hence, when used with short-term instructions (i.e., right now or over the past week), the PANAS is sensitive to fluctuations in mood.

Convergent validity has been found between the Positive Affect subscale of the PANAS and measures of social activity and diurnal variation in mood, while discriminant validity was found between the Positive Affect subscale and measures of stress, aversive events, general distress and dysfunction, and depression. The opposite was true for the Negative Affect subscales, with convergent validity being established between Negative Affect and measures of stress, aversive events, depression, and general distress and dysfunction, and discriminant validity with measures of social activity and diurnal variation in mood (Watson et al., 1988).

3.4 SATISFACTION WITH LIFE SCALE

The Satisfaction with Life Scale (Diener et al., 1985) can be utilized in therapy to better understand general levels of client life satisfaction as they cognitively (versus emotionally) reflect on their experiences in the world thus far. Emotional well-being is often defined as the combination of positive affect (in the absence of negative affect) and general satisfaction with life (appreciation of life's rewards; Bryant and Veroff, 1982; Lucas et al., 1996; Shmotkin, 1998). Hence, by combining the use of the PANAS (Watson et al., 1988) and the Satisfaction with Life Scale (Diener et al., 1985), therapists can get an idea of where a client stands in terms of an overall level of emotional well-being. The Satisfaction with Life Scale (Diener et al., 1985) can also be used within therapy to explore the strengths and resources the client possesses that have contributed to areas of satisfaction while also exploring what may be getting in the way of complete satisfaction. The information from such discussions can be used in treatment and long-term goal planning. The five-item Satisfaction with Life Scale (Diener et al., 1985) is provided in Worksheet 3.2.

Worksheet 3.2   Satisfaction with Life Scale (Diener et al., 1985)

Below are five statements that you may agree or disagree with. Using the 1–7 scale below, indicate your agreement with each item by placing the appropriate number on the line preceeding that item.

1	2	3	4	5	6	7
Strongly disagree	Moderately disagree	Slightly disagree	Neither agree nor disagree	Slightly agree	Moderately agree	Strongly agree

_____1. In most ways, my life is close to my ideal.

_____2. The conditions of my life are excellent.

_____3. I am completely satisfied with my life.

_____4. So far, I have gotten the important things I want in my life.

_____5. If I could live my life over, I would change nothing.

Scoring instructions
Total up the scores on all five items. Scores can range from a low of 5 to a high of 35. Higher scores indicate higher levels of life satisfaction. Scores can be interpreted according to the following rubric:

30–35	Extremely satisfied; much above average
25–29	Very satisfied, above average
20–24	Somewhat satisfied; average for American adults
15–19	Slightly dissatisfied, a bit below average
10–14	Dissatisfied, clearly below average
5–9	Very dissatisfied, much below average

3.4.1 Psychometric Properties of the Satisfaction with Life Scale

The Satisfaction with Life Scale is reported to have very good internal consistency, with an alpha of 0.87 and excellent test–retest reliability, with a correlation of 0.82 across a two-month time period. Concurrent validity has been established for this measure as well, with scores on the Satisfaction with Life Scale correlating positively with scores on nine other measures of well-being and a self-esteem inventory. Negative correlations were also found between the Satisfaction with Life Scale and measures of neuroticism, emotionality, and a checklist of clinical symptoms (Diener et al., 1985).

3.5 FORDYCE EMOTIONS QUESTIONNAIRE

The Fordyce Emotions Questionnaire (Fordyce, 1988) is a very brief measure of current happiness. Research supports that this questionnaire is a valid measure of emotional well-being and global health. The Fordyce Emotions Questionnaire can be used to understand client baseline mood levels and to track changes in client happiness over time. A potential downfall of this measure is the general nature of it. Some clients will likely find it hard to answer the items in a general sense. If this is the case, a discussion of how the client's answers would differ based on different life domains can provide additional useful information for therapists as they engage in client conceptualization and treatment planning. Worksheet 3.3 contains the items and scoring directions for the Fordyce Emotions Questionnaire.

Worksheet 3.3 The Fordyce Emotions Questionnaire (Fordyce, 1988)

In general, how happy or unhappy do you usually feel? Circle the number from the scale below that best describes your average happiness:

0= Extremely unhappy (utterly depressed, completely down)

1= Very unhappy (depressed, spirits very low)

2= Pretty unhappy (somewhat "blue", spirits down)

3= Mildly unhappy (just a bit low)

4= Slightly unhappy (just a bit below neutral)

5= Neutral (not particularly happy or unhappy)

6= Slightly happy (just a bit above neutral)

7= Mildly happy (feeling fairly good and somewhat cheerful)

8= Pretty happy (spirits high, feeling good)

9= Very happy (feeling really good, elated!)

10= Extremely happy (feeling ecstatic, joyous, fantastic!)

Consider your emotions a moment further. On the average, what percent of the time do you feel happy? What percent of the time do you feel unhappy? What percent of the time do you feel neutral (neither happy nor unhappy)? Write the percentage of time that you feel happy, unhappy, and neutral below. **Make sure that the three numbers add up to 100%.**

On average:

The percent of the time I feel happy=   _____%

The percent of the time I feel unhappy=   _____%

The percent of the time I feel neutral=   _____%

Scoring information

Scores range from 0 to 10 with higher scores indicating greater levels of happiness. The average score for American adults is 6.92 ($SD = 1.75$). The average score on time happy is 54.13% ($SD = 21.52$); unhappy is 20.44% ($SD = 14.69$); and neutral is 25.43% ($SD = 16.52$).

Scale reproduced with permission of the author.

3.5.1 Psychometric Properties of the Fordyce Emotions Questionnaire

The Fordyce Emotions Questionnaire has been demonstrated to have good reliability in a multitude of studies. For example, test–retest coefficients have been found to be as high as 0.98 over a two-day period, 0.86 to 0.88 over a two-week period, 0.81 over a one-month time interval, and between 0.62 and 0.67 over a four-month interval (Fordyce, 1987). Convergent validity has also been established with very strong, positive correlations being found between the Fordyce Emotions Questionnaire and a multitude of measures of happiness and well-being. Likewise, strong, negative correlations have been found for the Fordyce Emotions Questionnaire and measures of depression and negative affect (Fordyce, 1988).

3.6 STEEN HAPPINESS INDEX/AUTHENTIC HAPPINESS INVENTORY

The Steen Happiness Index (SHI; Seligman et al., 2005) was developed to "capture week-by-week upward changes in happiness" (p. 414). The measure was designed to be an opposite to the Beck Depression Inventory (BDI; Beck et al., 1961) in that it is meant to be sensitive to changes in levels of happiness. More specifically, the SHI (Seligman et al., 2005) evaluates changes in happiness based on how one experiences positive emotions, engagement, and a sense of meaning in life. Therapists who are interested in measuring potential increases in client happiness levels over time or upon completion of positive psychology exercises and interventions may find this measure useful. It is important to note, however, that the scale is still under development and therefore complete validity and reliability data is unavailable. The original SHI (Seligman et al., 2005) consisted of 20 items that included five statements from which respondents must choose in order to describe themselves in the present. A sample item from this measure is as follows (Seligman et al., 2005):

A. Most of the time I am bored (1)
B. Most of the time I am neither bored nor interested in what I am doing (2)
C. Most of the time I am interested in what I am doing (3)
D. Most of the time I am quite interested in what I am doing (4)
E. Most of the time I am fascinated by what I am doing (5)

The SHI (Seligman et al., 2005) currently appears to be referred to as the Authentic Happiness Inventory and has changed from a 20-item to a 24-item inventory. The Authentic Happiness Inventory can be accessed for no fee on-line at www.authentichappiness.org.

3.7 HOPE SCALE

Hope, according to Snyder (1994), is a cognitive model comprising three components: goals, agency, and pathways. Goals are considered the targets or end-points of mental action sequences, and as such form the anchor of hope theory (Snyder et al., 2000). Pathways, which are the routes toward desired goals, are necessary to attain goals and navigate around obstacles. Finally, agency is considered the determination and energy necessary to begin and sustain movement toward goals (Snyder et al., 2000). Use of the Adult Trait Hope Scale (Snyder et al., 1991) in a therapeutic context can result in a better understanding of the strengths and weaknesses clients possess related to setting and attaining goals in life. The Adult State Hope Scale (Snyder et al., 1996) can be used to measure the goal-directed thinking of clients at a given moment in time. This scale consists of 6 items that can be completed in less than five minutes and scored in a minute or less. The Domain Specific Hope Scale (Sympson, 1999) can be used to understand client abilities and deficits related to goal setting in specific contexts such as school, work, and leisure, as well as social, romantic, and family relationships. Finally, a children's version, a young children's version, and a Spanish language version of the Hope Scale are also available (see Lopez et al., 2000). Worksheets 3.4, 3.5, and 3.6 contain the Adult Trait Hope, Adult State Hope, and the Adult Domain Specific Hope Scales and scoring information.

Worksheet 3.4 The Adult Trait Hope Scale (Snyder et al., 1991)

Directions: Read each item carefully. Using the scale shown below, please circle the number next to each item that best describes YOU.

1	2	3	4	5	6	7	8
Definitely False	Mostly False	Somewhat False	Slightly False	Slightly True	Somewhat True	Mostly True	Definitely True

1 2 3 4 5 6 7 8	1. I can think of many ways to get out of a jam
1 2 3 4 5 6 7 8	2. I energetically pursue my goals
1 2 3 4 5 6 7 8	3. I feel tired most of the time
1 2 3 4 5 6 7 8	4. There are lots of ways around any problem
1 2 3 4 5 6 7 8	5. I am easily downed in an argument
1 2 3 4 5 6 7 8	6. I can think of many ways to get the things in life that are most important to me
1 2 3 4 5 6 7 8	7. I worry about my health
1 2 3 4 5 6 7 8	8. Even when others get discouraged, I know I can find a way to solve the problem
1 2 3 4 5 6 7 8	9. My past experiences have prepared me for my future
1 2 3 4 5 6 7 8	10. I've been pretty successful in life
1 2 3 4 5 6 7 8	11. I usually find myself worrying about something
1 2 3 4 5 6 7 8	12. I meet the goals that I set for myself

Scoring information

Pathways subscale score: Add items 1, 4, 6, and 8. Scores on this subscale can range from 4 to 32, with higher scores indicating higher levels of pathways thinking.

Agency subscale score: Add items 2, 9, 10, and 12. Scores on this subscale can range from 4 to 32, with higher scores indicating higher levels of agency thinking.

Total hope score: Add the pathways and Agency subscales together. Scores can range from 8 to 64, with higher scores representing higher hope levels.

Worksheet 3.5   The Adult State Hope Scale (Snyder et al., 1996)

Read each item carefully. Using the scale shown below, please select the number that best describes *how you think about yourself right now* and put that number in the blank before each sentence. Please take a few moments to focus on yourself and what is going on in *your life at this moment.* Once you have this "here and now" set, go ahead and answer each item according to the following scale:

1	2	3	4	5	6	7	8
Definitely False	Mostly False	Somewhat False	Slightly False	Slightly True	Somewhat True	Mostly True	Definitely True

_____ 1. If I should find myself in a jam, I could think of many ways to get out of it

_____ 2. At the present time, I am energetically pursuing my goals

_____ 3. There are lots of ways around any problem that I am facing now

_____ 4. Right now, I see myself as being pretty successful

_____ 5. I can think of many ways to reach my current goals

_____ 6. At this time, I am meeting the goals that I have set for myself

Scoring information

Pathways subscale score: Add items 1, 3, and 5. Scores on this subscale can range from 3 to 24, with higher scores indicating higher levels of pathways thinking.

Agency subscale score: Add items 2, 4, and 6. Scores on this subscale can range from 3 to 24, with higher scores indicating higher levels of agency thinking.

Total hope score: Add the pathways and Agency subscales together. Scores can range from 6 to 48, with higher scores representing higher hope levels.

Worksheet 3.6   The Domain Specific Hope Scale (Sympson, 1999)

Please take a moment to contemplate each of the following life areas before you answer the questions in each section. If a particular question does not apply to you at this time, try to answer it as you would if they did fit your situation (e.g., you don't have a job right now so think of your last job). Using the scale below, select the number that best describes your response to each question.

1	2	3	4	5	6	7	8
Definitely False	Mostly False	Somewhat False	Slightly False	Slightly True	Somewhat True	Mostly True	Definitely True

Please take a moment to contemplate your social life. Think about your friendships and acquaintances and how you interact with others. Once you have this in mind, answer the following questions using the scale above.

Social relationships (friendships, casual acquaintances)

_____ 1. I can think of many ways to make friends

_____ 2. I actively pursue friendships

_____ 3. There are lots of ways to meet new people

_____ 4. I can think of many ways to be included in the groups that are important to me

_____ 5. I've been pretty successful where friendships are concerned

_____ 6. Even when someone seems unapproachable, I know I can find a way to break the ice

_____ 7. My past social experiences have prepared me to make friends in the future

_____ 8. When I meet someone I want to be friends with, I usually succeed

Academics (school, coursework)

1	2	3	4	5	6	7	8
Definitely False	Mostly False	Somewhat False	Slightly False	Slightly True	Somewhat True	Mostly True	Definitely True

Please take a moment to contemplate your academic life. Think about your classes and your coursework. Once you have this in mind, answer the following questions using the scale above.

_____ 1. I can think of lots of ways to make good grades

_____ 2. I energetically pursue my school work

_____ 3. There are lots of ways to meet the challenges of any class

_____ 4. Even if the course is difficult, I know I can find a way to succeed

_____ 5. I've been pretty successful in school

_____ 6. I can think of lots of ways to do well in classes that are important to me

_____ 7. My past academic experiences have prepared me well for future success

_____ 8. I get the grades that I want in my classes

_____ 9. If you read this question, place an X on the line

Romantic relationships

Please take a moment to contemplate your love life. Think about your romantic relationships. Once you have this in mind, answer the following questions using the scale above.

_____ 1. I can think of many ways to get to know someone I am attracted to

_____ 2. When I am interested in someone romantically, I actively pursue him or her

_____ 3. There are lots of ways to convince someone to go out with me

_____ 4. I can think of many ways to keep someone interested in me when they are important

_____ 5. I've been pretty successful in my romantic relationships

_____ 6. Even when someone doesn't seem interested, I know I can find a way to get their attention

_____ 7. My past romantic relationships have prepared me well for future involvements

_____ 8. I can usually get a date when I set my mind to it

Family life

1	2	3	4	5	6	7	8
Definitely False	Mostly False	Somewhat False	Slightly False	Slightly True	Somewhat True	Mostly True	Definitely True

Please take a moment to contemplate your family life. Think about your family members. Once you have this in mind, answer the following questions using the scale above.

_____ 1. I can think of lots of things I enjoy doing with my family

_____ 2. I energetically work on maintaining family relationships

_____ 3. I can think of many ways to include my family in things that are important to me

_____ 4. If you read this question, place an X on the line

_____ 5. I have a pretty successful family life

_____ 6. Even when we disagree, I know my family can find a way to solve our problems

_____ 7. I have the kind of relationships that I want with family members

_____ 8. There are lots of ways to communicate my feelings to family members

_____ 9. My experiences with my family have prepared me for a family of my own

Work

Please take a moment to contemplate your working life. Think about your job and job history. Once you have this in mind, answer the following questions using the scale above.

_____ 1. I can think of many ways to find a job

_____ 2. I am energetic at work

_____ 3. There are lots of ways to succeed at work

_____ 4. Even if it's a lousy job, I can usually find something good about it

_____ 5. I have a good work record

_____ 6. My previous work experiences have helped prepare me for future success

_____ 7. I can always find a job if I set my mind to it

_____ 8. I can think of lots of ways to impress my boss if the job is important to me.

Leisure activities

1	2	3	4	5	6	7	8
Definitely False	Mostly False	Somewhat False	Slightly False	Slightly True	Somewhat True	Mostly True	Definitely True

Please take a moment to contemplate your leisure time. Think about the activities that you enjoy doing in your spare time. For some this may be sports or music or art. Once you have this in mind, answer the following questions using the scale above.

_____ 1. I can think of many satisfying things to do in my spare time

_____ 2. I energetically pursue my leisure time activities

_____ 3. If my planned leisure time activities fall through, I can find something else to do that I enjoy

_____ 4. I can think of lots of ways to make time for the activities that are important to me

_____ 5. Even if others don't think my activities are important, I still enjoy doing them

_____ 6. My experiences with hobbies and other leisure time activities are important to my future

_____ 7. I have satisfying activities that I do in my leisure time

_____ 8. When I try to perform well in leisure time activities, I usually succeed

Scoring information

Domain specific hope scores are obtained by summing the eight items within each domain. Scores can range from 8 to 64, with higher scores indicating higher levels of hope within each domain.

Total domain specific hope can be tallied by adding the scores from each of the 6 domains. Scores can range from 48 to 384, with higher scores indicating higher levels of total hope across domains.

Scale reproduced with permission of the author.

3.7.1 Psychometric Properties for the Adult Trait Hope Scale

According to norms reported by Snyder and colleagues (1991), average scores on the Adult Trait Hope Scale for college and noncollege samples of adults are approximately 48, with significantly lower Hope Scale scores for individuals who are inpatients at psychiatric hospitals or those who are seeking psychological treatment (Snyder, 1995). Hope scores of women and men were virtually the same across the samples used to develop norms.

Studies reported by Snyder et al. (1991) attest to the acceptable psychometric properties of the Adult Trait Hope Scale. For the total scale, internal consistency alphas range from 0.74 to 0.84. The four pathway items have been shown to correlate highly with one another, as do the four agency items, and factor analytic techniques have confirmed the theoretical model of the two factors (Babyak et al., 1993). Test–retest reliability, which was measured in four samples, was reported at 0.85 over a 3-week interval, 0.73 over an 8-week interval, and 0.76 and 0.82 over 10-week intervals.

Concurrent validity has been established between the Adult Trait Hope Scale and measures of optimism, expectancy for attaining goals, and self esteem ($r = 0.50$–0.60). Discriminant validity has been reported between the Adult Trait Hope Scale and measures of hopelessness ($r = -0.51$) and depression ($r = -0.42$; Snyder et al., 1991).

3.7.2 Psychometric Properties for the Adult State Hope Scale

The Adult State Hope Scale has adequate internal consistency reliability, with alphas between 0.79 and 0.95 being reported for total hope, alphas of 0.76–0.95 for the agency subscale, and alphas from 0.59 to 0.93 for the pathways subscale (Snyder et al., 1996). Because of the different situations in which the State Hope Scale is used as a measure, test–retest data is expected to vary. Indeed, in a study that lasted four weeks, test–retest correlations ranged from 0.48 to 0.93 on any two days measured throughout the study (e.g., days 1 and 30 or days 29 and 30; Snyder et al., 1996).

Concurrent validity has been established between the Adult State Hope Scale and a state self-esteem inventory ($r = 0.45$–0.75) and with the Positive Affect subscale of the momentary PANAS ($r = 0.48$–0.65). Discriminant validity was established between the Adult Sate Hope Scale and the Negative Affect subscale of the momentary PANAS ($r = -0.37$ to -0.50; Snyder et al., 1996).

3.7.3 Psychometric Properties of the Domain Specific Hope Scale

The mean total score for college-age adults on the Domain Specific Hope Scale is 302.88 ($SD = 36.03$). Average scores on each of the specific domains are as follows: 50.20 ($SD = 9.04$) for social hope; 49.38 ($SD = 9.24$) for academic hope; 52.32 ($SD = 10.12$) for family hope; 53.67 ($SD = 8.25$) for work hope; and 53.66 ($SD = 7.09$) for leisure hope (Sympson, 1999).

The Domain Specific Hope Scale has been found to have sufficient internal consistency reliability, with an overall alpha of 0.93, and alphas ranging from 0.86 to 0.93 for the domain subscales. Concurrent validity was established between the Domain Specific Hope Scale and a wide variety of measures of similar constructs. For example, the Family subscale of the Domain Specific Hope Scale correlated positively with scales of perceived social support from family ($r = 0.64$) and friends ($r = 0.46$). Similar findings were established for each of the other domains measured on this scale. Likewise, discriminant validity was established between the various domains of the Domain Specific Hope Scale and measures of loneliness and other conceptually opposite constructs. Finally, Domain Specific Total Hope scores were negatively correlated ($r = -0.45$) with scores on the Beck Depression Inventory (Sympson, 1999).

3.8 PERSONAL GROWTH INITIATIVE SCALE

Personal growth initiative, as operationalized by Robitschek (1998), is active, intentional engagement in changing and developing as a person, which is made up of both cognitive and behavioral components and an overall orientation toward change, and it may embody that potent client factor that leads to change. The behavioral components consist of seeking out opportunities to grow and then capitalizing on those opportunities that arise (Robitschek, 2001). Indeed, Robitschek (2001) reports that "the salient aspect of personal growth initiative is the intentionality of engaging in the change process, rather than mere awareness that the change process is occurring" (p. 7). Robitschek and Kashubeck (1999) found a strong negative relationship between personal growth initiative and psychological distress and a strong positive relationship between personal growth initiative and psychological well-being. The 9-item Personal Growth Initiative Scale (PGIS; Robitschek, 1998) and scoring instructions are contained in Worksheet 3.7.

Worksheet 3.7   The Personal Growth Initiative Scale (Robitschek, 1998)

Using the scale below, circle the number which best describes the extent to which you agree or disagree with each statement.

1	2	3	4	5	6
Definitely disagree	Mostly disagree	Somewhat disagree	Somewhat agree	Mostly agree	Definitely agree

1. I know how to change specific things that I want to change in my life
   1 2 3 4 5 6

2. I have a good sense of where I am headed in my life   1 2 3 4 5 6

3. If I want to change something in my life, I initiate the transition process
   1 2 3 4 5 6

4. I can choose the role that I want to have in a group   1 2 3 4 5 6

5. I know what I need to do to get started toward reaching my goals
   1 2 3 4 5 6

6. I have a specific action plan to help me reach my goals   1 2 3 4 5 6

7. I take charge of my life   1 2 3 4 5 6

8. I know what my unique contribution to the world might be   1 2 3 4 5 6

9. I have a plan for making my life more balanced   1 2 3 4 5 6

Scoring information
Personal Growth Initiative can be determined by summing the scores on all 9 items. Scores can range from 9 to 54, with higher scores indicating greater levels of intentional self-change.

Scale reproduced with permission of the author.

3.8.1 Psychometric Properties of the Personal Growth Initiative Scale

Validation studies of the PGIS yielded internal consistency estimates ranging from 0.78 to 0.90 in college students and adults. Test–retest reliability estimates were 0.84 for one week, 0.73 for four weeks, and 0.74 for eight weeks (Robitschek, 1998, 1999). Construct validity was supported by factor analysis which confirmed a single factor for the PGIS. Support for convergent and discriminant validity of the PGIS also exists, with PGIS scores being positively related with assertiveness, instrumentality and an internal locus of control, and negatively related to chance locus of control (Robitschek, 1998, 1999).

3.9 WHERE TO FIND OTHER POSITIVE PSYCHOLOGY MEASURES

Comprehensive information on other positive psychological tests, measures, and ways of assessing client strengths is available in the text entitled *Positive Psychological Assessment: A Handbook of Models and Measures* (Lopez and Snyder, 2003). Among the many useful resources in this text are chapters devoted to the measurement of constructs such as gratitude, forgiveness, optimism, creativity, emotional intelligence, self-esteem, career self-efficacy, empathy, attachment security, positive coping, and environmental well-being.

3.10 PROVIDING ASSESSMENT FEEDBACK

The process of positive psychological assessment and an understanding of the utility of positive psychological tests and measures would not be complete without a discussion of how the test results should be reported. Indeed, a major component of practicing therapy from a positive psychological perspective is to provide feedback on assessment results to clients and other mental health providers in a balanced way. More specifically, equal time and equal space should be devoted to reporting and naming client strengths, abilities, and environmental resources, as that which is devoted to noting weaknesses, deficits, and destructive forces in the environment (Lopez et al., 2003; Snyder et al., 2003a; Wright and Lopez, 2002). Indeed, the process of labeling clients is full of inherent power as well as problems. These issues are explored in the following section.

3.11 THE POWER OF LABELS AND NAMING

Labels are very powerful, especially when applied to people. Within a therapeutic context, it seems that the most commonly used labels are diagnoses of pathology based on the *Diagnostic and Statistical Manual of Mental Disorders* (*DSM;* American Psychiatric Association, 2000). Although clients can find relief or a sense of validation of their problematic experiences through an accurate diagnostic label, some consider a diagnosis to be negative, especially if the labels are inaccurate or if clients (or others with whom the clients interact) misinterpret the meaning of the label that has been applied. Some of the biggest problems that can occur when labels (especially labels related to negative functioning) are applied to clients include miscommunication, deindividuation, and self-fulfilling prophecies.

3.11.1 Miscommunication

Although labeling can provide a common nomenclature for mental health practitioners to use to communicate with one another and their clients, counting on labels to convey meaning is not always reliable (Maddux, 2002; Snyder et al., 2003a). Unfortunately, most people assume that others share their meanings; however, that often is not the case. This "shared meaning assumption" often goes unnoticed, hence miscommunications often go undetected (Snyder et al., 2003a). In addition, when labeling clients, many therapists have the tendency to believe that the client is now better understood by virtue of his or her label (Maddux, 2002). In other words, the label is often erroneously seen as being very meaningful. In reality, the label is only a starting point for describing the client; full understanding of clients cannot be achieved through the use of labels as verbal shortcuts (Snyder et al., 2003a).

3.11.2 Deindividuation

The application of labels to individuals results in the creation on in-groups and out-groups (Wright, 1988; Wright and Lopez, 2002). Those who are labeled make up the "in-group", whereas those who do not receive the label constitute the "out-group." People often fail to see the differences that exist among members of a labeled group, while at the same time overemphasizing the differences that exist between members of the labeled and unlabeled groups. This phenomenon is known as deindividuation and can be very harmful, as prejudices often develop via this process (Wright and Lopez, 2002). Indeed, prejudice occurs when people focus on one dimension of an individual, label that person as part of an in-group based on that dimension, and then assign different, negative behaviors to people in that in-group versus those who are part of the out-group.

To clarify how miscommunication and deindividuation can be harmful in a therapeutic context, let's consider the application of *DSM* diagnostic labels. Classifying clients based upon *DSM* diagnostic labels can result in unintentional errors and biases on the part of clinicians, despite the popular notion that such labels serve to enhance therapist understanding of clients and to facilitate professional communications (Maddux, 2002). These problems arise due to the fact that the *DSM* system is based on the assumption that all people who enter clinical settings are diagnosable and that there is a true dichotomy between normal and abnormal functioning. The criteria, however, for normality and abnormality are extremely vague (Maddux, 2002; Snyder et al., 2003a). As such, the criteria for assigning distinct, categorical diagnostic labels are vague as well. For example, according to the *DSM-IV-TR* (American Psychiatric Association, 2000), one can be diagnosed with Obsessive-Compulsive Personality Disorder if he or she meets criteria for four out of eight possible symptoms. Assume that two clients are assessed and one is found to meet the criteria for symptoms 1 through 4 and the other for symptoms 5 through 8. Both of these clients are labeled with

Obsessive-Compulsive Personality Disorder, yet they do not overlap on a single symptom. As a result of deindividuation, most people will ignore the differences between these two people who are perceived to be members of the same in-group (i.e., clients with Obsessive-Compulsive Personality Disorder), while highlighting the differences between these individuals and those without the label that make up the out-group (i.e., those with healthy personalities).

Indeed, the process of deindividuation may lead to dehumanization, whereby the client is seen as being equivalent to the disorder label (Wright and Lopez, 2002). Through simple observations of the language used by many therapists as they refer to their clients, the process of dehumanization via the application of diagnostic labels becomes clear. For instance, have you ever heard a colleague discussing his or her "borderline client"? What about references to "alcoholics," "schizophrenics," "anorexics," or "depressives"? Such language signifies that what is most important about these clients is their pathology and that which leads to their categorization as a member of an in-group, rather than who the person is as a whole human being. Putting the client first (i.e., "a client with borderline personality disorder") and seeing their disorder as only one aspect of who they are as a person is much more humane. Hence, if labels must be applied, clinicians are encouraged to develop an oral and written vocabulary in which people-first language is utilized in order to offset this tendency to deindividuate and dehumanize (Snyder et al., 2003a).

In addition to the aforementioned issues, the process of labeling and deindividuation can also affect a therapist's ability to appropriately assess the environment in which a client functions. This is likely a result of the fundamental attribution error as previously discussed in Chapter 2. Clinicians, as members of the out-group, are more likely to pathologize the experiences of their clients who are members of the in-group, leading them to look for the source of the client's problems within the client while ignoring the role of environmental factors in contributing to the perceived problems of the in-group (Wright and Lopez, 2002). Such a system provides fertile ground for misunderstanding clients (research supports that people make poor decisions under conditions of uncertainty) and for transferring this potentially inaccurate client assessment to others through relying on the diagnostic label as a shortcut for communication.

3.11.3 Self-Fulfilling Prophecy

The process of labeling often shapes the perceptions and beliefs of both those who assign labels to others, as well as those to whom the labels are assigned (Snyder et al., 2003a). In other words, labels influence how a person treats the labeled individual and even how the individual with the label comes to view him or herself. Through the self-fulfilling prophecy process, labels may be internalized and then affect behavior and motivation. This can be especially problematic when the labels applied are negative and/or inaccurate.

The use of *DSM* diagnostic labels in therapeutic contexts can potentially skew the perceptions of therapists and clients. This is most likely to occur when all of the behaviors of a client are interpreted in light of the label. A powerful example of the self-fulfilling prophecy in action for mental health professionals comes from the popular "On Being Sane in Insane Places" study by Rosenhan (1973). In this study, Rosenhan assigned 8 research assistants who did not meet criteria for any diagnostic label to present at different mental health hospitals in five different states reporting that they thought they needed to be admitted because they were hearing voices saying "hollow", "empty", and "thud". Beyond making up this symptom and using false names and employment histories, all the other information the research assistants provided was true. In addition, upon admittance to the hospitals, the assistants were told to act how they normally would act and to report that the voices were no longer being heard. Despite the fact that the research assistants had no pathology, all of them were admitted and all but one were given labels of schizophrenia (the other was diagnosed with bipolar disorder). All of their behaviors and background histories were interpreted in such a way as to coincide with a schizophrenia diagnosis. The research assistants were hospitalized for an average of 19 days, with the shortest stay being 7 days and the longest 52. Rosenhan (1973) concluded that clients in mental health hospitals are at risk of being misunderstood by practitioners who underestimate the power of labels to distort their subsequent observations of client behaviors and the meaning behind such behaviors.

Indeed, as in the study noted above, many clinicians and clients succumb to the self-fulfilling prophecy when they highlight or pay special attention to information that is consistent with the deviant label (i.e., that which is negative) while that which is not consistent (i.e., that which is positive) is overlooked. It is possible, therefore, that a well-intentioned practitioner may develop a negative hypothesis about a client's functioning, gather and attend to information that supports this hypothesis, and to find support from the client who readily agrees with the assessment of the professional whom the client sees as an expert. Hence, a negative collaborative illusion is developed and internalized by both the clinician and the client, which serves to affect how the clinician treats the client as well as how the client thinks about him or herself and subsequently his or her behaviors and motivations (Wright and Lopez, 2002).

3.12 POSITIVE EFFECTS OF LABELING

Although there are many potential problems associated with labeling people, positive outcomes can be achieved through the labeling process as well. Labels can have positive effects and be very enabling when they are used to identify more than just problems or deficits in human functioning. Indeed, when strengths and resources are labeled in addition to weaknesses and deficits, even the labeling of psychological disorders can have positive effects (Snyder et al., 2003a).

3.12.1 Labeling Strengths

It is commonly believed that once a person is assigned a label that others can better understand the person and that his or her label carries with it deep meaning. Such power is often detrimental when labeling weakness or deficits; however, when the valence of the label is changed and positive strengths and resources are being described, the power of the label is then strongly positive. Indeed, by explicitly naming human strengths, the person labeled as well as those who are informed of his or her label come to find merit in the label (Snyder et al., 2003a). Hence, a therapist who indicates, for example, that in addition to meeting criteria for a *DSM* diagnostic label of major depressive disorder, that the client also has high levels of resilience, personal growth initiative, and social intelligence, and is a loving parent who is holding down a stable job with the help of a supportive social network, assists the client in seeing him or herself as more than just the symptoms of pathology that are present. Indeed, the client will actually find merit in the strengths that were reported, rather than assuming that everyone has those qualities or simply failing to realize that he or she has strengths. Human strengths become salient when named.

3.12.2 Self-Fulfilling Prophecy

The self-fulfilling prophecy becomes a potential asset when people are labeled as having talents, strengths, abilities, and positive resources. Just as clients who are labeled with disorders may come to internalize their negative labels, so too may clients come to internalize positive labels. Just as therapists may inadvertently change the way they treat a client based on the *DSM* diagnostic label applied, so too may a therapist change the way the client is treated based on the positive label applied. Such a process may serve to further enhance the labeled strengths, and as the client becomes more cognizant of his or her potential, the client may also become more interested in nurturing these talents and strengths, and more confident in utilizing these skills and positive resources in the pursuit of complete mental health.

The application of positive labels to diagnostic assessment can counteract the many negative effects of negative labels as described previously. In addition, clinicians can capitalize on the positive effects of labeling, even when helping clients to overcome areas of problem and weakness. Indeed, labeling the positive produces a more balanced, well-rounded conceptualization of the client whose makeup may have previously been closely linked by both the client and therapist only to the presenting problem(s). Additionally, the labeling of assets and strengths may provide clinicians with a starting point from which to build a treatment plan and can serve as sources of motivation for clients to work from in the therapeutic treatment process (Snyder et al., 2003a).

In the following chapters, a number of positive psychological interventions and exercises are explained, followed by information on how therapists can decide upon and carry out positive psychology-infused treatment plans.

Chapter 4

Positive Psychological Interventions

Research to date reveals a number of positive psychological approaches to therapy and specific activities and exercises based on the principles of positive psychology that therapists can utilize in their treatment of clients. The overarching practices of Strengths-Based Counseling, Strengths-Centered Therapy, Positive Psychotherapy, Quality of Life Therapy, Well-Being Therapy, and Hope Therapy are reviewed first. Then, a variety of individual exercises designed to promote one or more positive psychology constructs are defined.

4.1 POSITIVE PSYCHOLOGICAL MODELS OF THERAPY

4.1.1 Strengths-Based Counseling

Strengths-Based Counseling is a model for conducting therapy based on the premises of counseling psychology, prevention, positive psychology, positive youth development, social work, solution-focused therapy, and narrative therapy (Smith, 2006). Although the model was created specifically for use with adolescents, the principles appear applicable for use with adult populations as well. The model is based on 12 propositions (see Table 4.1) that outline the basic principles of Strength-Based Counseling, which is then carried out in a series of ten stages.

The first three stages of Strengths-Based Counseling (i.e., building a therapeutic alliance, identifying strengths, and assessing presenting problems) are focused on the creation of a strong therapeutic alliance via helping clients to identify and use their strengths and competencies to confront their struggles. At the same time, a thorough assessment of client perceptions of their problems should occur (Smith, 2006). Smith (2006) notes that the assessment of client problems may be achieved through asking questions such as: "What's your theory about why you have this problem?" and "If there were one question that you were hoping I would ask you, what would that question be?" (p. 41). Therapists can help clients to identify their strengths by teaching them to narrate or reframe their life stories from a strengths perspective (i.e., helping clients to view themselves as survivors rather than victims of poor parenting). During these stages, practitioners are also encouraged to help their clients uncover strengths at the biological (i.e., rest, nutrition, exercise), psychological (i.e., both cognitive strengths such as

TABLE 4.1 Twelve Propositions that Outline the Basic Principles of Strength-Based Counseling (Smith, 2006).

1. Humans are self-righting organisms who are constantly working to adapt to their environments. Strengths develop as people try to right themselves.
2. Strengths develop as a result of internal and external forces and as part of the human driving force to meet basic psychological needs.
3. All people have the capacity for strength development and for growth and change. Strength development is a lifelong process that is influenced by the interaction of individual's heredity and the cultural, social, economic, and political environments in which they find themselves. All people have a reservoir of strengths, some of which have been tapped and others have been left unexplored and unrecognized. Strengths can be learned or taught. All people also have a natural drive for positive growth and a natural tendency to seek the realization and/or expression of their strengths and competencies.
4. Strength levels vary, ranging on a continuum from low to high.
5. Strength is the end product of a dialectical process involving a person's struggle with adversity. (Strengths can develop out of adversities.)
6. Strengths act as buffers against mental illness. All people possess the potential to experience mental disorder. Mental illness occurs when strengths are insufficient to deal with threats to psychological well-being.
7. People are motivated to change during counseling when practitioners focus on their strengths rather than deficits.
8. Encouragement is a key source or form of positive regard that the therapist intentionally provides to effect behavioral change in the client.
9. In Strength-Based Counseling, therapists consciously and intentionally honor client efforts and struggles to deal with their problems or presenting issues. Clients who feel they have been intentionally validated are theorized to achieve their counseling goals at a higher rate than those who have not been so validated by their counselors.
10. Strengths-based counselors understand that people are motivated to change dysfunctional or self-defeating behavior because they hope that doing so will effect the desired life changes and anticipated rewards. Those with higher hope are hypothesized to achieve their counseling goals at a higher rate than those lacking hope.
11. The strength-based counselor understands the process of healing from pain and adversity and designates counseling sessions to help clients heal from their pain.
12. The strength-based counselor assumes that race, class, and gender are organizing elements in every counseling interaction.

problem-solving abilities and emotional strengths such as self-esteem), social (i.e., connections with friends and family), cultural (i.e., beliefs, values, positive ethnic identity), economic (i.e., being employed, sufficient money for covering basic needs), and political (i.e., equal opportunity) levels. Indeed, many of the goals of the first three stages of Strengths-Based Counseling will likely be achieved via carrying out the multiculturally encompassing, positive psychological assessment process as previously described in Chapter 2.

In stage four, therapists set out to encourage and instill a sense of hope in clients by focusing on and providing feedback to clients based upon their efforts or improvements, rather than the outcomes of their efforts (Smith, 2006). For example, a client who is working to improve relationships with colleagues in the workplace is reinforced for such efforts, even if the relationships remain strained. The client is also encouraged simply for attending therapy and working to make progress. This is the case, regardless of whether or not a client is voluntarily seeking services.

In stage five, therapists help clients to frame solutions to their problems via solution-building conversations. The focus of such conversations is on how clients are addressing their problems rather than on the problems themselves (Smith, 2006). In other words, the client who is working to improve relationships with colleagues in the workplace would be asked to discuss what would be different or better at work if relations with colleagues improved and how he or she could contribute to such improvements, rather than focusing on the problems that are currently resulting from the strained relationships. Smith (2006) suggests that the following questions can be useful for framing solutions in therapy: "How have you been trying to solve this problem? What works for you, even for a little while? Is there ever a time you remember when the problem did not exist? What was going on in your life when the problem did not exist?" (p. 43). The principles of solution-focused interviewing are key at this stage of the Strengths-Based Counseling process. (For a more detailed review of solution-focused therapy, see De Jong and Berg, 2002.)

Stage six, building strength and competence, fosters the development of internal and external client assets by helping clients to realize that they have the power to effect important changes in their lives. This is accomplished via building upon and fostering personal strengths and environmental resources throughout the therapeutic process. Indeed, according to Walsh (1998), client strengths that are commonly built through the process of therapy include courage, insight, optimism, perseverance, and finding a sense of meaning and purpose in life.

Stages seven through nine, empowering, changing, and building resilience, are designed to promote agency and facilitate goal pursuits. Major components of these stages are: (a) to help clients develop an awareness of how their problems do not necessarily reside within them; (b) to help them see that change is a process, not an isolated event; (c) to utilize strengths to facilitate change; and (d) to view mistakes that occur en route to change as opportunities for learning, rather than as failures. During these stages, clients are also encouraged to realize that they have the ability to choose how they will view their adversities in life. Smith (2006) offers the following steps for helping a client to reframe a traumatic event: "(a) recognition [of the traumatic event], (b) acceptance, (c) understanding, (d) learning there is always choice for how to view adversity, (e) changing the meaning that is ascribed to an event, (f) deriving lessons from the painful event, (g) redefining ourselves around our strengths and multiple talents, and (h) taking constructive action around our new strength-based identities" (p. 47).

Finally, stage ten, evaluating and terminating, allows the therapist and client to identify the strengths that were most valuable to the change process and to honor the progress that has been made (Smith, 2006).

Although this Strengths-Based Counseling model is lacking a bit in terms of specific strengths-enhancing techniques, it does provide therapists with a guiding framework for practicing from a strengths-based perspective. To this end, Smith (2006) proposes that all therapists examine where they fall on a continuum of strength-based counselor skill competencies. The continuum ranges from deficit-based destructiveness to strength-based proficiency (see Worksheet 4.1). As you set out on your journey to incorporate positive psychology into the counseling room, self-evaluation of your level of strengths-based competence is advised.

4.1.2 Strength-Centered Therapy

Strength-Centered Therapy (Wong, 2006) is a model of counseling, grounded in social constructionism (the idea that knowledge is a product of social consensus) and designed to leverage character strengths and virtues (as defined by Peterson and Seligman, 2004) in the change process. A key aspect of Strength-Centered Therapy is the social constructivistic notion that the subjective views of clients regarding their own pathology and well-being are more important in therapy than the expert opinions of mental health providers. Hence, in this approach, therapists do not serve as experts who provide information to clients; rather, clients and therapists work together to make meaning of client experiences (Wong, 2006).

Over the course of Strength-Centered Therapy, practitioners and clients work together to develop new meanings for client experiences and to expand client strength vocabularies in order to help clients learn to attach their life experiences to that which is positive and adaptive. Strength-Centered Therapy employs weekly sessions during which clients are assumed to cycle and recycle through four phases (Explicitizing, Envisioning, Empowering, and Evolving) over the course of a few weeks or months (Wong, 2006).

In the first phase of Strength-Centered Therapy, Explicitizing, therapists work to help clients name their existing character strengths. Explicitizing strengths should be done carefully, so as not to ignore or overlook the presenting problems and concerns for which clients often come to therapy (Wong, 2006). This can be achieved through validating the client's concerns in a way that also highlights strengths. For example, a client who comes to therapy feeling very sad and depressed can have those feelings validated while at the same time pointing out the strength of hope that he or she possesses, by virtue of the fact that he or she has shown up for therapy. Indeed, at some level, the client must believe that things can get better or they would not be in the therapy room. Likewise, it may have taken courage and bravery to come to therapy in the first place, another important strength of character to be pointed out.

Reframing an apparent character flaw as a strength also may prove to be an effective strategy for naming the best characteristics in people (Gelso and

Worksheet 4.1

Strengths-Based Competence Continuum for Therapists (Smith, 2006)
Rate where you fall on the continuum below, based upon the descriptions of each anchor point:

Deficit-based therapist	Strength-based precompetent therapist	Strength-based competent therapist	Strength-based proficient therapist
• focuses entirely on client problems, weaknesses, and deficits	• beginning to develop an awareness that traditional counseling approaches have focused on the deficit model	• has some training in strength-based counseling	• thoroughly grounded in the tenets of positive psychology, risk and protective factors, resiliency, and hope
• clients leave therapy feeling drained	• consciously and unconsciously searching for a better and different way of working with clients, but formal training may have provided few clues in this direction	• understands strength-based counseling and can assess the impact of this approach on clients' lives	• skilled in risk assessment and has mastered a core body of strength-based counseling techniques, such as encouraging, instilling hope, and reframing
• client self-concept and self-efficacy may be lowered due to problem-focus		• understands that trauma, abuse, illness, and struggle may be injurious but that they may also be sources of challenge and opportunity	• knows how to conduct strength-based assessments
• diagnostic labels are applied which may devalue clients	• realizing the limitations of the disease model for clients in general, but especially those from minority groups or those who are at risk		• knows how to help clients develop competencies related to their goals and strengths
• may believe that childhood trauma is a predictor of adult pathology	• may have already tried to modify one's counseling practice	• is culturally aware; understands one's own as well as clients' cultures	
• lacks encouraging and hope-instilling counseling skills	• beginning to actively seek knowledge and training about positive ways to work with clients	• knowledge of strength-based assessment techniques is limited	• understands that all people have strengths and that individuals' motivations may be enhanced when those around them highlight their strengths
• devalues or is unaware of client strengths or resiliency	• can only articulate vague notions of strength-based counseling	• at this stage one has adopted part of the philosophy of the strength perspective, but cannot consistently obtain the results one desires with clients	• focuses on solutions
	• may go back to the deficit-based model if one has a few negative trial experiences with strengths-based work	• vacillates between using a deficit model and a strength-based model	• is genuine and competent
			• listens, understands, and converses in the language of their clients as opposed to the language of theory

Woodhouse, 2003). For example, a child with attention deficit disorder whose teachers call him "a dreamer who does not stay focused on the topic at hand," may be assisted in seeing how this weakness or area of concern by his teachers is also a sign of his potential ability to be creative, which can be a strength if he uses it at appropriate times. The process of Explicitizing can be facilitated through the use of positive psychological assessment measures such as those previously reviewed in Chapter 3.

Phase 2 of Strength-Centered Therapy is the Envisioning phase. Here, clients identify the strengths they intentionally wish to develop and envision how these strengths could be useful for accomplishing their goals in therapy. Simply asking questions such as "What strengths would you like to develop?" or "What strengths would be useful for helping you to reach your therapy goals?" will likely get the Envisioning phase underway (Wong, 2006). Another approach that therapists can utilize at this phase is to engage clients in a sentence completion exercise whereby they are asked to complete the following sentence "I am more likely to achieve my goal of _____ if I am a(an) _____ person" (Wong, 2006). Many of the words used by clients to fill in the blanks are likely to be related to character strengths. Once these strengths have been named, therapists should encourage their clients to elaborate upon the meanings of the strengths they wish to develop, so as to be sure that therapist understanding of strength labels matches that of the client.

The Empowering phase is the third stage of Strength-Centered Therapy (Wong, 2006). In this phase clients experience a boost in motivation and a sense of empowerment as they begin to believe that using their strengths can positively affect their lives. This increase in motivation may be derived from the development of habits (e.g., volunteering at a local charity weekly to cultivate kindness and generosity) that lead to the effective use of strengths. Hence, therapists should work to creatively incorporate exercises and activities that capitalize upon and further develop existing client strengths. Wong (2006) also recommends that therapists ask their clients to consider connecting with people in their lives that can support them in the strengths-development process. Finally, at this phase, therapists should help clients to explore when their strengths will be useful and when exercising strengths can be problematic. For example, a client who is very cautious and prudent may find these strengths to be effective when applied to his sex life, financial planning, and choice of hobbies; however, should caution and prudence be applied in such a way that it keeps him from taking any risks, it may become a problem. For instance, if he does not apply for a promotion at work because there is a risk involved, namely, no guarantee that he will get it, the strength is no longer serving him well in that context. Similarly, a client who has honesty and genuineness as a strength might find her honesty to work well for her in a number of contexts; however, if she is totally honest about how her manager's new haircut looks terrible or how her supervisor has bad breath, she may find herself out of work. Combining honesty with social intelligence in this context is key.

Finally, the Evolving phase occurs during the termination stage of psychotherapy and involves the process of making strengths-development a never-ending process that transcends the formal psychotherapeutic process (Wong, 2006). Here, progress should be reviewed and celebrated and considered successes to build on. Working together, therapists and clients identify areas for further growth and discuss ways in which clients can use their strengths to address future problems or challenges that might arise.

4.1.3 Positive Psychotherapy

Positive Psychotherapy is an empirically validated approach to psychotherapy that attends specifically to building client strengths and positive emotions, and increasing meaning in the lives of clients in order to alleviate psychopathology and foster happiness (Rashid, 2008). Positive psychotherapists elicit and attend to positive emotions and memories in their discussions with clients while also engaging in discourse related to client problems with the goal of integrating the positive and negative together (Rashid, 2008). For example, in helping a client to overcome a trauma, one would also point out the strengths that have developed as a result of the adverse experience. Similarly, a client who feels depressed because she is harboring guilt for having hurt a family member might also be asked to consider times when she has engaged in helping, or prosocial behaviors toward her loved one.

There are several assumptions that Positive Psychotherapy is based upon (Rashid, 2008). The first assumption is that all people are prone to mental illness and also have an inherent capacity for happiness. Such happiness and pathology develop based upon the interactions between person and environment. Hence, positive psychotherapists view clients as autonomous and growth-oriented. The second assumption of Positive Psychotherapy is that client strengths and positive emotions are as genuine and real as weaknesses and negative emotions. As such, attending to the positives is crucial in establishing a strong therapeutic alliance and fully understanding a client's psychological repertoire that can be used as a foundation for treatment planning.

The theoretical underpinnings of Positive Psychotherapy stem from the work of Seligman (2002), who has proposed that happiness consists of the pleasant life, the engaged life, and the meaningful life. More specifically, the pleasant life is achieved when people are able to experience positive emotions about their past, present, and future lives. The engaged life is felt when one is deeply involved and absorbed in what one is doing in multiple life roles, including love, work, and play. The meaningful life is defined as using one's strengths in the service of something larger than oneself (Seligman, 2002).

The Pleasant Life

As previously noted, the pleasant life consists of positive emotions about the past, present, and future (Seligman, 2002). Positive emotions about the past include feelings of satisfaction, contentment, and serenity and positive emotions about the future include hope, optimism, faith, and trust. Positive emotions in the present are divided into the pleasures and gratifications. The pleasures are momentary experiences that people feel either through their five senses (i.e., tasting delicious food, smelling wonderful fragrances, or experiencing sexual feelings) or through more complicated and learned experiences (i.e., meditation, mindfulness, and relaxation exercises). The gratifications are not feelings, but rather, consist of activities that people like doing (i.e., sports, reading, or dancing).

The Engaged Life

Engagement in life overlaps with the concept of flow or optimal experience, as elucidated by Csikszentmihalyi (1990). Flow is defined as a psychological experience in which one is fully immersed in what he or she is doing. There are nine characteristics or conditions of flow that can help people understand when they have experienced flow and how to choose activities that will make flow more likely (Jackson and Csikszentmihalyi, 1999).

In order for flow to occur, one must perceive a challenge or opportunity for action that stretches (without overmatching or underutilizing) his or her existing skill level. This is referred to as the challenge–skills balance (Jackson and Csikszentmihalyi, 1999). In addition, flow becomes more likely when such challenging activities are intrinsically rewarding, require concentration, and have clear goals coupled with immediate feedback on progress. Under these conditions, people often enter into a subjective state in which there is a merging of action and awareness, deep, effortless involvement in the task at hand, intense focus in the moment, a loss of self-consciousness, a sense of control, and distortion of time (i.e., time seems to stop or pass more quickly than normal; Jackson and Csikszentmihalyi, 1999).

In Seligman's (2002) theory of happiness, he proposes that flow or the engaged life can be achieved through identifying and regularly utilizing salient strengths of character. In Positive Psychotherapy, engagement is indeed fostered by utilizing the signature strengths of clientele (Rashid, 2008).

The Meaningful Life

The meaningful life entails using one's highest strengths in order to belong to and serve something larger than oneself (Seligman, 2002). "People who successfully pursue activities that connect them to such larger goals achieve what we call the meaningful life" (Rashid, 2008, p. 198). Such connections can be accomplished through close interpersonal relations, civic engagement, careers experienced as callings, or through involvement in various positive institutions (i.e., churches, temples, mosques, or nonprofit, environmental, or humanitarian organizations; Rashid, 2008).

The Full Life

Positive Psychotherapy is built upon the aforementioned assumptions and theoretical foundation. When taken together, a full life includes pleasure, engagement, and meaning that is achieved via separate activities or a single activity. The empty life, which occurs when one or more of these elements of the full life are lacking, is hypothesized to be a partial cause of psychological problems (Rashid, 2008).

The Process of Positive Psychotherapy

Positive Psychotherapy has been presented by Rashid (2008) in a series of 14 "idealized" sessions. At each of the 14 sessions, a different theme or construct from positive psychology is addressed and homework assignments for clients are provided. *It is important to note that Positive Psychotherapy should be done in such a way as to match the needs of each individual client. In other words, the length of therapy, the exercises and homework assigned, and the focus of each session should be customized to meet current client needs* (Rashid, 2008). In addition, as with all interventions based on positive psychology, therapists who practice Positive Psychotherapy must be careful that they do not overlook or deny the negative, distressing, or troubling experiences that clients will likely report in therapy. Rather, therapists who practice this treatment approach should strive to completely validate negative client experiences while also working to build positive emotions, character strengths, and meaning in life.

The validity of Positive Psychotherapy has been tested in a number of research studies. Seligman et al. (2006) found that individual Positive Psychotherapy for clients with depression resulted in a reduction of depressive symptoms and to more cases of complete remission of depression symptomology in comparison to treatment-as-usual and treatment-as-usual in addition to antidepressant medication conditions. In addition to reducing symptoms of depression, Positive Psychotherapy also served to enhance symptoms of happiness. In another study, group Positive Psychotherapy was provided to college students with mild or moderate levels of depression. In this study, the students reported a greater reduction of depressive symptoms and greater increases in life satisfaction that lasted for an entire year in comparison to a no-treatment control group (Seligman et al., 2006). A brief version of Group Positive Psychotherapy with children in middle school lead to increases in well-being (Rashid and Anjum, 2007) and many of the homework exercises utilized in Positive Psychotherapy have been validated through a variety of web-based studies conducted by Seligman et al. (2005). Based on these studies, Rashid (2008) concludes that "Positive Psychotherapy has demonstrated efficacy, with large to medium effect sizes" (p. 205). The fourteen sessions of Positive Psychotherapy and related homework assignments are described in detail in the following section.

The Fourteen Sessions of "Idealized" Positive Psychotherapy

Building off the idea that psychopathology occurs or is maintained via a lack of positive resources in a client's life, session 1 is focused upon orienting clients to the framework of Positive Psychotherapy. In this session, the assumptions and roles of the positive psychotherapist are elucidated for clients and client responsibilities are discussed. Clients are then asked to write a one-page positive introduction of themselves in which they tell a story about a time when they were at their best (see Worksheet 4.2) to be discussed at session 2 (Rashid, 2008). In order for therapists to be able to recognize the strengths clients' reveal in their positive introductions, it is useful to be familiar with the 24 strengths from the VIA Inventory of Character Strengths (Peterson and Seligman, 2004), the 35 strengths from the Clifton StrengthsFinder 2.0 (Asplund et al., 2007; Rath, 2007), as well as cultural strengths as previously described in Chapter 2. Once familiar with these strength definitions, one might be amazed at how many strengths can be inferred from just one story. Figure 4.1 includes a sample positive introduction and the strengths that can be pointed out from just that one example.

Worksheet 4.2 Positive Introduction (Rashid, 2008) Instructions

Positive Introduction

Please write a one-page positive introduction of yourself to be reviewed at our next therapy session. The story you write should be a concrete story that shows you at your best and it should have a clear beginning and middle and finish with a strong ending. Please feel free to handwrite your story below or to type it up if you prefer.

Positive Introduction

Please write a one-page positive introduction of yourself to be reviewed at our next therapy session. The story you write should be a concrete story that shows you at your best and it should have a clear beginning and middle and finish with a strong ending. Please feel free to handwrite your story below or to type it up if you prefer.

A time when I was at my best was when I was a senior in high school. I was on a trip to Disney World in Florida with my high school band. I had a lot of good friends and a boyfriend who were on the same bus as I was and for the first 6 hours or so of the 20 hour trip, we were all just having a fun time. Then I noticed a boy on the bus who I did not recognize. He looked really small to be in high school, wore very thick glasses, and was sitting all by himself. I watched him out of the corner of my eye for a few more hours and finally decided to go sit by him since he had been by himself for the whole trip up to that point and I felt sorry for him. When I sat down, he looked surprised and my friends were looking at me strange as well. I think they were wondering why I was going over by that little "nerdy" looking boy. I ignored them and gently started asking the boy questions about who he was and if he was excited for the trip. He opened up pretty quickly and said his name was Adam and that he was only supposed to be in 8th grade, but he was intellectually gifted so he got moved up to high school a year early. Eventually he told me about a very sad situation regarding his home life with a younger brother who had cancer. I really felt like I bonded with him. When we finally got to Florida and then to Disney World, I noticed that he was about to walk off into the big amusement park all by himself. I could not imagine being alone in a big place like that for a whole day, so I decided to invite him along with myself and my friends. Again, some of my friends looked at me like I was strange for doing this, but I did not care. I figured they would either get over it or they could go off by themselves and I would just spend the day with Adam. I ended up spending a few more days with Adam as well. When we returned home, my band director pulled me aside and thanked me for taking the time and initiative to include Adam throughout the week and he noted that what I had done was one of the most mature and kindest things he had ever seen from a high school student. I knew after this experience that I wanted to pursue a career in the helping professions.

There are many client strengths that can be identified in this positive introduction story. Before reading the identified strengths below, try determining on your own the salient strengths of this client.

The strengths identified between the client and therapist in just this one positive introduction story were:

Values in Action strengths:
- Curiosity
- Authenticity
- Bravery
- Kindness
- Social Intelligence
- Fairness

Clifton StrengthsFinder strengths:
- Belief
- Command
- Communication
- Connectedness
- Empathy
- Includer
- Woo

FIGURE 4.1 Example of a completed positive introduction story and the identifiable client strengths in the story.

During session 2, positive introduction stories are reviewed and strengths within the story are identified and discussed. Helping clients to realize times in the past when they have used their strengths to experience a sense of engagement in life is the key. In order for clients to fully participate in this discussion, providing them with a copy of the definitions of the strengths as measured by the VIA (Peterson and Seligman, 2004), and the Clifton StrengthsFinder 2.0 (Asplund et al., 2007; Rath, 2007) Inventories (see Tables 3.1 and 3.2 in Chapter 3) and asking them which strengths they see in their stories is useful. Worksheet 4.3 can also be used to facilitate the discussion of client positive introductions. In this session, therapists also educate clients about the three routes to happiness and have them complete and discuss the Positive Psychotherapy Inventory (see Worksheet 4.4; Rashid, 2008; see Rashid and Anjum (2008) for the Positive Psychotherapy Inventory for Children). Finally, clients are asked to complete the Values-in-Action Inventory of Character Strengths (Peterson and Seligman, 2004; available on-line; see information on this measure in Chapter 3) as homework (Rashid, 2008).

Psychometric Properties of the Positive Psychotherapy Inventory

According to Rashid (2008), the Positive Psychotherapy Inventory was designed to measure happiness, similar to how the Beck Depression Inventory measures depression. The 21 self-report items of the Positive Psychotherapy Inventory assess the three routes to happiness (i.e., the pleasant, engaged, and meaningful lives) as elucidated by Seligman (2002). The Positive Psychotherapy Inventory has been shown to have good internal consistency reliability, with an overall alpha of 0.90 and subscale alphas of 0.78–0.80. Convergent validity has been found between the Positive Psychotherapy Inventory and measures of well-being such as the Satisfaction with Life Scale ($r = 0.68$), the Fordyce Emotions Questionnaire ($r = 0.56$) and the Positive Affectivity Scale from the PANAS ($r = 0.23$). Discriminent validity has been established between the Positive Psychotherapy Inventory and measures of depression, including the Beck Depression Inventory ($r = -0.62$) and the Zung Depression Rating Scale ($r = -0.57$). The Positive Psychotherapy Inventory has also been found to be sensitive to change, hence it appears to be useful as a therapy outcome measure (Rashid, 2008).

Worksheet 4.3 Review of Positive Introduction Story

This worksheet is to be completed during/after reviewing your positive introduction story with your therapist.

The strengths I can identify and that my therapist heard in my positive introduction are:

I first recognized these strengths in myself when:

Other areas/times in my life when I have used these identified strengths are:

How did it feel to write your positive introduction?

How did it feel to get feedback on it from your therapist?

Worksheet 4.4 The Positive Psychotherapy Inventory (Rashid, 2008)

Please read each group of statements carefully. Then, pick the one statement in each group that best describes you. Be sure to read all of the statements in each group before making your choice.

Some questions are regarding strengths. Strength refers to a stable trait which manifests through thoughts, feelings and actions, is morally valued and is beneficial to self and others. Examples of strengths include but are not limited to optimism, zest, spirituality, fairness, modesty, social intelligence, perseverance, curiosity, creativity, teamwork . . . etc.

In responding to statements regarding strengths, it is important that you distinguish between strengths, abilities and talents. Abilities and talents are attributes such as intelligence, perfect pitch, or athletic prowess. Strengths fall in a moral domain, whereas abilities and talents do not. Talents and abilities seem to have more tangible consequences (acclaim, wealth) than strengths. Someone who "does nothing" with a talent like high IQ or musical skill courts eventual disdain. We may experience dismay when extremely talented individuals like Judy Garland, Michael Jackson, and Elvis Presley, are overwhelmed by drugs and other problems. In contrast, we never hear the criticism that a person did nothing with her wisdom or kindness. Put simply, talents and abilities can be squandered, but strengths cannot. Nevertheless, strengths, abilities and talents are closely linked. Think of famous basketball player Michael Jordan. He is revered for his athletic ability but also for his refusal to lose.

1. **Joy**
   - **0.**   I rarely feel joyful
   - **1.**   I occasionally feel joyful
   - **2.**   I feel more joyful than joyless
   - **3.**   I usually feel joyful

2. **Knowing strengths**
   - **0.**   I do not know my strengths
   - **1.**   I have some idea about my strengths
   - **2.**   I know my strengths
   - **3.**   I am very well aware of my strengths

3. **Impact on society**
   - **0.**   What I do usually does not matter to society
   - **1.**   What I do occasionally matters to society
   - **2.**   What I do often matters to society
   - **3.**   What I do usually matters to society

4. Positive mood observed by others
   0. Others say I usually do not look happy
   1. Others say I occasionally look happy
   2. Others say I usually look happy
   3. Others say I look happy most of the time

5. Pursuing strength activities
   0. I usually do not pursue activities which use my strengths
   1. I occasionally pursue activities which use my strengths
   2. I often pursue activities which use my strengths
   3. I usually pursue activities which use my strengths

6. Sense of connection
   0. I do not feel connected to people with whom I regularly interact
   1. I occasionally feel connected to people with whom I regularly interact
   2. I often feel connected to people with whom I regularly interact
   3. I usually feel connected to people with whom I regularly interact

7. Gratitude
   0. I usually do not take time to think about the good things in my life
   1. I occasionally notice good things in my life and feel thankful
   2. I often notice good things in my life and feel thankful
   3. I feel grateful for many good things in my life almost every day

8. Solving problems using strengths
   0. I rarely use my strengths to solve problems
   1. I occasionally use my strengths to solve problems
   2. I often use my strengths to solve problems
   3. I usually use my strengths to solve problems

9. Sense of meaning
   0. I rarely feel like my life has purpose
   1. I occasionally feel like my life has purpose
   2. I often feel like my life has purpose
   3. I usually feel like my life has purpose

10. Relaxation
   0. I rarely feel relaxed
   1. I occasionally feel relaxed
   2. I often feel relaxed
   3. I usually feel relaxed

11. Concentration during strength activities

0. My concentration is poor during activities which use my strengths
1. My concentration is sometimes good and sometimes poor during activities which use my strengths
2. My concentration is usually good during activities which use my strengths
3. My concentration is excellent during activities which use my strengths

12. Religious or spiritual activities

0. I usually do not engage in religious or spiritual activities
1. I occasionally spend some time in religious or spiritual activities
2. I often spend some time in religious or spiritual activities
3. I usually spend some time every day in religious or spiritual activities

13. Savoring

0. I usually rush through things and don't slow down to enjoy them
1. I occasionally savor things that bring me pleasure
2. I savor at least one thing that brings me pleasure every day
3. I usually let myself get immersed in pleasant experiences so that I can savor them fully

14. Time during strength activities

0. Time passes slowly when I am engaged in activities that use my strengths
1. Time passes ordinarily when I am engaged in activities that use my strengths
2. Time passes quickly when I am engaged in activities that use my strengths
3. I lose the sense of time when I am engaged in activities that use my strengths

15. Closeness with loved ones

0. I usually do not feel close to my loved ones
1. I occasionally feel close to my loved ones
2. I often feel close to my loved ones
3. I usually feel close to my loved ones

16. Laughing/smiling

0. I usually do not laugh much
1. I occasionally laugh heartily
2. I often laugh heartily
3. I usually laugh heartily several times each day

17. Managing strength activities
0. It is usually hard for me to manage activities which use my strengths
1. I can occasionally manage activities which use my strengths
2. I often can manage well activities which use my strengths
3. Managing activities which use my strengths comes almost natural to me

18. Contributing to something larger
0. I rarely do things that contribute to a larger cause
1. I occasionally do things that contribute to a larger cause
2. I often do things that contribute to a larger cause
3. I usually do things that contribute to a larger cause

19. Zest
0. I usually have little or no energy
1. I occasionally feel energized
2. I often feel energized
3. I usually feel energized

20. Accomplishment in strength activities
0. I do not feel a sense of accomplishment when I spend time in activities which use my strengths
1. I occasionally feel a sense of accomplishment when I spend time in activities which use my strengths
2. I often feel a sense of accomplishment when I spend time in activities which use my strengths
3. I usually feel a sense of accomplishment when I spend time in activities which use my strengths

21. Using strengths to help others
0. I rarely use my strengths to help others
1. I occasionally use my strengths to help others, mostly when they ask
2. I often use my strengths to help others
3. I regularly use my strengths to help others

Scoring information
To obtain **Pleasant life** scores, add items 1, 4, 7, 10, 13, 16, and 19. Scores can range from 0 to 21, with higher scores indicating higher levels of pleasure. The average score for non-depressed adults is 13 and for depressed adults is 8.

To obtain **Engaged life** scores, add items 2, 5, 8, 11, 14, 17, and 20. Scores can range from 0 to 21, with higher scores indicating higher levels of engagement. The average score for non-depressed adults is 14 and for depressed adults is 10.

To obtain **Meaningful life** scores, add items 3, 6, 9, 12, 15, 18, and 21. Scores can range from 0 to 21, with higher scores indicating higher levels of meaning. The average score for non-depressed adults is 12 and for depressed adults is 9.

To obtain **Overall happiness** scores, add the totals from the pleasant life, engaged life, and meaningful life subscales. Scores can range from 0 to 63, with higher scores indicating higher levels of overall happiness. The average score for non-depressed adults is 39 and for depressed adults is 27.

Scores based on a normative study of 302 adults. For psychometric details please email (tayyab@psych.upenn.edu). Copyright by Tayyab Rashid; reproduced with permission of the author. This inventory can be used for research or clinical purposes without contacting the author.

Session 3 is designed to help clients cultivate their top strengths and positive emotions. In order to do so, therapists assist clients in formulating specific plans for putting strengths into action. Worksheet 4.5 can be utilized in the process. Figure 4.2 includes an example of a completed client strengths action plan. The connection between utilizing strengths and experiencing positive emotions can be made, and an explanation of the value of positive emotions, based on the Broaden and Build theory (Fredrickson, 1998, 2000, 2001) as described previously in Chapter 1 should be provided (see Worksheet 4.6). The homework for session 3 is for clients to start a gratitude journal, in which they are to document daily at least three good things that happened throughout the day (Rashid, 2008). This exercise should be on-going throughout the course of therapy and possibly beyond. Worksheet 4.7 can be copied and bound together for clients who may appreciate a bit more structure with this exercise. Alternatively, providing clients with a nice, hardcover journal or encouraging them to purchase one on their own often increases their motivation for maintaining gratitude journals for the long-term.

Putting Strengths Into Action Plan

My top five VIA strengths:

1. Creativity

2. Authenticity

3. Kindness

4. Open-mindedness

5. Love of learning

Which of your top five strengths are you currently using on a regular basis? Please briefly describe how you are currently using these strengths.

I think I use my open-mindedness strength all the time. I think I am very open-minded, as I am very accepting of other opinions and ideas and never try to push my values or beliefs onto others. Sometimes that is hard when dealing with my husband and my kids, but even in relation to them, I think I am very open-minded and accepting, even if they choose to do things that I do not necessarily think are best. I think I also use my strength of kindness often, as I always seem to be doing things for others. Mostly for my family, but for other people and groups too. I volunteer at a local homeless shelter at least once a month. I guess I am authentic, I mean, I never try to act fake or like someone I am not. I don't think I am using my strengths of creativity or love of learning very much anymore these days.

Are there ways in which you have used these strengths in the past that you are no longer engaging in now? If so, please list how and when you used to use these strengths.

Yes, when I was in high school I was very creative. I took all sorts of art classes and even though I was the only girl in the class, I took several semesters of shop because I liked to make things with my hands. I also participated on the debate team because it was fun to problem-solve and come up with creative solutions or arguments to the questions posed. It seems these days that I am so busy with work and parenting that I spend little time on creative tasks. I think my love of learning strength has not been used lately for the same reason. I remember, before the kids, spending many hours at the library or reading books at home. I don't think I have read a book, other than a fairy tale to my girls, for five years now! My husband and I used to travel as well. I loved learning about other cultures through our travels.

One way I can put my strength of creativity **into action this week is by:**

FIGURE 4.2 Sample completed client strengths action plan.

figuring out a creative way to find more time in my schedule so that I can also work on my love of learning strength! I really want to understand more about various world religions. I honestly do not really understand the differences between some of the major religions and think that this is important information to have. For example, when I watch the news coverage of events in the Middle East, they talk about Sunni's and Shiite's and I don't understand the differences. This week I will take the girls with me to the library and get them their very own library cards. We will go on a book hunt for a topic that each of them would like to learn about and then they can sit in the child's reading room area and read while I find a good book on religion. Then, I will use reading time and library book hunts as positive reinforcers for the girls when they behave. This should give me more time to readmyself.

Please designate a time in your schedule this week when you will put the above strengths action plan into action. After you have implemented your plan, please briefly respond to the following questions:

1. How did it feel to put your strength into action?

It felt pretty good! The plan actually worked and the girls thought the library was really cool. There is a reading/activity program for kids there that I was not even aware of that I can take the girls to each week for free. That is an hour each week that I can use to focus on my own reading in a quiet space. I talked to my husband about my plan to learn more about world religions and he brought up the idea of going on a trip this summer, maybe to China or India, to expose us to some places and cultures we have not yet been to. I did not think he would want to travel with the girls, but he thinks they are old enough now to start traveling. How exciting!

2. Did you face any challenges in planning or carrying out this action plan? If so, please briefly describe these challenges and how you overcame them.

Yes, at first the girls had no interest in the library. I think it helped when I reminded them of how much Belle, a character from one of their favorite kids' movies, loved the library and found books to be fascinating. That was creative on my part, wasn't it! I also found it a bit challenging to pick a book because once I got there, I realized there are tons of subjects I would love to learn more about.

3. Did you experience positive emotions either during or after carrying out this action plan? If so, please briefly describe the positive emotions and when they occurred.

Yes, I felt positive both during and after implementing this plan. I felt good about creatively finding more time for myself and fostering my strength of love of learning while hopefully also helping my girls to develop a passion for learning too!

FIGURE 4.2   (Continued)

Worksheet 4.5 Putting Strengths Into Action Plan

My top five VIA strengths:

1.

2.

3.

4.

5.

Which of your top five strengths are you currently using on a regular basis? Please briefly describe how you are currently using these strengths.

Are there ways in which you have used these strengths in the past that you are no longer engaging in now? If so, please list how and when you used to use these strengths.

One way I can put my strength of _____ into action this week is by:

Please designate a time in your schedule this week when you will put the above strengths action plan into action. After you have implemented your plan, please briefly respond to the following questions:

1. How did it feel to put your strength into action?

2. Did you face any challenges in planning or carrying out this action plan? If so, please briefly describe these challenges and how you overcame them.

3. Did you experience positive emotions either during or after carrying out this action plan? If so, please briefly describe the positive emotions and when they occurred.

Worksheet 4.6 An Explanation of the Broaden and Build Theory of Positive Emotions (Fredrickson, 1998, 2000, 2001)

When experiencing negative emotions, you are likely to see the world with tunnel vision. This can be very useful when you are in danger or are being attacked, as you need to take action quickly in such situations. The tunnel vision or narrowed mindset you experience when you feel emotions such as fear or anger allow you to take quick action to fight or flee. However, when such negative emotions are experienced in the absence of any real threat or danger, they are not as useful and may even become problematic.

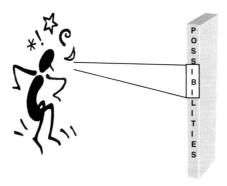

When experiencing positive emotions, the blinders come off and you are able to see all the possibilities that exist. In other words, positive emotions broaden your mindset rather than narrow it the way negative emotions do. Such a broadened mindset is very useful for a number of reasons. For example, when your mindset is broadened, you are likely to be better at problem-solving, to have better coping skills, to be more open to making friends, and to be more likely to engage in physical activities that build your physical health.

Worksheet 4.7 Gratitude Journal Instructions

Many people find it easier to think about the things that did not go well throughout their days rather than the many things that did go well. This tendency to focus on the negative while overlooking the positive is a bias in human thinking referred to as the fundamental negative bias. You are being asked to keep a journal for the next several weeks in which you will write down three good things that happened to you each day in order to manually override the fundamental negative bias. In addition to writing down at least three good things that happen, you are being asked to consider *why* those things happened. For example, did you do something to make it happen? Did someone else cause this good event to happen? Was it pure luck? Thinking about those things that go well in our lives helps us to feel more positive emotions and more satisfied with life while simultaneously building strengths such as gratitude and optimism.

The following chart can be copied and used for keeping your gratitude journal. If you prefer to keep a type-written journal or to purchase a separate notebook or diary, please feel free to do so.

Date	3 Good events	Why these good things happened
_____	1. 2. 3.	1. 2. 3.
_____	1. 2. 3.	1. 2. 3.
_____	1. 2. 3.	1. 2. 3.

Worksheet 4.8 Three Bad Memories (Rashid, 2008) Instructions

Memories can be very powerful. Indeed, memories of the past often affect us in the present. This is true regardless of whether those memories are good or bad. Please think about three bad memories from your past and write about those memories below. We will discuss this assignment further at our next therapy session.

Bad memory number 1:

How does this memory impact you in the present? Do you feel anger, sadness, or other symptoms of depression as a result of such memories? Please write out your thoughts on these questions here:

Bad memory number 2:

How does this memory impact you in the present? Do you feel anger, sadness, or other symptoms of depression as a result of such memories? Please write out your thoughts on these questions here:

Bad memory number 3:

How does this memory impact you in the present? Do you feel anger, sadness, or other symptoms of depression as a result of such memories? Please write out your thoughts on these questions here:

Session 4 is focused upon helping clients understand the role of memories, both good and bad, in the maintenance of depression symptoms. Clients are assisted in expressing anger, bitterness, and other negative emotions. Afterwards, the effects of these emotions on depression and well-being are discussed. Clients are instructed to write about three bad memories and the negative feelings associated with those memories, followed by an examination of how such memories maintain depression (Rashid, 2008). Worksheet 4.8 can be used to assist clients with this homework task.

> Resentment is like taking poison and waiting for the other man to die.
>
> Unknown

Session 5 is focused on the construct of forgiveness. Forgiveness is presented as a tool that can be utilized to undo anger, bitterness, and other negative emotions. For some, forgiveness even holds the power to transform negative emotions into positive ones. Homework for session 5 consists of having clients write a forgiveness letter to someone they are holding a grudge against. The letter should address the transgression that occurred and the feelings associated with the transgression. The client should then pledge to forgive the transgressor, if appropriate. However, the letter should not actually be delivered to the transgressor (Rashid, 2008). Worksheet 4.9 provides instructions to assist clients in the completion of this forgiveness homework.

Worksheet 4.9 Forgiveness Letter Instructions

Think of a person from your past who you are holding a grudge against or have been in conflict with. How is this grudge affecting you? How is it affecting the other person? Those who study forgiveness have discovered that forgiving does not mean forgetting, condoning, pardoning, or excusing the transgression and the goal of forgiveness is not necessarily reconciliation (Enright and Coyle, 1998; McCullough and Witvliet, 2002; Seligman, 2002). Rather, forgiveness is something you do for yourself in order to reduce your level of psychological distress through the release of toxic negative emotions. It has been said that the opposite of love is not hate (rather, it is indifference), since hating someone takes just as much energy as loving them, with the direction of the energy being the only difference. The negative energy and emotion that you put into not forgiving can, over time, cause major negative health outcomes while the person who committed the transgression against you suffers no further ill effects due to unforgiveness (van Oyen Witvliet et al., 2001). It seems that by not forgiving, you allow your transgressors to victimize you all over again and for an indefinite amount of time. Essentially, forgiveness allows you to take your power back. That being said, forgiveness is something that you must freely choose to do and something that will take hard work.

To help get you started down the path of forgiveness, you are being asked to write a letter in which you describe a transgression that has been committed against you and the emotions related to that transgression. Then, pledge to forgive the transgressor (if appropriate), but DO NOT SEND or discuss the contents of the letter with the person you write it to. The purpose of this exercise is to help you experience the power of forgiveness even in the absence of feedback. Hence, your letter can be written to someone whom you are no longer in contact with or someone who may have already passed away. Finally, some people hold unforgiveness toward themselves. If this is the case for you, writing a forgiveness letter to yourself is appropriate.

Please briefly respond to the following questions after you have written your forgiveness letter:

1.   What did it feel like to write your forgiveness letter?

2. Do you feel as if you are truly ready and willing to commit to
    forgiveness? Why or why not?

3. How did it feel to complete and read over the letter?

Because some clients do not hold grudges against others but rather, are harboring unforgiveness toward themselves, an alternative option for writing forgiveness letters is to have clients write forgiveness letters to themselves. Indeed, although not a formal strategy in Positive Psychotherapy, this can be a useful tool for helping clients to overcome guilt or shame. Finally, clients should also be reminded that writing forgiveness letters to people who have passed away but to whom they still hold a grudge against can also be therapeutic.

For those who have negative emotions about the past due to feeling wronged, betrayed, or cheated, finding forgiveness can be essential to freeing oneself of the burden of unforgiveness and for experiencing instead, positive emotions about the past. Although many people struggle to understand that forgiveness is something that can be done for oneself, rather than for the person who has done one wrong, research supports this notion. Indeed, forgiveness researchers state that forgiving does not mean forgetting, condoning, pardoning, or excusing the transgression and the goal of forgiveness is not necessarily reconciliation (Enright and Coyle, 1998; McCullough and Witvliet, 2002; Seligman, 2002). Rather, forgiveness is done to benefit the person who has been wronged in order to reduce his or her level of psychological distress through the release of toxic negative emotions. It has been said that the opposite of love is not hate (rather, it is indifference), since hating someone takes just as much energy as loving them, with the valence of the energy being the only difference. The negative energy and emotion that one puts into not forgiving can, over time, cause major negative health outcomes while the people who committed the transgression suffer no further ill effects due to unforgiveness (vanOyen Witvliet et al., 2001). It seems that by not forgiving, people allow their transgressors to victimize them all over again and for an indefinite amount of time. Essentially, forgiveness allows individuals to take their power back. Indeed, those who are able to forgive are found to have better mental and physical health outcomes in a variety of studies in comparison to those who hold onto unforgiveness (Maltby et al., 2001; Seybold et al., 2001; Touissant et al., 2001; Krause and Ellison, 2003; Kendler et al., 2003; Witvliet et al., 2004).

When working with clients on forgiveness, therapists should determine which model of forgiveness fits best with the worldview of each individual client. For example, Worthington has created a five-stage model of forgiveness known as the REACH model (Ripley and Worthington, 2002; Worthington, 1998, 2001; Worthington and Drinkard, 2000). REACH is an acronym that represents each of the five stages of forgiveness, namely, *R*ecall the hurt, *E*mpathize with the transgressor, offer an *A*ltruistic attitude of forgiveness, *C*ommit to forgive, and *H*old onto forgiveness. Another popular forgiveness model has been proposed by Baskin and Enright (2004). This model consists of 20 steps which are divided into 4 major phases. The phases include an uncovering phase (i.e., clients confront and work to release their anger), a decision phase (i.e., clients have a change of heart, conversion, or new insights that old resolution strategies are not working and consider forgiveness as an option), a work phase (i.e., clients reframe, find acceptance, and a sense of empathy for the offender), and an outcome phase (i.e., clients find meaning in the suffering and the forgiveness process). Baskin and Enright (2004) emphasize that forgiveness entails the *willful* giving up of resentment and is an act that must be freely chosen by the forgiver. In other words, therapists cannot and should not force clients to forgive, but rather, educate them about the power of forgiveness and provide them with techniques that can make forgiveness more likely (i.e., writing forgiveness letters).

> Gratitude unlocks the fullness of life. It turns what we have into enough, and more. It turns denial into acceptance, chaos into order, confusion into clarity .... It turns problems into gifts, failures into success, the unexpected into perfect timing, and mistakes into important events. Gratitude makes sense of our past, brings peace for today and creates a vision for tomorrow.
>
> Melodie Beattie

Gratitude is the focus of session 6. The discussion of the role of good and bad memories is revisited, this time with an emphasis on the affects of gratitude on such memories. Clients are instructed to write a detailed letter of gratitude to someone whom he or she has never properly thanked and then to deliver that letter in person to the intended recipient (Rashid, 2008). Instructions for the gratitude letter and delivery can be found in Worksheet 4.10.

Worksheet 4.10 Gratitude Letter and Delivery (Rashid, 2008) Instructions

The expression of gratitude is a powerful way for increasing your satisfaction in life and increasing positive emotions about the past. Although many people say "thank you" often, they fail to really express the depth of their gratitude to those for whom they are most thankful. Think of the people in your life to whom you are most grateful but to whom you have never formally expressed your gratitude toward or properly thanked. Write a detailed letter of gratitude toward this individual. Be sure the letter is concrete, in other words, be sure to name specific things the person did for you and how those things impacted your life. Rewrite the letter if necessary and when you are satisfied with the final copy, set up a meeting so that you can personally deliver your letter to the person to whom it was written, but do not tell them the purpose of the meeting in advance. When you meet with them, please read the letter to them or stay with them as they read the letter you have written.

Take some time to really think about and respond to the following questions after you have written and delivered your letter of gratitude:

1. How did you feel as you wrote your letter?

2. How did you feel as you prepared to deliver the letter? Was it easy or challenging?

3. How did the other person react to your expression of gratitude? And how were you affected by their reaction?

4. If the experience of expressing your gratitude indeed resulted in positive emotions, how long did those feelings last after you delivered your letter? As you recall this experience, how does it impact your present mood?

For those who are not satisfied with the past, but who are not harboring grudges or bitterness, finding ways to be more grateful may be the key to feeling more positive emotions about the past. In comparison to finding forgiveness, being more grateful does not seem to be as difficult for most people, though it does require conscious effort.

Gratefulness has been defined as a willingness to recognize that one has received a valuable positive outcome from another individual's kindness. There is also recognition that the individual intentionally provided this benefit, often at some personal cost (Emmons, 2007). "Being grateful is an acknowledgement that there are good and enjoyable things in the world" (Emmons, 2007, p. 5). Snyder and Lopez (2007) report that gratitude can also come from non-human actions or events. For example, many people experience gratitude for surviving traumatic events or getting through crises (Coffman, 1996; Affleck and Tennen, 1996). In general, people who are grateful see the world through a lens of abundance (vs. a lens of scarcity), where they look for what life is offering rather than what life is denying. They also see life as a gift, rather than as a burden, and overall feel more satisfaction than deprivation (Emmons, 2007). Finally, research has shown that being grateful has many benefits in terms of psychological (i.e., increased positive affect, more energy, enthusiasm, and attentiveness), physical (i.e., increased exercise, better sleep, and fewer illnesses), and interpersonal (i.e., feeling more connected and less lonely and isolated) outcomes (Emmons and McCullough, 2003).

There are several ways to increase one's level of gratitude. According to Snyder and Lopez (2007), gratitude entails consideration of those people and things that are often overlooked or taken for granted and purposefully learning how to give thanks for them. Appreciating those people who have made a difference, whether it large or small, is something one can do to find more gratitude in his or her own life. Hence, the reason that Positive Psychotherapy includes homework assignments such as writing and delivering letters of gratitude and keeping daily gratitude journals. Indeed, research has shown that participants who completed a gratitude letter and delivery exercise showed increases in happiness and decreases in symptoms of depression when measured at one week after letter delivery. Furthermore, these positive changes in affect were maintained at a one-month follow-up as well. By three months, however, participant emotion levels had returned to baseline levels (Seligman et al., 2005). Participants who completed gratitude journals each night for one full week also experienced higher levels of happiness and lower levels of depression at follow-up measured at one-month, three-month, and six-month intervals. It is important to note, however, that those participants who actively continued their assigned journaling exercise on their own beyond the prescribed one-week period mediated the long-term benefits in this study (Seligman et al., 2005).

Session 7 of Positive Psychotherapy consists of a mid-therapy check. In this session, therapists check in with clients on their progress with writing forgiveness and gratitude letters, gratitude journals, and putting their strengths into action based on their action plans that were started in session 2. Client feedback about the process of and their progress in therapy is discussed.

The eighth session of Positive Psychotherapy is about teaching clients to satisfice versus maximize (Schwartz et al., 2002). More specifically, clients are taught that while choice is crucial to well-being, too much choice can actually get in the way, especially for individuals who are almost always looking to get the best or to maximize. For those who strive to maximize, one must know what all the possibilities are, hence one must also pursue all the possible alternatives when making a choice or decision. Such a process can be extremely exhausting, especially in a world that is full of choices and options. Instead of maximizing, clients are encouraged to satisfice or to make a "good enough" choice or decision by searching through alternatives only until they find one that meets their needs. The goal is to help clients realize that they will be more satisfied when they satisfice instead of maximizing because maximizing often leads to frustration, regret that not every possible alternative could be considered, and a mismatch between expectations and reality (Schwartz et al., 2002).

The homework in session 8 is to have clients engage in a writing assignment in which they come up with ways to increase satisficing in their lives and to create a personal satisficing plan (Rashid, 2008). In addition, taking clients through a few decisions in which they strive to maximize and then a few in which they aim to satisfice can be useful. After these decisions have been made, examining the process and results of the two competing methods of decision-making is recommended (Schwartz et al., 2002). Worksheet 4.11 is designed to assist clients in the process of understanding and implementing satisficing in their own lives.

Worksheet 4.11 Satisficing Versus Maximizing Homework Instructions

Having choices is important to well-being; however, too much choice can actually get in the way, especially if you are a person who is almost always looking to get the best or to maximize. If you are a person who strives to maximize, you must know what all the possibilities are, hence, you must also pursue all the possible alternatives when making a choice or decision. Such a process can be extremely exhausting, especially in a world that is full of choices and options! Instead of maximizing, you are being encouraged to satisfice or to make a "good enough" choice or decision by searching through alternatives only until you find one that meets your needs. The goal is to help you realize that you will be more satisfied when you satisfice instead of maximizing because maximizing often leads to frustration, regret that not every possible alternative could be considered, and a mismatch between expectations and reality (Schwartz et al., 2002).

For this homework assignment, you are being asked to think and write about ways to increase satisficing in your own life and to create a personal satisficing plan.

1. Please write down an example of a decision that you have made in which your aim was to maximize (i.e., consider all the options and pick the best one).

2. How much time did it take to make this decision? Did you feel frustrated? Did you regret that you didn't look at every possible alternative?

3. Please write down an example of a decision that you made in which you satisficed (i.e., looked at only a limited number of options and stopped when you found something good enough).

4. How much time did it take to make this decision? Did you feel frustrated? Did you feel regret about not considering all the possible options?

5. How can you increase satisfcing when making decisions in your life? How will you catch yourself when you slip into maximizing mode?

Find the good. It's all around you. Find it, showcase it and you'll start believing in it.

Unknown

In session 9 of Positive Psychotherapy, the topics of optimism and hope are explored. This is especially useful for those clients who may be lacking in positive emotions related to the future. If clients do not naturally possess a high level of dispositional optimism, or the stable tendency to believe that good rather than bad things will happen (Carver and Sheier, 1985), they can work to learn to be optimistic (Seligman, 1991).

According to learned optimism theory, which is based on attributional style theory, there are several key differences between how pessimistic and optimistic people tend to think about the bad and good things that happen to them (Seligman, 1991, 1998; Seligman et al., 1995). More specifically, people who are optimistic make external, variable, and specific attributions for failure-like events rather than the internal, stable, and global attributions made by pessimists. For example, a client who is optimistic will explain a relationship breakup as being due to a poor match between herself and her partner (external), and something that is unlikely to happen in her next relationship (variable), as this negative event is confined to this particular relationship (specific). In contrast, a pessimistic client in the same situation is likely to view the breakup as her fault because she was not pretty enough, caring enough, or good at opening up to other people (internal), and she will predict that such a poor outcome is likely to occur in future relationships (stable), as this negative event is likely to be repeated should she even find another person to connect with (global). Though not emphasized as greatly by Seligman, the reverse is also true. When it comes to explaining successful events or outcomes, the optimist will attribute the success to internal, stable, and global factors while the pessimist will explain his or her success as the result of external, variable, and specific attributions.

Teaching clients about optimism and helping them to learn to be more optimistic can become easier to do once several misconceptions about optimism are refuted. It seems that some clients believe that optimists are simply naïve, dumb, dreamers, or living in a fantasy world. Helping clients to understand that optimists are not happy because they ignore the problems in their lives and the world or because they are too unintelligent to realize that everything is not rosy is important. An example of this comes from research by Aspinwall and colleagues (2001) in which optimists and pessimists were presented with frightening health information pertinent to their own lives (for example, the relationship between tanning and skin cancer for those who frequented tanning beds and the sunny beach). When asked one week later what they remembered about the health information they were presented with, it was the optimists, not the pessimists, who recalled more of the negative health information and rated that information as something that convinced them that changes in their health behaviors may be needed. These findings may also help us understand why optimists tend to live longer, healthier lives than pessimists (Ostir et al., 2000; Danner and Snowdon, 2001; Maruta et al., 2000). If optimists were truly naïve or dumb, they would not survive to old age.

What optimists do that allows them to be happier than pessimists is that they choose to focus on the positive as much as possible. It is vital to help clients see that optimism does not entail simply thinking positive thoughts. For example, a client can think positively all day long that he is going to be a professional basketball player, but if the individual is 35 years old and lacking in terms of height and coordination, there is no way that this is going to happen and eventually he is going to feel very unhappy since his "positive thinking" did not come true. In contrast, if this individual were to *focus on the positives that actually exist*, for example, his excellent understanding of the game of basketball and his ability to motivate others, he could make himself much happier than if he focuses on the negatives that actually exist. In this example, the client could utilize his existing skills to pursue a career in coaching instead of a career as a professional athlete. The classic example of the glass half-full or half-empty does a nice job of reminding us that optimists choose to focus on the realistic positive aspect of having half a glass of water left and the pessimist chooses to focus on the negative reality that half the glass of water is already gone.

> When one door closes another door opens; but we so often look so long and so regretfully upon the closed door, that we do not see the ones which open for us.
>
> Alexander Graham Bell

The homework assignment for session 9 of Positive Psychotherapy is for clients to complete a door opening and closing exercise. More specifically, they are asked to recall three times in their lives when they lost out on something important, when an important plan fell through, or when they experienced rejection and then to find the doors that later opened as a result of these seemingly negative events (Rashid, 2008). Worksheet 4.12 can be used to guide clients through this assignment.

Worksheet 4.12 One Door Closes, Another Door Opens Instructions (Rashid, 2008)

What optimists do that allows them to be happier than pessimists is that they choose to focus on the positive as much as possible. Optimism does not entail simply thinking positive thoughts, rather optimists *focus on the positives that actually exist.* The classic example of the glass half-full or half-empty does a nice job of reminding us that optimists choose to focus on the realistic positive aspect of having half a glass of water left and the pessimist chooses to focus on the negative reality that half the glass of water is already gone. Optimism does not make a person foolish or naïve.

This exercise is designed to help you think about times in your life when important doors have closed and what doors opened as a result.

Please write about three times in your life when you lost out on something important, when a big plan collapsed, or when you were rejected by someone. Then consider what doors opened after these important doors closed.

1. An important door that closed on me was:

and the door that opened as a result was:

2. An important door that closed on me was:

and the door that opened as a result was:

An important door that closed on me was:

and the door that opened as a result was:

Please reflect upon and briefly respond to the following questions:

1. How long after these doors closed were you able to see the doors that opened?

2. What, if anything, tends to get in the way of your ability to see the open doors?

3. What can you do in the future when doors close on you to more readily find the open doors?

Although not formally listed as a homework assignment in Positive Psychotherapy, another useful learned optimism exercise to use with clients is referred to by Seligman (2002) as ABCDE Disputation. In this exercise, clients are asked to think of an *Adverse* experience that lead them to think like a pessimist. They are then asked to write down their *B*eliefs about the adverse event and the *C*onsquences of these pessimistic beliefs. Next, they are asked to *D*ispute their current beliefs in order to feel more *E*nergized and optimistic about the adversity.

According to Seligman (2002), in order to be able to effectively dispute one's thoughts and beliefs in a variety of situations, one can set out to find concrete evidence that their beliefs are faulty. Essentially, learning to consider alternative explanations for adverse events and to choose the one that is most temporary and specific (rather than permanent and global) is key to increasing optimism. Becoming skilled at arguing with oneself is the key to the ABCDE technique. Indeed, the utility of this process has been well-documented, with an entire book being devoted to learned optimism and how to enhance it (see Seligman, 1991, 2002). Worksheet 4.13 can be used to help clients learn to dispute their pessimistic thoughts and therefore become more optimistic.

Worksheet 4.13 ABCDE Disputation (Seligman, 2002) Instructions

There are several key differences between how pessimistic and optimistic people tend to think about the bad and good things that happen to them (Seligman, 1991, 1998; Seligman et al., 1995). More specifically, people who are optimistic make external, variable, and specific attributions for failure-like events rather than the internal, stable, and global attributions made by pessimists. For example, a person who is optimistic will explain a relationship breakup as being due to a poor match between herself and her partner (external), and something that is unlikely to happen in her next relationship (variable), as this negative event is confined to this particular relationship (specific). In contrast, a pessimistic person in the same situation is likely to view the breakup as her fault because she was not pretty enough, caring enough, or good at opening up to other people (internal), and she will predict that such a poor outcome is likely to occur in future relationships (stable), as this negative event is likely to be repeated should she even find another person to connect with (global). When it comes to explaining successful events or outcomes, the optimist will attribute the success to internal, stable, and global factors while the pessimist will explain his or her success as the result of external, variable, and specific attributions.

Learning to consider alternative explanations for adverse events and to choose the one that is most variable and specific (rather than stable and global) is key to increasing optimism. In order to be able to effectively dispute your thoughts and beliefs in a variety of situations, you can set out to find concrete evidence that your beliefs are faulty. Becoming skilled at arguing with yourself is the key to the ABCDE technique (Seligman, 2002).

In order to effectively dispute your own pessimistic thoughts, you must first be able to recognize them and then to treat these thoughts as if someone else had said them to you. Indeed, we are often better able to dispute what other people say to us than what we say to ourselves (Seligman, 2002). One way to argue with yourself when you identify a pessimistic belief is to ask yourself the questions: "What is the evidence for the belief?" and "What alternative ways can I look at this situation?" When you identify a pessimistic belief that is warranted, you might then ask yourself "What does this negative event really mean – is the outcome as negative as I am making it out to be?" or ask yourself "How useful is it for me to dwell on this negative event or belief?" (Seligman, 2002).

In this exercise you are being asked to pay attention to any *A*dverse experiences that you have over the course of the next few weeks that lead you to think like a pessimist. Next, write down your *B*eliefs about the adverse events and the *C*onsquences of these pessimistic beliefs. Then vigorously *D*ispute your current beliefs in order to feel more *E*nergized and optimistic about the adversities. If you find it difficult to dispute the thoughts on your own, turning to a friend or a loved one for help in finding the disputation may be helpful. Please record at least five disputation examples in the spaces provided below.

Two examples of completed ABCDE disputation records are provided below for your reference. The first example is about a bad event and the second is about a good event.

Example 1: Negative event

Adversity: I received a negative review from my boss at work. She said that I am not outgoing enough to work the sales floor and therefore is going to have me work in the stockroom instead.

Beliefs: I have been working really hard and obviously it does not matter. I hate my boss and this stupid job. I don't want to see her or anyone at work for that matter. I am fed up with the whole thing.

Consequences: I got my review two days ago and am still furious. I really want to tell my boss off and then quit so that she can deal with covering my hours for the next week. I called in sick already yesterday since I could not fathom seeing her. I don't know what I am going to do tomorrow though. I am scheduled to work a double shift and don't have any more sick days left.

Disputation: Although I think my boss could have been more fair in my review, she is probably right that my personality is not as naturally outgoing as many of the other salespeople. I am not always comfortable talking to all of the customers and that probably shows through, but at the same time, I am not completely incapable as she made it seem. I guess she must see this on some level since she still wants me to work there, just in a different position. If she really disliked me, she could have just fired me. Maybe I am taking this too personally. I really do like my colleagues and the pay is pretty good. I guess in the stockroom I will have more time to interact with my colleagues and I don't have to worry so much about my wardrobe. Professional work clothes are expensive!

Energization: I feel much less angry. I am still a little bothered by how the review focused only on the negatives, but I know my boss had a lot of reviews to do that day so she was probably just trying to conserve time. It was hard to admit that I am not as outgoing as some of my colleagues, but I do realize that this is the case. I am actually looking forward to spending more time with my colleagues in the stock room and not feeling so on edge all the time.

Example 2: Positive event

Adversity: I wrote a paper for my English class and my professor thought it was excellent. He asked me to write another paper to submit for a writing competition. The winner of the competition will have his or her work published nationally.

Beliefs: Oh my goodness. I am terrified! I am not that good of a writer. I just got lucky on that last paper. There is no way that I am going to be able to write anything even close to being competitive with all the other entries. I am going to utterly disappoint my professor and probably end up with a poor grade in this class as a result. I wish he had never asked me to do this.

Consequences: I have writer's block and feel sick to my stomach. I don't even know where to begin. I just want to forget all about this.

Disputation: Wait a minute here, would a professor really tell me how good my work is if that were not true? What reason would he have for doing that? He has been teaching for almost 25 years so surely has seen a lot of papers and if he thinks mine is exceptional, then maybe it actually is. I have always gotten good grades in my English classes and on my papers for other classes too. Maybe I am not giving myself enough credit here. I already committed to doing this so I should just follow through. Even if I don't win, it will be a good experience to at least try.

Energization: I feel much more relaxed and able to think more clearly. I think I am over my writer's block too. I have a good idea of the topic I will write on and am going to head to the library right now to get a few more resources.

Please make at least five copies of the following chart in order to record at least five instances of ABCDE disputation in your own life.

ABCDE Disputation Record

Adversity:

Beliefs:

Consequences:

Disputation:

Energization:

It is important to recall the information related to cultural aspects of optimism and pessimism and about the benefits of defensive pessimism as noted in Chapter 3 before working with clients on the optimism exercises previously described. Indeed, such optimism exercises could be ineffective or even problematic if used inappropriately.

A noble person attracts noble people, and knows how to hold onto them.

Goethe

Love and attachment are the foci of Session 10 of Positive Psychotherapy. Clients are assisted in understanding how engagement and meaning in life might be experienced through relationships and connections with others. In particular, clients are asked to consider how they respond to the positive events in the lives of those that they care about (Rashid, 2008).

According to Gable and colleagues (2004), there are four possible ways in which one can respond to the good events in the lives of those with whom one interacts. Table 4.2 provides examples of these four response styles. Of the four styles, only the active–constructive style benefits both the individual one is interacting with, as well as the relationship between the two parties. Indeed, research supports that those who interact with others in active–constructive ways report higher levels of daily happiness, more satisfaction, more trust and

TABLE 4.2 Four Styles of Interpersonal Responding to the Good Events in Others' Lives (Gable et al., 2004).

Situation: a husband responds to his wife's good news that she is being considered for a promotion.

	Constructive	Destructive
Active	"That is wonderful! I am so happy for you. You would be excellent in that new position." (responding enthusiastically; maintaining eye contact, smiling, displaying positive emotions)	"If you get the promotion, you are going to have to be at work all week and on Saturday mornings too." (pointing out the downside; displaying negative nonverbal cues)
Passive	"That's nice that you are being considered for the promotion." (happy, but lacking enthusiasm/ downplaying; little to no active emotional expression)	"A promotion, huh? Well, hurry up and get changed so we can get some dinner. I'm starving." (lacking interest; displaying little to no eye contact, turning away, leaving the room)

Only the active-constructive style of responding benefits both the individual with the good news and the relationship (Gable et al., 2004).

intimacy within their relationships, and less conflicts (Gable et al., 2004). In contrast, the other three response styles are negatively related to well-being for both the person with the good news and one's relationship with that individual.

In order to get better at active–constructive responding, clients can consciously work on becoming aware of their usual style of responding by keeping a daily log of interpersonal interactions. If a person is not often engaging in the active–constructive style, he or she can write down what could have been said to make the response active and constructive and then consciously think about responding in this way in the future. In addition, if one has access to the person who they failed to respond to in an active–constructive manner, the individual can intentionally seek out the person whose good news had been shared and apologize for not being more enthusiastic the first time. Finally, clients can practice this response style by purposefully trying to elicit information about the positive events in the lives of those with whom they interact on a daily basis. Worksheet 4.14 can be provided to help clients learn to become better at active–constructive responding.

Worksheet 4.14 Active–Constructive Responding (Gable et al., 2004) Homework Instructions

When other people you care about tell you good news, how do you typically respond? There are four possible ways in which you can respond to the good events in the lives of those with whom you interact. See the chart below for examples of these response styles.

Situation: A husband responds to his wife's good news that she is being considered for a promotion.

	Constructive	Destructive
Active	*"That is wonderful! I am so happy for you. You would be excellent in that new position."* **(responding enthusiastically; maintaining eye contact, smiling, displaying positive emotions)**	*"If you get the promotion, you are going to have to be at work all week and on Saturday mornings too."* **(pointing out the downside; displaying negative nonverbal cues)**
Passive	*"That's nice that you are being considered for the promotion."* **(happy, but lacking enthusiasm/downplaying; little to no active emotional expression)**	*"A promotion, huh? Well, hurry up and get changed so we can get some dinner. I'm starving."* **(lacking interest; displaying little to no eye contact, turning away, leaving the room)**

Of the four styles, only the active–constructive style benefits both the individual you are interacting with, as well as your relationship with that person. In contrast, the other three response styles are negatively related to well-being for both the person with the good news and your relationship with that individual (Gable et al., 2004).

In order to get better at active–constructive responding, you can consciously work on becoming aware of your usual style of responding by keeping a daily log of your interpersonal interactions. If you are not often engaging in the active–constructive style, you can write down what could have been said to make the response active and constructive and then consciously think about responding in this way in the future. In addition, if you have access to the person/people who you failed to respond to in an active–constructive manner, you can intentionally seek out the person/people whose good news had been shared and apologize for not being more enthusiastic the first time. Finally, you can practice this response style by purposefully trying to elicit information about the positive events in the lives of those with whom you interact on a daily basis.

The chart on the next page has been designed in order to help you get started on becoming better at active–constructive responding. Over the course of the next week, please listen carefully for others to report positive events to you and go out of your way to respond enthusiastically to their good news. As noted above, if in retrospect you realize that you failed to respond actively and constructively to someone's good news, please consider seeking out the person and apologizing for not responding more enthusiastically and be sure to respond in this manner the next time they share their good news.

Finally, you are encouraged to take note of how those in your personal life respond when you share good news with them. If you identify that your friends, family, or significant others fail to respond in the active–constructive style, you might want to teach them about the value of active–constructive responding and how to implement it. Indeed, many people are willing and able to use the active–constructive response style once they understand the importance of this response style in terms of relationship enhancement.

Active–Constructive Responding Log

Positive event reported	Reported by	My response (verbatim)	Type of response (active/passive; constructive/destructive)	Others' reaction to my response	What I could have said/did that would have been better

In addition to helping clients to become better at active–constructing responding, therapists can also encourage clients to think about how those in their personal lives respond to their good events. When clients identify that their significant others fail to respond in the active–constructive style, they can be encouraged to ask for what they need. Indeed, clients can teach those in their lives about the value of active–constructive responding and how easy it is to implement once one is aware of the utility of this response style in terms of relationship enhancement.

Therapists are also highly encouraged to practice active–constructive responding in their work with clients. Indeed, responding in this manner to the positive events reported by clients serves not only to model this important relationship-enhancing behavior, but to strengthen the therapeutic bond as well.

In addition to the active–constructive responding homework, clients are provided with a strengths-date exercise in session 9 (Rashid, 2008). In this homework assignment, clients are asked to set up a date with a significant other that will capitalize upon the strengths of both the client and his or her partner. In order to complete this exercise, it is useful if both the client and the client's partner have completed the VIA Inventory of Character Strengths (Peterson and Seligman, 2004) and know each other's top five strengths. Worksheet 4.15 can be used in the strengths-date planning process. The worksheet includes several example strengths dates as well to help clients in their own date planning.

Worksheet 4.15 Strengths Date Exercise (Rashid, 2008) Instructions

One way to enhance your relationship and to increase positive emotions for yourself and your significant other is through understanding, recognizing, and celebrating one another's character strengths (Rashid, 2008). One way to do this is through planning a strengths date.

In order to complete a strengths date, please be sure that you and your significant other have completed the VIA Inventory of Character Strengths on-line at www.authentichappiness.org or www.viacharacter.org and know each other's top five strengths from this measure. Then, together plan a date that will allow you both to capitalize upon one or more of your signature strengths. Several examples of strengths dates are provided for you below.

Strengths Date Example 1: Tahlia and Jace
Tahlia's strengths:

- Capacity to love and be loved
- Creativity
- Open-mindedness
- Appreciation of beauty and excellence
- Hope

Jace's strengths:

- Humor
- Teamwork
- Zest
- Love of learning
- Curiosity

Strengths date plan: In order to capitalize on Tahlia's strengths of appreciation of beauty and excellence and open-mindedness and Jace's strengths of love of learning and curiosity we will go to the traveling "Bodies: The Exhibition" show that is coming to our local museum next month. This exhibition is something neither of us has been to before. It is an exhibition designed to help people better understand the human body and how it functions. They have actually preserved whole-body specimens and individual organs so that people can see how their bodies really work! People who have seen it say it is fascinating so we are looking forward to seeing for ourselves.

Strengths Date Example 2: Ceanna and Briella
Ceanna's strengths:

- Fairness
- Gratitude
- Teamwork
- Kindness
- Perspective

Briella's strengths

- Forgiveness
- Modesty
- Curiosity
- Leadership
- Social intelligence

Strengths date plan: In order to capitalize on Ceanna's strengths of kindness and teamwork and Briella's strengths of leadership and social intelligence, we are going to volunteer with the local girl scouts to co-lead a troop outing for one weekend next month. Briella will use her social intelligence and leadership skills to plan the events of the outing and to motivate all the girls to fully participate. Ceanna will use her teamwork strength to make sure the girls work together to accomplish the tasks and activities that Briella plans. Ceanna will also be capitalizing on her kindness strength since this entire plan is altruistic in nature.....we are doing this voluntarily. Although they offer a small stipend for leaders, we are not going to accept it.

Use the worksheet below to guide you and your significant other through planning, implementing, and reflecting upon your own strengths date.

Strengths Date Planning Worksheet

Top five strengths for _____:

1.

2.

3.

4.

5.

Top five strengths for _____:

1.

2.

3.

4.

5.

Strengths date plan:

Please briefly respond to the following questions after carrying out your strengths date:

Was your date enjoyable? Did you and your significant other experience positive emotions during and/or after the date? Briefly describe your response below.

Do you feel as if you and your significant other grew closer or have a better understanding of one another as a result of this exercise? Briefly describe your response below.

Did your strengths date go as planned? Did you feel as if your strengths and the strengths of your partner were both put into action during your date? Please briefly describe your response below.

Although not a formal aspect of Positive Psychotherapy, following the suggestions of well-known relationship researcher, John Gottman, is also recommended for clients who are looking specifically to enhance interpersonal relationships with significant others. According to Gottman and Silver (1999), marriages and romantic relationships that flourish have partners who commit five hours per week to engaging in behaviors that build the strength of their relationship. In fact, Gottman refers to these behaviors, listed in Table 4.3, as the "magic five hours." These crucial behaviors for creating successful relationships are likely done naturally by many couples; however, for those who may feel that there is room for improvement in their current relationship, examining Worksheet 4.16 may be very informative. If one can identify any of the magic five hour behaviors as lacking, extra effort can be made to incorporate these activities on a regular basis. Reviewing the list with one's partner may be all that is needed in order to make changes for implementing these relatively simple, yet highly important relationship-enhancing behaviors.

TABLE 4.3 "Magic Five Hours" for Relationship Enhancement (Gottman and Silver, 1999).

Intimate relationships that flourish have partners who devote 5 hours per week to enhancing the emotional connection that keeps the relationship alive as follows:

1. Partings	2 minutes per work day × 5 days a week = 10 minutes • Find one thing out about what your partner is going to do that day
2. Reunions	20 minutes per work day × 5 days a week = 1 hour 40 minutes • Find out how your partner's day went
3. Admiration/appreciation	5 minutes × 7 days a week = 35 minutes • Find one thing to admire or appreciate about your partner each day and share this admiration with him or her
4. Affection	5 minutes × 7 days a week = 35 minutes • Kissing, touching, playfulness
5. Date	2 hours per week = 2 hours • Alone time with just your partner

---

Worksheet 4.16 Implementing the "Magic Five Hours" for Relationship Enhancement (Gottman and Silver, 1999)

Marriages and romantic relationships that flourish have partners who commit five hours per week to engaging in behaviors that build the strength of their relationship. In fact, these behaviors, listed in the chart below, are referred to as the "Magic Five Hours" (Gottman and Silver, 1999).

These crucial behaviors for creating successful relationships are likely done naturally by many couples; however, if you feel as if there is room for improvement in your current relationship, carefully review the chart below with your partner in order to identify whether or not any of the magic five hour behaviors are lacking in your relationship. If you find one or more of these behaviors to be lacking, vow to make an extra effort to incorporate these activities into your interactions on a regular basis.

Intimate relationships that flourish have partners who devote 5 hours per week to enhancing the emotional connection that keeps the relationship alive as follows:

1. **Partings** – 2 minutes per work day × 5 days a week = 10 minutes
   - Find one thing out about what your partner is going to do that day

2. **Reunions** – 20 minutes per work day × 5 days a week = 1 hour 40 minutes
   - Find out how your partner's day went

3. **Admiration/appreciation** – 5 minutes × 7 days a week = 35 minutes
   - Find one thing to admire or appreciate about your partner each day and share this admiration with him or her

4. **Affection** – 5 minutes × 7 days a week = 35 minutes
   - Kissing, touching, playfulness

5. **Date** – 2 hours per week = 2 hours
   - Alone time with just your partner

Session 11 of Positive Psychotherapy is designed to enhance meaning through helping clients realize the importance of understanding and acknowledging the highest strengths of one's family members (Rashid, 2008). Indeed, such recognition of family members' strengths not only serves to increase appreciation for one another amongst family members and to forge stronger connections, but potentially to help clients gain new insights into behaviors of family members that were previously misunderstood. For example, when a wife discovers that several of the top strengths for her husband are honesty, justice, and fairness, she is better able to understand why he drives all the way across town to return the extra dollar he was accidentally given when checking out at the grocery store, even though he will spend over a dollar in gas in the process of returning this money. Rather than seeing his behavior as illogical, she can see that he is simply acting according to his strengths of character. Likewise, parents who come to understand that a signature strength for their child is curiosity and interest in the world are better able to tolerate and even come to enjoy the abundance of questions posed by their child about how and why things work the way that they do.

A family tree of strengths assignment is provided as homework following this session (Rashid, 2008). In order to complete this homework, clients must ask family members to complete the VIA Strengths Inventory (Peterson and Seligman, 2004) on-line and to use the results to create a strengths family tree that will then be discussed in a family meeting. Worksheet 4.17 is designed to assist clients in the process of making their strengths family trees.

Worksheet 4.17 Family Tree of Strengths Homework Assignment Instructions (Rashid, 2008)

One way to enhance meaning in your life is through realizing the importance of understanding and acknowledging the highest strengths of your family members and how you fit into your larger family network (Rashid, 2008). When you recognize the strengths of your family members, you are more likely to better appreciate one another and to build stronger connections. In addition, learning about one another's strengths may potentially help you to gain new insights into behaviors of your family members that you previously misunderstood. For example, when a wife discovers that several of the top strengths for her husband are honesty, justice, and fairness, she is better able to understand why he drives all the way across town to return the extra dollar he was accidentally given when checking out at the grocery store, even though he will spend over a dollar in gas in the process of returning this money. Rather than seeing his behavior as illogical, she can see that he is simply acting according to his strengths of character. Likewise, parents who come to understand that a signature strength for their child is curiosity and interest in the world are better able to tolerate and even come to enjoy the abundance of questions posed by their child about how and why things work the way that they do.

This family tree of strengths assignment is designed to help you and your family members gain greater insight into each other's strengths. In order to complete this homework, please ask your family members to complete the VIA Strengths Inventory or the Children's Strength Survey on-line at www.authentichappiness.org or www.viacharacter.org and to use the results to create a strengths family tree. After the family tree is complete, arrange for a family meeting in which you discuss one another's strengths. The following questions may be useful for guiding this family discussion:

1. Can we find any patterns in terms of the strengths in our family?

2. Can you identify the people in our family who have helped you to develop your strengths?

3. Do you have any strengths that no one else in the family has among their top five?

4. How can we use our strengths together in order to make our family relationships stronger?

5. Are there any behaviors that you understand differently about your mom, dad, sister, brother, etc…now that you know what his or her strengths are?

He who allows his day to pass by without practicing generosity and enjoying life's pleasures is like a blacksmith's bellows: he breathes but does not live.

Proverbs

Session 12 of Positive Psychotherapy is used to introduce clients to the concept of savoring (Rashid, 2008). Enhancing positive emotions in the present can be achieved by partaking in pleasurable activities and by finding activities that fully engage clients and utilize their personal strengths (Seligman, 2002). For example, clients might eat their favorite food for dinner or indulge in a favorite desert. Relaxing in a warm bath, getting a massage, or listening to one's favorite music can enhance positive emotions for some. Ultimately, there is an endless range of possibilities when it comes to activities that can enhance positive emotions in the present. In order to feel more momentary positive emotion in one's life, however, there are several key concepts clients need to consider, namely, habituation and savoring (Seligman, 2002).

Habituation has to do with the fact that if one continuously engages in the same pleasurable activity, it is no longer going to produce the positive emotion that it once produced. For example, if a client eats his favorite desert every night for two weeks, it is no longer going to be a treat, and may even become something that is unpleasant. So, to avoid habituation, clients should be taught to space out and mix up the pleasurable activities in which one engages. In addition, engaging in specific savoring techniques can enhance positive experiences as well (Seligman, 2002; Bryant and Veroff, 2002).

In order to help clients practice engaging in and savoring the pleasures, they are instructed to complete a savoring homework assignment in which they plan and implement a pleasurable activity while intentionally engaging in savoring techniques (Rashid, 2008). Savoring entails being aware of pleasures and purposefully paying attention to the experience of pleasure (Bryant and Veroff, 2002). There are four kinds of savoring, namely, basking (i.e., receiving congratulations or praise), thanksgiving (i.e., expressing gratitude for positive experiences), marveling (i.e., getting caught up in the experience of wonder or awe), and luxuriating (i.e., indulging the senses). In order to savor an event or activity, the following techniques can be utilized: (a) share the experience with others, (b) make mental notes of the event and reminisce about the event after it is over, (c) congratulate oneself or take pride in what has happened, (d) be mindful of important elements of the event while blocking out distractions and kill-joy thinking, and (e) let oneself get totally absorbed in the event (Bryant and Veroff, 2002; Seligman, 2002). Worksheet 4.18 is provided as a guide for clients in completing this savoring activity.

Worksheet 4.18   Savoring Assignment (Rashid, 2008) Instructions

One way to increase positive emotions is to savor the pleasures in life. You are being asked to plan and implement at least one pleasurable activity while intentionally engaging in savoring techniques (Rashid, 2008). Savoring entails being aware of pleasures and purposefully paying attention to the experience of pleasure (Bryant and Veroff, 2002).

In order to savor an event or activity, the following techniques can be utilized (Bryant and Veroff, 2002; Seligman, 2002):

Share the experience with others – tell others about the pleasurable experience before it takes place, engage in the experience with others if possible, and reminisce about the positive experience with others after it is over.

Memory-building – Make mental notes of the event as it is happening and later reminisce about the event once it is over. If possible, you might also take photos or purchase souvenirs that represent the positive event.

Self-congratulation – Congratulate yourself or take pride in what has happened.

Sharpen your perceptions – Be mindful of important elements of the event while blocking out distractions or kill-joy thinking. (**Kill-joy thinking** is one way to kill savoring. This type of thinking occurs when you begin to think about how the positive event is not as good as someone else's or how it could be better, when you begin to think of things you could/should be doing instead, or when you get distracted by thoughts unrelated to the pleasurable experience.)

Absorption – Let yourself get totally absorbed in the event.

In the space provided below, please write out your plan for savoring a positive experience. If possible, engaging in pleasurable activities for a half day or full day is recommended (Seligman, 2002). Be sure to build these pleasurable activities into your schedule and resist the urge to put them off in order to get other tasks completed.

On _____ (date), the pleasurable experience(s) I plan to engage in are:

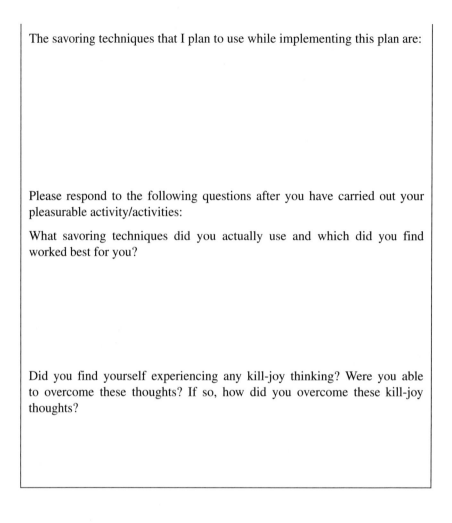

The savoring techniques that I plan to use while implementing this plan are:

Please respond to the following questions after you have carried out your pleasurable activity/activities:

What savoring techniques did you actually use and which did you find worked best for you?

Did you find yourself experiencing any kill-joy thinking? Were you able to overcome these thoughts? If so, how did you overcome these kill-joy thoughts?

It is one of the most beautiful compensations in life... we can never help another without helping ourselves.

Ralph Waldo Emerson

Finding meaning through implementing signature strengths in order to serve others is the goal of session 13. In this session, therapists engage clients in discussions of ways in which their top five strengths from the VIA Strengths Inventory (Peterson and Seligman, 2004) can be utilized to help others. Clients are then encouraged to "give the gift of time by doing something that requires a fair amount of time and whose creation calls on signature strengths, such as mentoring a child or doing community service" (Rashid, 2008, p. 202). This homework assignment can be facilitated through the use of Worksheet 4.19.

Worksheet 4.19 Giving the Gift of Time (Rashid, 2008) Instructions

One way to enhance your sense of meaning and purpose in life is to use your signature strengths in order to serve others (Rashid, 2008). Although giving your time to help others may not seem enjoyable on the surface, most people find a deep sense of gratification and purpose *after* they have given this precious gift to another. This worksheet has been designed to help you think of ways in which your top five strengths from the VIA Strengths Inventory (Peterson and Seligman, 2004) can be utilized to help others.

My top Five VIA strengths:

1.

2.

3.

4.

5.

Formal volunteer experiences (for example, helping to build homes for low-income families in need with your local chapter of Habitat for Humanity, helping to prepare meals for homeless residents at a local soup kitchen or homeless shelter, participating in outreach services through a religious organization, serving as a big brother or big sister at your local big brothers/big sisters organization, leading a girls or boys scout troop, etc....) that would capitalize upon one or more of my strengths are:

Informal acts of kindness (for example, helping teach your next door neighbor's child how to play a new sport, playing music for residents in senior living facilities, or offering to watch your neighbor's pet and mow her grass while on vacation) that would capitalize on my strengths are:

How will you give the gift of time to another between now and your next therapy session?

Please respond to the following questions *after* you have given the gift of time:

1. How did it feel to give the gift of time to another?

2. Did you actually use your strengths in the process of giving your gift of time?

3. How did the person (or people) you gave your gift of time to respond to your actions?

4. Did you experience a sense of meaning or connection to something larger than yourself through this activity? Please briefly explain your response to this question below.

In the 14th and final session of Positive Psychotherapy, the full life is discussed (see the explanation of the full life as described previously in this chapter). Clients are asked to come to this session having re-taken the Positive Psychotherapy Inventory (see Worksheet 4.4) which is discussed in comparison to the results from this measure taken earlier at session 2. Discussion of any homework assignments that were not previously reviewed takes place and the progress or gains made throughout the Positive Psychotherapy sessions are made explicit.

Finally, therapists provide clients with a plan for maintaining or continuing to strengthen the skills and lessons learned throughout this treatment regimen (Rashid, 2008).

4.1.4 Quality of Life Therapy

Quality of Life Therapy has been described as a comprehensive approach to blending the tenets of positive psychology with cognitive therapy in order to help clients discover and proceed toward their needs, goals, and wishes in important areas of life in order to live a life of quality and satisfaction (Frisch, 2006). Indeed, Quality of Life Therapy is so comprehensive that all of the components of this treatment approach cannot be explained within the context of this text. However, an overview is provided and those therapists interested in learning more about Quality of Life Therapy can refer directly to Frisch (2006) for more details.

Quality of Life Therapy emphasizes a whole life or life goal perspective (Frisch, 2006). More specifically, at each stage of treatment a direct connection is made between the client's life goals, needs, and wishes and the interventions being used. In addition, clients are conceptualized in a complete way that incorporates both their strengths and weaknesses in 16 areas of everyday life functioning as well as any actual psychopathology they may be experiencing. Table 4.4 includes the 16 areas of life functioning that are major foci of this treatment approach and can be measured using the Quality of Life Inventory (QOLI; Frisch, 1994).

Quality of Life Therapy is built upon a five-fold model of life satisfaction referred to as the CASIO model (Frisch, 2006). Central to this model is the idea that satisfaction in any given area of life is made up of four components, namely, 1) the objective *C*ircumstances or *C*haracteristics of the life area; 2) the subjective *A*ttitudes, perceptions, and interpretations held by a client regarding the life area; 3) a client's evaluation of fulfillment in the life area based on his or her *S*tandards of what constitutes fulfillment in that life domain; and 4) the value or *I*mportance the client places on the life area in terms of his or her overall well-being. The "O" in this CASIO model represents the *O*verall satisfaction a client experiences in life. A client's overall satisfaction levels can be increased by raising satisfaction in each of the 16 life areas noted in Table 4.4 (Frisch, 2006).

Clients in Quality of Life Therapy are guided to gain more satisfaction in the important domains of their lives by considering how to get their most important goals and needs fulfilled by following the CASIO model. For example, if clients find that they are dissatisfied in one or more important life areas, Quality of Life therapists would assist the clients to consider ways in which they could *C*hange their circumstances, for example, by changing careers, relationships, or moving, or by seeking out support or assistance to help with the source of the dissatisfaction. Next, clients are asked to consider how they can change their *A*ttitudes about the situation in order to fix

TABLE 4.4   The 16 Areas of Everyday Life Functioning that are the Foci of Quality of Life Therapy (Frisch, 2006).

Area of life functioning	Definition
Health	Being physically fit, not sick, and without pain or disability.
Self-esteem	Liking and respecting yourself in light of your strengths and weaknesses, successes and failures, and ability to handle problems.
Goals-and-values/Spiritual life	(A person's goals-and-values or philosophy of life may or may not include spiritual life.) Goals-and-values are your beliefs about what matters most in life and how you should live, both now and in the future. This includes your goals in life, what you think is right or wrong, and the purpose or meaning of life as you see it. Spiritual life may or may not be an important part of a person's goals-and-values. Spiritual life refers to spiritual or religious beliefs or practices that you pursue on your own or as part of a like-minded spiritual community.
Money (or standard of living)	The money you earn, the things you own (like a car or furniture), and believing that you will have the money and things that you need in the future.
Work	Your career or how you spend most of your time. You may work at a job, at home taking care of your family, or at school as a student. Work includes your duties on the job, the money you earn (if any), and the people you work with.
Play (or recreation)	What you do in your free time to relax, have fun, or improve yourself. This could include watching movies, visiting friends, or pursuing a hobby like sports or gardening.
Learning	Gaining new skills or information about things that interest you. Learning can come from reading books or taking classes on subjects like history, car repair, or using a computer.
Creativity	Using your imagination to come up with new and clever ways to solve everyday problems or to pursue a hobby like painting, photography, or needlework. This can include decorating your home, playing the guitar, or finding a new way to solve a problem at work.
Helping (social service and civic action)	Helping others (not just friends or relatives) in need or helping to make your community a better place to live. Helping can be done on your own or in a group like a church, a neighborhood association, or a political party. Helping can include doing volunteer work at a school or giving money to a good cause.

TABLE 4.4 (Continued)

Area of life functioning	Definition
Love (or love relationship)	A very close romantic relationship with another person. Love usually includes sexual feelings and feeling loved, cared for, and understood.
Friends (or friendships)	People (not relatives) you know well and care about who have interests and opinions like yours. Friends have fun together, talk about personal problems, and help each other out.
Children	How you get along with your child (or children). How you get along as you care for, visit, or play with your child (or children).
Relatives	How you get along with your parents, grandparents, brothers, sisters, aunts, uncles, and in-laws. How you get along when you are doing things together like visiting, talking on the telephone, or helping each other.
Home	Where you live. Your house or apartment and the yard around it. How nice it looks, how big it is, and your rent or house payment.
Neighborhood	The area around your home. How nice it looks, the amount of crime in the area, and how well you like your neighbors.
Community	The whole city, town, or rural area where you live (not just your neighborhood). Community includes how nice the area looks, the amount of crime, and how well you like the people. It also includes places to go for fun like parks, concerts, sporting events, and restaurants. You may also consider the cost of things you need to buy, the availability of jobs, the government, schools, taxes, and pollution.

Reproduced with permission from John Wiley & Sons.

any errors in thinking or cognitive distortions from which the clients may be working. The third component of change is to have clients reevaluate and restructure their goals and *S*tandards for fulfillment in a particular life domain such that their standards are in line with reality. Changing priorities or the *I*mportance that is placed on each life area is the fourth change strategy of Quality of Life Therapy. Here, clients are asked to consider changing what they think is most important in life by focusing on what is most under their control and deemphasizing those aspects that are outside of their control. Finally, clients are guided to increase their *O*verall level of life satisfaction by attending to those specific life areas that they may be overlooking because they are not of immediate concern (Frisch, 2006). For example, a client who has come to therapy because of problems related to work might be able to boost her overall level of life satisfaction by focusing on her satisfaction in relationships and love while simultaneously working on the dissatisfaction related to her career.

In addition to the CASIO model and associated change strategies for enhancing life satisfaction, Quality of Life Therapy emphasizes the need for clients to engage in self-care, to make time for themselves each day in order to relax, to process stressors and worries, and to focus on their key life goals that provide a sense of meaning and purpose in their lives. A vast number of client exercises and homework assignments (i.e., "mindful breathing and the guide for worry warts," "play it again technique," the "five minutes to joy technique," and "mental health day or hour technique") are provided by Frisch (2006) to help therapists assist their clients in achieving lasting happiness, contentment, and satisfaction with life in general. In addition, Frisch (2006) provides a number of area-specific intervention strategies and exercises (i.e., the "emotional honesty" and "find a friend, find a mate" principles for relationship enhancement) for use with clients who are struggling to find satisfaction in one or more of the 16 life areas emphasized in this treatment protocol.

4.1.5 Well-Being Therapy

Well-Being Therapy is a brief (8 session), structured, directive, and problem-oriented treatment program based upon Ryff's (1989) cognitive model of psychological well-being that utilizes client self-observations, structured journaling, and client and therapist interactions in order to increase client well-being (Ruini and Fava, 2004). Ryff's (1989) model of psychological well-being contains six dimensions, including environmental mastery, personal growth, purpose in life, autonomy, self-acceptance, and positive relations with others. The goal of therapists who practice Well-Being Therapy is to help clients move from low to high levels of functioning in each of the six domains of psychological well-being as described in Table 4.5 (Ruini and Fava, 2004).

In order to help clients move from impaired to optimal levels of psychological well-being, therapists help clients identify current and previous well-being experiences in their lives, no matter how brief those well-being experiences may have been (Ruini and Fava, 2004). Clients are given a homework assignment that entails writing about their well-being experiences and the circumstances of such experiences in a structured diary. Each experience that is written down is also to be evaluated by the client on a scale from 1 to 100, with 1 representing the complete absence of well-being and 100 the most intense well-being possible (Ruini and Fava, 2004). Worksheet 4.20 can be copied, bound together, and provided to clients for completing this homework task. In addition to using this structured journaling technique to help clients

TABLE 4.5 Desired Changes in Psychological Well-Being (Ryff, 1989) for Clients Participating in Well-Being Therapy (Ruini and Fava, 2004).

Psychological well-being dimensions	Impaired level functioning	Optimal level functioning
Environmental mastery	The client has or feels difficulties in managing everyday affairs; feels unable to change or improve surrounding context; is unaware of surrounding opportunities; lacks sense of control over external world.	The client has a sense of mastery and competence in managing the environment; controls external activities; makes effective use of surrounding opportunities; is able to create or choose contexts suitable to personal needs and values.
Personal growth	The client has a sense of personal stagnation; lacks a sense of improvement or expansion over time; feels bored and uninterested with life; feels unable to develop new attitudes or behaviors.	The client has a feeling of continued development; sees self as growing and expanding; is open to new experiences; has a sense of realizing own potential; sees improvement in self and behavior over time.
Purpose in life	The client lacks a sense of meaning in life; has few goals or aims, lacks a sense of direction, does not see purpose in past life; has no outlooks or beliefs that give life meaning.	The client has goals in life and a sense of directedness; feels there is meaning to present and past life; holds beliefs that give life purpose; has aims and objectives for living.
Autonomy	The client is overconcerned with the expectations and evaluations of others; relies on judgment of others to make important decisions; conforms to social pressures to think or act in certain ways.	The client is self-determining and independent; able to resist social pressures; regulates behavior from within; evaluates self by personal standards.
Self-acceptance	The client feels dissatisfied with self; is disappointed with what has occurred in past life; is troubled about certain personal qualities; wishes to be different from what he or she is.	The client has a positive attitude toward the self; accepts his or her good and bad qualities; feels positive about his or her past life.
Positive relations with others	The client has few close, trusting relationships with others; finds it difficult to be open and is isolated and frustrated in interpersonal relationships; is not willing to make compromises to sustain important ties with others.	The client has warm and trusting relationships with others; is concerned about the welfare of others; is capable of strong empathy, affection, and intimacy; understands the give and take of human relationships.

Reproduced with permission from John Wiley & Sons.

become more aware of instances of psychological well-being in their lives, results from the psychological well-being portion of the Mental Health Continuum – Long Form (see Worksheet 2.5) can be used to assess client levels of psychological well-being. Indeed, the psychological well-being subscale on the MHC-LF measure was also developed based upon Ryff's (1989) conceptualization.

Worksheet 4.20   Well-Being Diary Instructions

In order to help you experience more well-being in your life, you are being asked to keep a well-being diary. Please identify and write about current and/or previous well-being experiences in your life, no matter how brief those well-being experiences may have been (Ruini and Fava, 2004). After writing about each experience and the circumstances that brought about those experiences, please rate each experience on a scale of 1 to 100, with 0 representing the complete absence of well-being and 100 the most intense well-being possible.

The following chart can be copied, bound together, and then used as a guide for you in completing this diary assignment.

Well-being experience:

Please write about your well-being experience below. Be sure to include when this experience occurred, the circumstances that lead to the well-being experience, the role you or others played in making this experience occur, and how you felt during and after this well-being experience.

Well-being rating for this well-being experience:

(Rating scale = 1 to 100, with 1 representing the complete absence of well-being and 100 the most intense well-being possible.)

After clients have become thoroughly aware of instances of well-being in their lives, the next phase of treatment entails helping clients to identify the thoughts and beliefs they have that get in the way of experiencing well-being, as well as the feelings associated with well-being (Ruini and Fava, 2004). This phase of treatment is similar to the identification of automatic thoughts (Beck et al., 1979) or irrational beliefs (Ellis and Becker, 1982) in popular cognitive therapy treatment programs; however, in Well-Being Therapy, the self-observation of client thoughts is based upon instances of well-being rather than instances of distress (Ruini and Fava, 2004). This is vital information for therapists who conduct Well-Being Therapy to elicit from clients, as it allows therapists to discover those areas of psychological well-being that are free of irrational or automatic thoughts as well as those areas that are highly affected by such faulty thinking.

Once therapists and clients understand which areas of psychological well-being are affected and unaffected by negative thinking, therapists can help clients to challenge or refute their faulty thinking by asking what evidence exists to support their current beliefs while also encouraging behaviors and actions that are likely to elicit feelings of well-being. Finally, therapists should educate clients about the six dimensions of psychological well-being (see Table 4.5) and help them to make connections regarding their own functioning in each of these domains. For those dimensions that are problematic for clients, errors in thinking and alternative interpretations should continue to be explored and discussed. In general, the key techniques in helping clients overcome deficits in psychological well-being include cognitive restructuring of automatic thoughts, scheduling of activities that will produce a sense of mastery or pleasure, assertiveness training, and problem-solving (Ruini and Fava, 2004).

Attending to Culture in Well-Being Therapy

When conducting Well-Being Therapy (Ruini and Fava, 2004), it is important to consider the cultural factors that may impact client well-being. For example, striving for autonomy may not lead to greater well-being for clients from collectivistic cultures. Indeed, striving for autonomy within a collectivistic family or community may actually lead to more problems. Likewise, control over one's environment or external activities may not be a desired or useful goal for clients from cultural contexts in which they were taught to let things happen naturally and to focus on the here and now.

4.1.6 Hope Therapy

The grand essentials of happiness are: something to do, something to love, and something to hope for.

Allan K. Chalmers

As noted in Chapter 3, hope consists of one's perceptions of his or her abilities to create clear goals, to develop plans for reaching those goals (pathways thinking), and to find and maintain the energy and motivation necessary for following through with goal pursuits (agency thinking). Goals can be anything clients desire to experience, create, get, do, or become, hence, they may be major, lifelong goals or more minor, short-term goals. In order for clients to achieve their goals, both pathways and agency thinking are necessary (Lopez et al., 2004).

Hope theory posits that emotions follow from one's thoughts regarding goal pursuits. More specifically, "emotions are a by-product of goal-directed thought – positive emotions reflecting perceived success in the pursuit of goals, and negative emotions reflecting perceived failures" (Snyder, 2000, p. 11). Indeed, research supports this postulate as both correlational and causal designs have shown that blocked goal pursuits are related to negative emotional responses (Snyder et al., 1996) and problems that arise in the process of goal attainment undermine well-being (Diener, 1984; Emmons, 1986), whereas there is no support for low well-being impeding later goal pursuits (Brunstein, 1993; Little, 1989).

According to Snyder and colleagues (2000), higher hope is related to benefits across a wide range of therapy outcome indicators. More specifically, research shows that high-hope individuals have more positive and less negative thoughts and see themselves in a more favorable light than those with low-hope (Snyder et al., 1996). In addition, high-hope people have higher self-esteem, and report having more energy and confidence, and being more challenged by their goals than those with lower hope (Snyder et al., 1996). In contrast, low-hope people tend to think negatively about their goal pursuits, often feeling overwhelmed by them. Low hope individuals often present themselves in a self-effacing manner, and they are especially prone to recalling personal weaknesses (Snyder et al., 2000).

Hopeful, goal-directed thinking is important in predicting outcomes in therapy (Snyder et al., 2000). During the first four weeks of psychological treatment, many clients improve considerably (Howard et al., 1993; Ilardi and Craighead, 1994). Indeed, even without actual treatment, the mere promise of therapy can set a positive change process into motion, for example, 40% to 66% of clients have reported feeling better before their initial counseling sessions (Lawson, 1994; Weiner-Davis et al., 1987). In addition, 56% to 71% of the overall change variance in psychotherapy has been found in the early stages of treatment (Fennell and Teasdale, 1987; Howard et al., 1993).

Snyder and colleagues (2000) suggest that these findings of improvement before and shortly after the start of counseling are due to an increase in agency thinking. First, the very decision to seek therapy "represents a new determination to achieve a specific goal of 'getting better.' As such, a spark in agency thinking propels the new client toward the goal of improvement" (Snyder et al., 1999, p. 184). Second, the sense of motivation the therapist conveys to the client is often infectious, raising the client's agency self-perceptions and capabilities. Indeed, higher levels of agency in therapists is positively related to higher levels of agency in clients (Crouch, 1989, as cited in Snyder et al., 2000). Third, the establishment of a therapeutic alliance early in counseling also serves as a potential agency-enhancing function for the client, since feeling cared for may help clients feel more motivated to make needed life changes (Snyder et al., 2000).

The decision to seek counseling not only leads to increased agency thinking, but also to increased pathways thinking. "To initiate psychotherapy reflects a momentous decision, in which the client typically taps into the rich societal lore about psychotherapy as a vehicle for making improvements. This thought – that therapy actually may help – is perhaps the first pathways-enhancing thought in the sequence of psychotherapy" (Snyder et al., 2000, p. 135). When therapy is underway, pathways thinking can also be enhanced by therapists in a number of ways. Details about hope enhancement will be described in the Hope Enhancing section below.

Hope Therapy is designed to capitalize upon hope in the therapy process, as hope seems to be a malleable strength that can indeed serve as an important therapeutic change agent (Lopez et al., 2004). Therapists who practice Hope Therapy help clients to conceptualize clearer goals, to learn how to produce multiple pathways to reach goals, and to generate the mental energy needed to sustain goal pursuits in order to positively change client self-perceptions regarding their abilities to engage in goal-directed and agentic thinking (Lopez et al., 2000b).

There are multiple principles that underpin Hope Therapy, including the fact that Hope Therapy is designed to be a brief, semi-structured form of therapy in which the primary focus is upon current goals. In addition, in order to enhance hope, therapists help clients to focus on goals, possibilities, and past successes rather than on problems or failures. There are four major components of Hope Therapy, namely, Hope Finding, Hope Bonding, Hope Enhancing, and Hope Reminding. Various strategies for accentuating hope in each of these components of Hope Therapy are described in the following sections. However, before exploring the stages of Hope Therapy, Lopez and colleagues (2000b) recommend that therapists who practice from this perspective make sure they fully understand hope theory, assess their own hope levels, and work to increase hope if necessary. Indeed, since hope begets hope, being a hopeful helper who models and transfers hope to clients is crucial to conducting Hope Therapy.

Hope Finding

Hope Finding entails discovering the hope that each client possesses that can be built upon in the therapeutic change process. Each client will likely have a different way of experiencing hope, since hope can be trait-like (i.e., being hopeful about goals in general), domain-specific (i.e., being hopeful about a particular life domain), or goal-specific (i.e., being hopeful about one specific goal; Lopez et al., 2004).

Assessing and identifying the type(s) of hope present for clients can be done by having clients complete one or more measures of hope as presented in Chapter 3. In addition, hope can be determined through narrative approaches or through hope profiling (Lopez et al., 2004).

When implementing narrative strategies for hope finding, therapists educate clients about goals, agency, and pathways thinking through sharing stories of hopeful characters. Eventually, clients are asked to tell stories from their own lives in which the components of hope can be identified and made explicit. Many times, clients tell stories of hope without even realizing it; hence, astute therapists will be able to point out the components of hope in a client's life even if the client was not specifically asked to share a hopeful life experience story.

Therapists can increase client willingness to engage in the use of narratives in Hope Therapy by providing clients with a rationale for doing so. More specifically, explaining to clients that the goal of this therapeutic technique is to help uncover times when clients have been hopeful so that they realize that they have this ability is key. In order to avoid demoralization, therapists should also be clear that hope finding is often difficult at first and something that may take time (Lopez et al., 2000b).

Lopez and colleagues (2004) encourage therapists to consider the 14 aspects of client narratives noted in Table 4.6 when using this hope finding strategy. In addition, therapists should be willing to pose these questions to clients in order to direct their attention to the hopeful elements of their stories, while also making connections between past stories and current issues (Lopez et al., 2000b).

TABLE 4.6 The 14 Aspects of Client Narratives to Attend to in Hope Finding (Lopez et al., 2004).

1. How did the client generate goals?
2. What was the motivation?
3. How attainable or realistic were the goals?
4. How were the goals perceived?
5. What was the client's mood/attitude during the process?
6. How was the movement toward goals initiated?
7. How was the movement toward goals maintained?
8. What were the biggest barriers to reaching the goals?
9. What emotions did these barriers elicit?
10. How were barriers overcome, and what steps were taken to reach the goals?
11. Were the goals attained?
12. How does the client feel about the outcome?
13. If the client were to attempt the same goal today, what would he or she do differently?
14. Can the client recast the experience in more hopeful terms (i.e., by identifying lessons learned that can facilitate future efforts)?

Hope profiling is another narrative technique for identifying hope that clients can be assigned to complete outside of therapy sessions. Clients are asked to write approximately five short stories about their previous or current goal pursuits. They can also be encouraged to write stories about a variety of life domains (i.e., work-related, family-related, sport-related, etc.). These stories are then reviewed within the therapeutic context and utilized to help clients see that they have the resources needed to make life changes (Lopez et al., 2004). Worksheet 4.21 can be copied, bound together, and provided to clients to guide them in the hope profiling process. In addition, having a copy of the questions in Table 4.6 handy when conducting the in-session review of client hope stories is advised.

Worksheet 4.21 Hope Profiling (Lopez et al., 2004) Instructions

Hope narratives

In order to help you identify that you have the resources needed for making changes you desire in your life, you are being asked to write five short stories about your past or current goal pursuits. As you write your stories, please consider including information about how you developed your goals, the path or paths you followed in working toward your goals, what, if any, barriers you encountered on the way to your goals, and where your motivation to work on your goals came from. Feel free to write about goal pursuits in your various life domains (for example, work-related goal pursuits, family-related goal pursuits, recreational goal pursuits, and so on.) You can copy and then write your stories on the page below or type them up on separate pages and bring them with you to our next therapy session.

Goal pursuit story number _____:

Hope Bonding

The goal of Hope Bonding is to foster a strong, hopeful working alliance with clients. Indeed, there appears to be much overlap between the three components of hope and the three components of the working alliance as defined by Bordin (1979). More specifically, working alliance goals seem to overlap with the goal component of hope, the tasks component of the working alliance relates to pathways thinking, and the bond component of the working alliance corresponds to agency thinking (Lopez et al., 2000b; Magyar-Moe et al., 2001). Given the extensive research that supports the relationships between the working alliance, hope, and positive therapeutic outcomes, working to build hopeful alliances is key in Hope Therapy.

Hopeful alliances become more likely when therapists engage clients in their own treatment planning and therapeutic outcome goal-setting (Lopez et al., 2004). Indeed, many clients feel more comfortable in therapy and with their therapists if they have a sense of why they are being asked to engage in various discussions, activities, and homework assignments. Once therapeutic goals have been established through collaborations between therapists and clients, generating a variety of pathways to goal attainment, again in conjunction with clients, also serves to strengthen the therapeutic bond while simultaneously building hope.

More generally, hopeful alliances are also more likely to be fostered when therapists are able to establish trust, be empathic, and understand clients in their totality and within their cultural contexts while also modeling hopeful behaviors and using hopeful language (Lopez et al., 2000b).

Hope Enhancing

The goal of Hope Enhancing is to increase hopeful thinking in clients who may be lacking hope in general or in a specific life domain. In order to enhance hope, clients should have their current level of trait hope evaluated using the Adult Trait Hope Scale (Snyder et al., 1991; see Worksheet 3.4). Therapists should provide feedback to clients on this assessment and educate them about hope theory and the role of hope in the therapy process. In particular, pointing out the components of hope that are strengths for clients as well as those that leave room for improvement should occur. Hope Therapy provides several techniques that can be followed for enhancing those component(s) of hope that clients are lacking.

There are two Hope Therapy techniques that can be utilized for helping clients who struggle with the process of goal development. Indeed, for some, developing goals is not easy because they are uncertain about where to begin. Hence, therapists can help provide structure for goal development by asking clients to create lists of their various life domains, prioritizing which are most important, and rating their current levels of satisfaction within each domain.

Next, positive, specific, and workable goals are developed for each life domain (Lopez et al., 2004). This is done collaboratively between clients and therapists.

The goal is to help clients state their goals as precisely as possible (Lopez et al., 2000b). For example, a client who says he wants to be happier could be asked questions such as "How would your life be different if you were happier?" or "If you were feeling happier, what would you be doing that you are not currently doing?"

Clients should also be guided in stating their goals positively, as this often facilitates pathways planning and helps to shift the focus from reducing negative to increasing positive behaviors (Lopez et al., 2000b). For example, rather than having a goal to lose weight, a client could be assisted to make the goal of working out more often and eating healthier. These positively framed goals could then be made even more explicit by defining exactly how often the client will work out and what healthier eating entails. Likewise, helping a client set a goal to be more spontaneous and try new things rather than to avoid being so regimented and structured provides more options for determining the pathways to take en route to this goal.

Several strategies for helping clients who struggle with the pathways component of hope include teaching clients how to break pathways planning down into a series of smaller steps and to be creative and flexible in their thinking about how goals can be attained (Lopez et al., 2000). Lopez and colleagues (2000b) suggest using the "making an internal movie" technique for developing pathways thinking, based on the work of Walter and Pellar (1992). More specifically, clients are asked to mentally picture the steps needed to approach a goal as if they were watching themselves in a movie. Through this process, they can identify on their own (or if shared out loud with their therapist, can be assisted in identifying) whether or not the pathways chosen are likely to lead to success and if not, they can mentally rewind and choose an alternative pathway. In addition, they can envision obstacles that may arise and devise pathways for navigating these barriers in their goal pursuits.

Another technique for building pathways thinking is for therapists to challenge clients to come up with as many possible routes to a goal as possible (Lopez et al., 2000b). This could be accomplished via a written homework exercise, through discussion between clients and therapists, or through client discussions or consultations with trusted others outside of the therapeutic context.

Clients who struggle with the agency component of hope can be assisted to increase their motivation to work toward goals by coming to understand what, in general, serves to motivate them (Lopez et al., 2000b). Asking questions about what has motivated clients in the past and how they have overcome barriers before can prove useful. In addition, teaching clients to engage in positive rather than negative self-talk about their abilities to successfully pursue goals while also learning to enjoy the process of working toward goals rather than focusing only on the outcomes is advised (Snyder, 1994). Worksheet 4.22 has been designed to facilitate the goal structuring process as outlined in this section.

Worksheet 4.22 Structuring Goals

This worksheet has been designed to help you through the process of developing goals. In order to help you figure out where to begin in terms of creating goals for your life, please think about the major domains of life, as listed below, and then indicate which areas are most important for you in the chart provided.

Life domains
- Home/family
- Work
- School
- Social relationships
- Romantic relationships
- Hobbies
- Religion/spirituality
- Physical health
- Civic engagement (i.e., volunteering/helping others)
- Sports
- Arts/music
- Other: _____
- Other: _____

List the life domains that are most important in your life in the spaces below. List them from most to least important. If a domain does not apply, do not include it in your list. Next, rate how satisfied you are with your life in each of these domains on a scale from 1 (not satisfied at all) to 10 (extremely satisfied).

	Rank ordering of life domains	Satisfaction rating (1–10)
Most important	1.	
	2.	
	3.	
	4.	
	5.	
	6.	
	7.	
	8.	
	9.	
	10.	
	11.	
	12.	

Now, based on the chart above, choose an important life domain that is in need of improvement and respond to the questions below.

Life domain chosen:

The aspect of this life domain that I would like to work on is:

Next, state your goal for this life domain as specifically as you can and be sure to phrase it in positive terms. (For example, if your physical health goal is to lose weight, you might precisely and positively define your goal as follows: My goal is to become healthier by working out for at least 30 minutes a day, three days per week and eating at least four fruits or vegetables per day.)

My goal, stated precisely and positively is:

The first step I need to take to put this goal into action is:

I will find the motivation to work toward my goal by:

The challenges that I might face as I work toward this goal are:

I will overcome these potential challenges by:

Throughout the process of structuring your goals, remember to break large goals down into a series of smaller goals and do not put too much pressure on yourself to accomplish large goals all at once. Also, if your plan for reaching a goal fails, do not get down on yourself or give up. Rather, learn from it and create an alternative plan for reaching your goal. If your goal is truly blocked, find a substitute goal to focus upon. As you work toward your goals, be sure to enjoy the process and be kind to yourself. Talk to yourself in positive terms and remind yourself of your past goal successes, especially if you find yourself losing motivation (Lopez et al., 2004).

Once goal, pathway, and agency planning are complete, clients are encouraged to visualize and mentally rehearse their goal pursuits and then to actually put these plans into action. Therapists continuously check in with clients on their goal progress and help clients adjust or modify any problems related to goal attainment that may be identified along the way (Lopez et al., 2004).

Hope Reminding

Hope Reminding consists of teaching clients how to self-monitor their own hopeful thinking and use of hope enhancing techniques so that they can sustain high hope levels independent of their therapists (Lopez et al., 2004). Hope Reminding can be carried out by providing clients with mini-assignments or interventions such as: (a) having them review their personal hope stories as generated during the Hope Finding phase of therapy; (b) finding a "hope buddy" in their personal life that they can turn to for assistance in goal planning or for reinforcement when goal pursuits become difficult; (c) reflecting upon successful goal pursuits and what they did that lead to the success; or (d) completing automatic thought records in order to understand and confront barrier thoughts (Lopez et al., 2004).

In preparation for terminating Hope Therapy, therapists should assist clients in developing post-treatment goals and remind clients that they will have setbacks from time to time and to plan for these occasional backslides. In addition, encouraging clients to make time for daily hope check-ups is encouraged for maintaining the progress made in Hope Therapy. More specifically, daily hope check-ups consist of having clients set a simple goal for the day, a slightly more challenging goal for the week, and an assessment of progress on post-treatment or long-term goals (Lopez et al., 2000b). Worksheet 4.23 can be copied, bound together, and provided to clients to assist them in following through with these daily hope check-ups. Finally, it is suggested that therapists schedule brief Hope Therapy booster sessions at 3, 6, and 9 months following the end of therapy (Lopez et al., 2000b). Alternatively, having clients complete hope letters to themselves at the end of therapy and then sending these letters as hope reminders to clients at 3, 6, and 9 month intervals can also be effective. Worksheet 4.24 can be used to guide clients in writing hope letters.

Worksheet 4.23 Post-Treatment Goal Planning for Terminating Hope Therapy

My Goals now that Hope Therapy is Complete

Now that your therapy is almost complete, it is important that you can continue to plan and implement successful goal pursuits on your own. Remember, you will likely have setbacks from time to time, so planning for them is important as well. In the spaces provided below, please list the goals you plan to continue to work on even after our last therapy session:

Goals I plan to work on after therapy ends:

One way to maintain the progress you have made in Hope Therapy is to make time each day for daily hope check-ups. Daily hope check-ups consist of writing a simple goal for the day, a slightly more challenging goal for the week, and then briefly assessing your progress on the goals you listed above (Lopez et al., 2000b). The following chart can be copied, bound together, and used to guide your daily hope check-ups.

Daily Hope Check-Up Log

Date: _____

My goal for the day (simple)	My goal for the week (somewhat challenging)	Status of my progress on my major life goals (challenging)

Worksheet 4.24 Hope Letter Instructions

In order to help you stay on track and motivated to work toward your goals upon the completion of Hope Therapy, you are being asked to write yourself a hope letter. In this letter, you should indicate what the goals are that you plan to continue working on even when you are no longer meeting regularly with your hope therapist. You will then make three copies of this letter and place them into three separate envelopes. Address each envelope to yourself and bring them with you to your last therapy session. Your therapist will then mail you one of these hope letters at 3, 6, and 9 months from the date of your last therapy session. When you receive your letters, you will be able to check in with yourself on your goal pursuits. If you find that you have been doing well, you should congratulate yourself and use this as motivation to continue moving forward. If, however, you find that you have lost motivation for your goal pursuits or are struggling to find ways to reach your goals, you might decide to change your goal pursuits and/or seek extra assistance from your therapist at that time.

Attending to Culture in Hope Therapy

As with all positive psychological interventions, it is important for therapists to be sensitive to the cultural contexts in which clients exist when implementing Hope Therapy. Although there is evidence that hope is prevalent across time, cultures, and ethnic groups, it is also the case that more barriers arise in the goal pursuits for some members of minority groups (Lopez et al., 2000c). Indeed, all people come across obstacles in the process of working toward their life goals and those who are high in hope are able to perceive these obstacles as challenges to be overcome. However, members of various religious backgrounds, ethnic and racial groups, immigrants, and gender and sexual minority groups are prone to experiencing larger impediments to their goals on a more frequent basis due to such factors as prejudice, racism, sexism, stereotyping, poverty, acculturation stress, language barriers, and more. These obstacles exist on various levels, including the interpersonal, societal, and institutional (Lopez et al., 2000c).

Therapists who want to be sure that they conduct Hope Therapy in a culturally appropriate manner are advised to be aware of the fact that various obstacles are more likely to be encountered by members of diverse groups. In addition, helping clients to develop goals within the context of their cultural frameworks and examining factors that are likely to make goals more or less available or attainable is key. Finally, providing culture-specific examples of hope during the narrative work of the Hope Finding phase is recommended (Lopez et al., 2000c).

4.2 POSITIVE PSYCHOLOGY EXERCISES

There are a number of exercises designed to foster various positive psychological constructs and strengths that can be used alone or in conjunction with the aforementioned positive psychological treatment models. These exercises are described in the following sections.

4.2.1 Forgiveness Exercises

There are a number of exercises that can be used to foster forgiveness in addition to the writing of forgiveness letters, as previously described in the section on Positive Psychotherapy (see session 5) in this chapter. More specifically, therapists can help clients work toward forgiveness by engaging them in emotional storytelling, finding benefits in adversity, and letting go of grudges activities.

Emotional Storytelling

Emotional storytelling consists of having clients systematically write down the emotional upheaval they feel after experiencing a traumatic event over the course of several timed writing sessions in order to process intense negative emotions. This technique was popularized by Pennebaker (1997) and has since been referred to as the Pennebaker paradigm. Instructions for completing emotional storytelling and the rationale for this technique are available in Worksheet 4.25.

According to Niederhoffer and Pennebaker (2002), putting emotion-laden experiences into words helps clients to stop avoiding their thoughts and feelings, to start to frame these thoughts and feelings into meaningful frameworks that allow them to make better sense of the traumatic events, and to reintegrate themselves back into their daily lives and social networks without constantly being distracted by their negative emotions.

Some therapists and clients may wonder why emotional storytelling is a positive psychology exercise since the process of writing about emotional upheaval often has the short-term effect of making clients feel worse, as they are focusing on the negatives in their lives. Indeed, many research participants report feeling anxious, sad, depressed, and frustrated upon writing their stories (Pennebaker, 1989). However, in the long-term, many positive health benefits have been found in association with emotional storytelling (Pennebaker et al., 1988; Petrie et al., 1998) for a diversity of people including "all social classes and major racial and ethnic groups in the United States, as well as samples in Mexico City, French-speaking Belgium, the Netherlands, Spain, and Japan" (Niederhoffer and Pennebaker, 2002, p. 575). In addition, participants in emotional storytelling research studies report that despite the initial sadness, anxiety, and frustration experienced after engaging in writing their negative life stories, the writing

Worksheet 4.25 Emotional Storytelling Instructions

Research shows that when people experience traumas or any sort of event that results in lingering negative emotions, writing about these negative events can be very helpful (Niederhoffer and Pennebaker, 2002). It seems that putting your emotion-laden experiences into words helps you to stop avoiding your thoughts and feelings and to start to make sense of the negative events. When you free yourself up from these negative experiences, you are more likely to be able to focus on your daily life goals and activities without being distracted by negative emotions. Essentially, emotional storytelling can be viewed as a first step in the process of finding forgiveness.

This worksheet has been designed to help you engage in emotional storytelling. For the next four days, please find a quiet space to sit down and write about a negative event or trauma in your life and the emotions you feel regarding this experience. Please include your innermost thoughts and feelings regarding the event. Set a timer and write for 15 minutes each day. Do not be distracted by spelling, grammar, or punctuation. If possible, spend some time relaxing after you are done writing, rather than moving directly into a new activity. Be prepared to discuss your emotional storytelling writing experience at your next therapy session.

It is important to note that the process of writing about emotional upheaval may have the short-term effect of making you feel worse, as you will be focusing on the negatives in your life. However, research shows that in the long-term, this process of emotional storytelling has many positive health benefits (Pennebaker et al., 1988; Petrie et al., 1998).

experience was also very valuable and meaningful. Indeed, 98% of participants indicate that they would participate in emotional storytelling research again if given the opportunity to do so (Pennebaker, 1997).

Emotional storytelling can be viewed as a first step in the process of finding forgiveness, given that recalling the hurt is a first step in most models of forgiveness, followed by making meaning out of the transgression experience. Emotional storytelling is one way to help clients progress to the point where they are truly ready to let go of grudges and find forgiveness so that they can experience more positive emotions and satisfaction with life.

Finding Benefits in Adversity

King and Miner (2000) suggest that an alternative to Pennebaker's emotional storytelling entails having clients write about the benefits that have resulted from their traumatic experiences. Indeed, a variety of researchers have found positive relationships between finding meaning in traumatic experiences and effective coping, psychological adjustment, higher self-esteem, and fewer symptoms of depression (Janoff-Bulman, 1992; Taylor, 1983; Tennen et al., 1991a,b; Freedman and Enright, 1996). King and Miner (2000) found that individuals who were instructed to write about only the positive aspects of negative or traumatic events (i.e., writing about the positive aspects of and how one has grown or benefited as a result of a negative event) for 20 minutes a day for three days showed the same health benefits as those who were instructed to write about their most traumatic life experiences. Hence, having clients write about the perceived benefits of their negative experiences may be a great alternative to having them experience or re-experience the pain of their past traumas through emotional storytelling. Worksheet 4.26 provides instructions for clients to follow in completing this benefit-finding writing activity.

Worksheet 4.26 Benefit-Finding Writing Activity Instructions

Research shows that writing about the benefits that have resulted from negative or traumatic experiences helps people to cope more effectively and to overcome their traumas (King and Miner, 2002). This, of course, results in greater levels of positive emotion and life satisfaction.

This worksheet has been designed to help you find the benefits in the adversity or adversities you have experienced. For the next three days, please find a quiet space to sit down and write **only the positive aspects of** a negative event or trauma in your life. Consider how you have grown or benefitted in some way as a result of this negative event. Set a timer and write for 20 minutes each day. Do not be distracted by spelling, grammar, or punctuation. If possible, spend some time relaxing after you are done writing, rather than moving directly into a new activity. Be prepared to discuss your benefit-finding writing experience at your next therapy session.

Letting Go of Grudges

Reivich (2004) has created a forgiveness exercise that works off the principles of both gratitude and forgiveness. More specifically, clients are asked to think about a person that they are holding a grudge against and then to recall and write down as many things as they can about that person for which they are grateful. The idea is that seeing the person in his or her entirety and recalling gratitude will loosen the grudge and allow the process of forgiveness to proceed. Instructions for this letting go of grudges activity can be found on Worksheet 4.27.

Worksheet 4.27 Letting Go of Grudges (Reivich, 2004) Activity Instructions

Think of a person from your past who you are holding a grudge against or have been in conflict with. How is this grudge affecting you? How is it affecting the other person? Those who study forgiveness have discovered that forgiving does not mean forgetting, condoning, pardoning, or excusing the transgression and the goal of forgiveness is not necessarily reconciliation (Enright and Coyle, 1998; McCullough and Witvliet, 2002; Seligman, 2002). Rather, forgiveness is something you do for yourself in order to reduce your level of psychological distress through the release of toxic negative emotions. It has been said that the opposite of love is not hate (rather, it is indifference), since hating someone takes just as much energy as loving them, with the direction of the energy being the only difference. The negative energy and emotion that you put into not forgiving can, over time, cause major negative health outcomes while the person who committed the transgression against you suffers no further ill effects due to unforgiveness (vanOyen Witvliet et al., 2001). It seems that by not forgiving, you allow your transgressors to victimize you all over again and for an indefinite amount of time. Essentially, forgiveness allows you to take your power back. That being said, forgiveness is something that you must freely choose to do and something that will take hard work.

To help get you started down the path of forgiveness, you are being asked to participate in a forgiveness exercise that works off of the principles of both gratitude and forgiveness. Think about a person you are holding a grudge against and then recall and write down as many things as you can about that person for which you are grateful. The idea is that seeing the person in his or her entirety and recalling gratitude will loosen the grudge and allow the process of forgiveness to proceed.

Locate the center circle on the next page. In that circle, briefly describe what the person you are holding a grudge against did that led you to become angry or hurt by them.

Next, write one word or sentence that describes some aspect or characteristic of the person you are holding your grudge against for which you are grateful. These could be things that he or she has said or done for you. They may be very important or more minor, and they could be things in the present or things from the past.

After completing this activity, take some time to reflect on the questions that follow.

Letting Go of Grudges Exercise

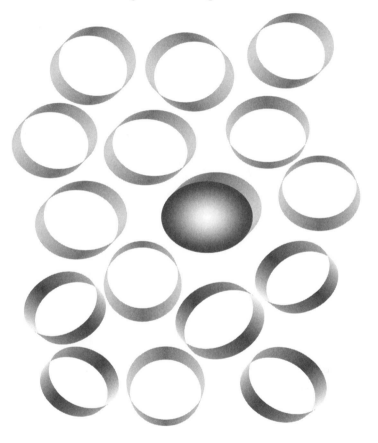

Letting Go of Grudges Activity Reaction Questions

1. As you look at the grudge surrounded by the sea of gratitude, are you able to see the situation differently? Do you feel any differently about the person? Why or why not?

2. Do you feel any more ready or willing to work toward forgiveness (remember, forgiveness is for you, not the person who wronged you)? Why or why not?

3. If the person who wronged you is someone you would like to continue a relationship with, do you feel as if you are now in a better position to work toward reconciliation? Why or why not?

4.2.2 Gratitude Exercises

In addition to writing and delivering gratitude letters and keeping gratitude journals, as previously described in the section on Positive Psychotherapy (see session 6) in this chapter, several other exercises that may serve to increase gratitude and thereby life satisfaction are reviewed below. Such interventions include couples or family gratitude journals and gratitude jars.

Couples or Family Gratitude Journals

In addition to keeping an individual daily gratitude journal, some clients may find it useful to engage in gratitude activities that involve their significant others or family members. For example, clients who are working on strengthening their marriages or partnerships may find that keeping a gratitude journal with their significant other is useful not only for increasing gratitude, but also for increasing appreciation for one another. Couples are instructed to write down and share three things each day that they are thankful for regarding their partner. The same activity can be extended to include children or other family members as well. Worksheet 4.28 can be copied, bound together, and provided to clients who might benefit from couples or family gratitude journaling exercises.

Worksheet 4.28 Couples or Family Gratitude Journal Instructions

Many people find it easier to attend to the things that they are irritated with regarding their partners or family members while taking for granted the good things that their loved ones do. This tendency to focus on the negatives while overlooking the positives is a bias in human thinking referred to as the fundamental negative bias. You are being asked to keep a journal for the next several weeks in which you and your partner and/or other family members will write down three things that you are grateful toward one another for in order to manually override the fundamental negative bias. In addition to writing down three things you appreciate about your loved one(s), be sure to spend some time sharing your gratitude entries with your loved one(s) each day.

The following chart can be copied and used for keeping your couples or family gratitude journal. If you prefer to keep a type-written journal or to purchase a separate notebook or diary for yourself and each of your loved ones, please feel free to do so.

Date	3 Things I admired today in _____ (fill in the name of the loved one you are writing about here)	3 Things I admired today in _____ (fill in the name of the loved one you are writing about here)	3 Things I admired today in _____ (fill in the name of the loved one you are writing about here)
_____	1. 2. 3.	1. 2. 3.	1. 2. 3.
_____	1. 2. 3.	1. 2. 3.	1. 2. 3.
_____	1. 2. 3.	1. 2. 3.	1. 2. 3.

Gratitude Jars

Gratitude has been posited to be a motive for altruism or prosocial behaviors (Bartlett and DeSteno, 2006). One activity that clients can engage in that serves to foster both gratitude and altruism is the gratitude jar activity. Clients can be provided with a gratitude jar that is designed to hold coins or be instructed to create their own gratitude jars. Each time they find themselves being grateful for something that happened in their lives, they are to put a set amount of money in the jar (e.g., 10 or 25 cents) for each gratitude experience that they have. When the jar is full, they are to take the money to a favorite charity or other cherished organization so that their gratitude can serve to foster gratitude in others. Worksheet 4.29 provides directions for keeping a gratitude jar.

Gratitude jars can be kept by clients alone or in conjunction with family members, roommates, or others who reside with them. In the workplace, gratitude jars can be utilized among coworkers with the emphasis being on finding things to be grateful for specifically within the workplace. Similarly, gratitude jars could be used within other group settings such as the classroom or with athletic teams.

Worksheet 4.29 Gratitude Jar Instructions

Many people find it easier to think about the things that did not go well throughout their days rather than the many things that did go well. This tendency to focus on the negative while overlooking the positive is a bias in human thinking referred to as the fundamental negative bias. You are being asked to keep a gratitude jar for the next several weeks in order to manually override the fundamental negative bias.

Here is what you will need to do in order to implement this gratitude jar activity. Find or create a jar or other container that is suitable for holding coins. Label the jar, your "gratitude jar" and put it in a place you will see each day. Every time you find yourself being thankful or grateful for something that happens in your life, put a set amount of money in the jar (1, 5, 10, or 25 cents will do) for each gratitude experience that you have. When the jar is full, take the money to your favorite charity or other cherished organization so that your gratitude can serve to foster gratitude in others.

(If you prefer, you can keep your gratitude jar in conjunction with family members, roommates, or others who reside with you.)

4.2.3 Altruism Exercises

In order to help clients find more meaning in their lives and to experience first-hand how tending to the welfare of others is more satisfying than focusing on pleasure for oneself, clients can be assigned an exercise designed by Seligman called Fun versus Philanthropy (Peterson, 2006). This exercise entails having clients engage in one activity purely for fun or pleasure and then another activity designed to benefit another person. They are then asked to reflect on the similarities and differences between these two experiences. Typically, clients will report that both events lead to positive emotions, but the benefits of the philanthropic activity are longer lasting (Peterson, 2006). Instructions for the Fun versus Philanthropy exercise can be found on Worksheet 4.30.

Altruism can also be fostered by encouraging clients to seek out and participate in volunteer activities in their local communities. Indeed, research shows that volunteering is related to higher levels of life satisfaction, good health (Dulin and Hill, 2003; Hunter and Linn, 1981; Krause et al., 1999; Morrow-Howell et al., 2003), and reductions in symptoms of depression and anxiety (Della Fave and Mossimini, 1992). In addition, Myers (2004) reports that when people feel happy they are more willing to help others and vice versa – when people help others, they are more likely to feel happy. Salovey (1990) describes this relationship between helping and happiness as the "feel-good, do-good phenomenon."

4.2.4 Flow Exercises

Flow, as described previously in this chapter, can be fostered through helping clients to utilize their signature strengths on a regular basis. Hence, one exercise that may produce flow is the Putting Strengths Into Action activity as previously described on Worksheet 4.5. Another way to enhance flow is to help clients to recall previous flow experiences. Explaining the components of flow to clients and then asking them to recall flow experiences in their own lives may serve to spark ideas of activities they can engage in that will lead to more flow. In addition, this activity helps them to realize that flow is something they are capable of experiencing, even if they have not recently done so. Worksheet 4.31 can be utilized in helping clients to recall previous flow states.

Another exercise that can serve to help clients identify flow experiences is referred to as the Top Ten Evaluation Activity (Freemire, 2004 personal communication). In this exercise, clients are asked to write down their top ten favorite things to do and then to evaluate which of those top ten activities meet criteria for flow, which they are currently doing and which they are not currently doing, and what may be getting in the way of pursuing these cherished experiences. Instructions for completing the Top Ten Evaluation Activity are provided in Worksheet 4.32.

Worksheet 4.30 Fun versus Philanthropy (Seligman) Instructions

In order to help you find more meaning in your life and to experience first-hand how tending to the welfare of others is more satisfying than focusing on pleasure for yourself, you are being asked to complete a Fun versus Philanthropy exercise (Seligman).

Over the course of the next week, please participate in one activity purely for fun or pleasure and then another activity purely to benefit another person. After you have completed these activities, respond to the following questions:

1. What was your pleasurable activity?

2. What was your philanthropic activity?

3. What similarities can you identify between how these activities made you feel?

4. What differences can you identify between how these activities made you feel?

5. Assuming you felt positive emotions about both of these experiences, which activity resulted in positive emotions that lasted longer or are more lingering? Why do you think this was the case?

Worksheet 4.31 Recalling Flow Experiences Instructions

Flow is defined as a psychological experience in which one is fully immersed in what he or she is doing. Often, athletes, musicians, and other performers refer to flow as "being in the zone." There are 9 characteristics or conditions of flow that can help you understand when you have experienced flow and how to choose activities that will make flow more likely for you in the future (Jackson and Csikszentmihalyi, 1999). The 9 characteristics of flow are:

1. There is a balance between your skill level and the challenge or opportunity you are taking on (the activity is not underutilizing, nor overtaxing your skills)

2. The challenge or opportunity is rewarding

3. The challenge or opportunity has clear goals

4. You receive immediate feedback on your progress as you engage in the challenge or opportunity

5. You feel a sense of deep, effortless involvement

6. You feel completely absorbed in and focused upon the task at hand

7. You are not concerned with what others are thinking or about being judged (your sense of self vanishes)

8. You feel a sense of control

9. Time seems distorted (for example, time seems to stop or to pass more quickly than normal)

Think of a time when you were totally involved in what you were doing – a time when you felt strong and positive, not worried about yourself or about failing. In the space below, describe the situation as fully as possible: When and where you were? Who were you with? What was happening? How did the experience start? Use as many senses as you can to recall/imagine the event. Jot down thoughts, feelings, and impressions of the experience, including how you felt after the experience was over.

Worksheet 4.32 Top Ten Evaluation Activity (Freemire) Instructions

Flow is defined as a psychological experience in which one is fully immersed in what he or she is doing. Often, athletes, musicians, and other performers refer to flow as "being in the zone." There are 9 characteristics or conditions of flow that can help you understand when you have experienced flow and how to choose activities that will make flow more likely for you in the future (Jackson and Csikszentmihalyi, 1999). The 9 characteristics of flow are:

1. There is a balance between your skill level and the challenge or opportunity you are taking on (the activity is not underutilizing, nor overtaxing your skills)

2. The challenge or opportunity is rewarding

3. The challenge or opportunity has clear goals

4. You receive immediate feedback on your progress as you engage in the challenge or opportunity

5. You feel a sense of deep, effortless involvement

6. You feel completely absorbed in and focused upon the task at hand

7. You are not concerned with what others are thinking or about being judged (your sense of self vanishes)

8. You feel a sense of control

9. Time seems distorted (for example, time seems to stop or to pass more quickly than normal)

In order to help you identify flow experiences in your own life, please write down your top ten favorite things to do.

1.

2.

3.

4.

5.

6.

7.

8.

9.

10.

Now, review each of the items on your top ten list in comparison to the 9 criteria of flow as described above. Put a star next to each activity that meets the criteria for flow. Then respond to the following questions:

1. Are you currently doing any of these activities in your life?

2. Do you want to increase the time you spend in doing any of these activities? If so, which ones?

3. What, if anything, is interfering with your ability to engage in these activities more? How can you overcome these barriers?

4. Which, if any, of your top strengths do you use when engaging in these flow activities?

4.2.5 Gainful Employment Exercises

> The return from your work must be the satisfaction which that work brings you and the world's need of that work. With this, life is heaven, or as near heaven as you can get. Without this with work which you despise, which bores you, and which the world does not need, this life is hell.
>
> William Edward Burghardt Du Bois

Because work is such a large part of life and therefore has a large impact upon well-being, clients in therapy may need assistance in finding work that could be characterized as gainful employment (Snyder and Lopez, 2007). Those who are gainfully employed are people who look forward to going to work rather than dreading it. More specifically, gainful employment consists of holding a job that: (1) provides a sense of engagement and involvement; (2) allows one to find a sense of purpose in life via providing a product or service; (3) leads to a sense of performing well and meeting goals; (4) includes companionship with and loyalty to colleagues, supervisors, and companies; (5) provides variety in job duties; (6) provides a safe working environment; (7) provides minimal income for oneself and family; and (8) leads to happiness and satisfaction.

Snyder and Lopez (2007) created a measure of gainful employment that can be utilized to help clients see what they value most in the workplace and how well their current job fits their value system. This measure and instructions for scoring and interpretation are provided in Worksheet 4.33. A sample completed measure of gainful employment for a client who is **not** gainfully employed is provided in Figure 4.3.

Importance ratings:	Job grading scale:
0 = None	F = 0
1 = Very little	D = 1
2 = Some	C = 2
3 = Very much	B = 3
4 = Extremely	A = 4

Components of Gainful Employment	Importance Rating	Job Grade	Importance × Job Grade
Variety in duties performed	3	1	3
Safe working environment	4	4	16
Income for self and family	4	3	12
Deriving purpose in providing a product or service	3	0	0
Happiness and satisfaction	4	1	4
Engagement and involvement	3	1	3
Sense of performing well and meeting goals	3	3	9
Companionship and loyalty to coworkers and bosses	3	3	9
Totals	Importance Total = 27		Importance × Grade Total = 56
Averages	Average Importance = 3.375		Average Importance × Job Grade = 2.074

FIGURE 4.3 Sample completed measure of gainful employment (Snyder and Lopez, 2007). The client in this example is **not** currently gainfully employed. This can be determined by her higher "Average Importance" score in comparison to her "Average Importance × Job Grade" score. Further review of this measure reveals that areas she could focus upon to make her current job better are finding a sense of purpose in the work she does and finding ways to better utilize her strengths in the workplace in order to feel more engaged and involved.

Worksheet 4.33 Gainful Employment Measure (Snyder and Lopez, 2007)

The following measure can be used to help you see what you value most in the workplace and how well your current job fits your value system. If there is a good fit between your workplace values and the reality of your workplace, you are likely to be gainfully employed.

Importance Ratings:	Job Grading Scale:
0 = None	F = 0
1 = Very Little	D = 1
2 = Some	C = 2
3 = Very Much	B = 3
4 = Extremely	A = 4

Components of Gainful Employment	Importance Rating	Job Grade	Importance × Job Grade
Variety in duties performed			
Safe working environment			
Income for self and family			
Deriving purpose in providing a product or service			
Happiness and satisfaction			
Engagement and involvement			
Sense of performing well and meeting goals			
Companionship and loyalty to coworkers and bosses			
Totals	Importance Total = _____		Importance × Job Grade Total = _____
Averages	Average Importance = _____		Average Importance × Job Grade = _____

In the "Importance Rating" column, list how important each of the components of gainful employment are to you based on the rating scale above. Then total your scores in that column. Next, in the "Job Grade" column, rate how well your current job meets each of the criteria of gainful employment using the scale above. Next, multiply your scores in the "Importance Rating" and "Job Grade" columns and put the result in the "Importance × Job Grade" column. Now, total these scores. You should now have a "Total Importance Score" and a "Total Importance × Job Grade Score." To get your "Average Importance Score," divide your "Total Importance Score" by 8. You should come up with a number between 0 and 4.0. To get your "Average Importance × Job Grade Score," divide your "Total Importance × Job Grade Score" by your "Total Importance Score." You should end up with a number between 0 and 4.0.

If your "Average Importance × Job Grade Score" is greater than or equal to your "Average Importance Score", you are considered to be gainfully employed. Congratulations!

If your "Average Importance × Job Grade Score" is less than your "Average Importance Score", you are **not** considered to be gainfully employed. You may find it useful to review the chart above in order to find the areas of greatest mismatch between your values in the workplace and what your job actually provides. Are there ways you can re-craft your work, ask for what you need, or change your way of viewing your work or going about your job in order to find a greater fit? Is there another job or career that you can think of that would be a better match for you? Please discuss these questions with your therapist at your next therapy session.

Measure reproduced with permission from Shane Lopez.

Several of the components of gainful employment and exercises to help increase them are provided in the following sections.

Engagement and Involvement at Work

Engagement in the workplace is most likely to take place when clients feel as if their needs are being met and that there is a match between their strengths, skills, abilities, and personality and the job requirements (War, 1999). When clients feel they have the opportunity to do what they do best on a daily basis in the workplace, they are also more likely to report feeling engaged (Harter and Schmidt, 2002).

A sense of engagement in the workplace overlaps with the concept of flow (Snyder and Lopez, 2007). As previously described, flow is related to the regular implementation of top strengths. In order to help clients to experience more engagement or flow in the workplace, therapists can help them to recall their top strengths from the Values in Action Inventory of Character Strengths (Peterson and Seligman, 2004) and the Clifton StrengthsFinder 2.0 (Asplund et al., 2007; Rath, 2007) and then discover ways in which these strengths could be utilized more often in the workplace. If clients are unable to discover ways to implement their strengths regularly at work, they might consider other careers that would be a better fit. Therapists can guide clients through this process by assisting them in the completion of a Workplace Strengths Action Plan. Instructions for this activity are provided in Worksheet 4.34. An example of a completed Workplace Strengths Action Plan is provided in Figure 4.4.

Workplace Strengths Action Plan

You are most likely to feel engaged and involved in the workplace when there is a match between your strengths, skills, abilities, and personality and the job requirements (War, 1999) and when you feel that you have the opportunity to do what you do best at work on a daily basis (Harter and Schmidt, 2002). This worksheet has been designed in order to help you to experience more engagement or flow in the workplace.

My Top Five Strengths from the Values in Action Inventory of Character Strengths:

1. Leadership
2. Humor
3. Modesty
4. Social intelligence
5. Persistence

My Top Five Strengths from the Clifton Strengthsfinder 2.0:

1. Achiever
2. Consistency
3. Developer
4. Empathy
5. Maximizer

1. Please look over your top five strengths from the VIA Strength Survey and the StrengthsFinder 2.0. Which, if any, of your strengths are you currently using on a regular basis in your work? Briefly explain how you are regularly using these strengths.

I am currently using my persistence, consistency, and achiever strengths, as I have been at this job for 11 years now. I have been recognized on several occasions for my loyalty to my work and my diligence in getting tasks done. I believe I also use modesty often, as I never brag about myself or my abilities and am quite humble when others point out my talents or a job well done. I also use humor a lot. Since I sit at the reception desk, I interact with a lot of people and I find that if I use a little humor, it lightens the mood for both my coworkers and our customers, since this can definitely become a pretty high stress place. I enjoy being able to put a smile on someone's face, especially if their day is not going so well. I guess I am using my empathy and social intelligence strengths in this process as well. I didn't realize that until just now!

FIGURE 4.4   Sample completed Workplace Strengths Action Plan.

2. How can you re-craft your work so that you can capitalize on more of your strengths?

Well, when I look over my other strengths, they all seem to be related to being a good leader. Strengths like leadership, maximizer, and developer. I don't feel like I really have a chance to use these strengths in my current position. I really do not have anyone to mentor or lead in my position. I wonder if I could ask my manager for an opportunity to train and mentor colleagues who will be taking on positions similar to mine at some of our other branches. That would be ideal. If this is not possible, however, I wonder if I could start some sort of informal mentoring program with some of the newer employees that we could conduct over the lunch hour. Even if the employees don't work in my area, I have a lot of knowledge and background information on our company that they might find really informative and useful.

3. Write out a specific plan for implementing one strength that you are not currently using at work.

In order to implement my strength of leadership, I will go to my manager on Monday morning and ask if I can serve as a trainer for other receptionists/office administrators that are being hired to work at surrounding branches of the company. I think I will bring the results from my VIA and StrengthsFinder measures so that she has a better understanding of why I would be good in such a role. I think I can provide her with some examples of my leadership abilities from roles I have taken on with several volunteer organizations in my free time.

4. What, if anything, do you need from your colleagues/managers to make this (see questions 2 and 3) happen?

In order to implement my plan, I would need my manager to agree to give me a chance to be a trainer. Since I would not have as much time to do my daily work if I am working on training another, I may also need to work overtime (another thing my manager would have to approve) or I would need to have colleagues cover some of my duties from time to time. I would also need to rearrange my car pool schedule a bit, so would need the colleagues in my car pool arrangement to be willing to potentially fill in for me on days I am supposed to drive if I need to go to a different branch for that day.

FIGURE 4.4 (Continued)

Worksheet 4.34 Workplace Strengths Action Plan Instructions

You are most likely to feel engaged and involved in the workplace when there is a match between your strengths, skills, abilities, and personality and the job requirements (War, 1999) and when you feel that you have the opportunity to do what you do best at work on a daily basis (Harter and Schmidt, 2002).

This worksheet has been designed in order to help you to experience more engagement or flow in the workplace.

My Top Five Strengths from the Values in Action Inventory of Character Strengths:

1.

2.

3.

4.

5.

My top five strengths from the Clifton StrengthsFinder 2.0:

1.

2.

3.

4.

5.

1. Please look over your top five strengths from the VIA Strength Survey and the StrengthsFinder 2.0. Which, if any, of your strengths are you currently using on a regular basis in your work? Briefly explain how you are regularly using these strengths.

2. How can you re-craft your work so that you can capitalize on more of your strengths?

3. Write out a specific plan for implementing one strength that you are not currently using at work.

4. What, if anything, do you need from your colleagues/managers to make this (see questions 2 and 3) happen?

Please repeat questions 2 and 3, taking into consideration the rest of your strengths.

Finding Purpose in Life via Providing a Product or Service

Clients who are able to find a sense of purpose in their lives through the work they do are also more likely to be happy and satisfied with their work. In order to help clients discover what their purpose is related to the workplace, having them complete a personal work mission statement may prove to be useful (Clifton and Nelson, 1992). Personal work mission statements essentially entail having clients write out why they do what they do in order to help them realize that they can make a difference in the workplace and beyond. Worksheet 4.35 can be used to guide clients in the development of their personal work mission statements.

Worksheet 4.35 Personal Work Mission Statement (Clifton and Nelson, 1992) Instructions

People who are able to find a sense of purpose in their lives through the work they do are also more likely to be happy and satisfied with their work. One way that you can discover what your purpose is related to the workplace, is to develop a Personal Work Mission Statement.

Personal work mission statements are rare because as a society, we do not typically promote them. We promote the development of personal goals, but rarely do we acknowledge the value of a personal mission. In order to find the work that you do to be positive, it helps to have a personal mission or sense of meaning for what you do. Essentially, a personal mission statement will explain why you do what you do. Your mission statement, when put together with your strengths, becomes your fuel for achievement and well-being (Clifton and Nelson, 1992).

Please answer the following questions. Write fast, don't worry about spelling, grammar, or logic. The objective is to let your thoughts flow. When you are done, go back and edit this to create your own personal work mission statement.

1. What is it that you believe you do that makes a difference to other people?

2. Why do you do what you do?

3. What is it that you believe you do that makes a difference to customers and/or colleagues at your workplace?

4. Why do you do what you do at your workplace?

5. What strengths do you possess that you put into action while doing what you do?

My Personal Work Mission Statement (Note: your mission statement can be as long or short as you want it to be. Once you have it complete, claim it! Realize that you can make a difference in the workplace and beyond by living your mission statement and using your strengths.):

Note: For those who like examples, a few typical personal work mission statements include:

- Police Officer: To help people understand lawfulness and to provide them security in their neighborhood communities.
- Life Insurance Agent: To provide financial security to families.
- Garbage Collector: To provide a clean and beautiful place for people to enjoy life.
- Clothing Salesperson: To help people look and feel their best.

Income for Self and Family

Those who are gainfully employed make an income that can support the needs of themselves and their families; however, most people overestimate the role of money in predicting happiness. Money is a strong predictor of happiness for those who go from living at or below the poverty line to above it, but for those above the poverty line, more money does not predict enduring happiness (Seligman, 2002). Therefore, Myers (2004) suggests that people will be happier if they realize that lasting happiness does not come from financial success. Hence, when assisting clients to choose a career or decide whether or not to accept a promotion, therapists are encouraged to help clients make sure that the pursuit of a higher income does not undermine important life and family pleasures or obligations (Snyder and Lopez, 2007).

4.3 A NOTE ON USING POSITIVE PSYCHOLOGICAL INTERVENTIONS AND EXERCISES

You may have noticed that there are many worksheets provided in this chapter that have the potential to become overwhelming for clients should they be assigned every activity. Chances are that most clients will not have a need to complete each activity, therefore carefully picking and choosing among the worksheets that are most relevant for each individual client is recommended. If you prefer, you might provide a client with all of the worksheets and review them together with the client to identify which he or she is most interested in completing. Finally, if you recognize that a client needs some assistance in completing the assigned activities, you might consider doing part or all of the activity or activities together during therapy sessions.

To better ensure that clients will follow through on the homework assignments they are given, providing clients with a three-ring binder that they can use for neatly storing their worksheets is recommended. In addition, providing clients with copies of the handouts that have already been three-hole punched will make this task even more convenient for them. When clients bring back their completed worksheets for discussion in therapy, therapists should make a copy of the completed assignment to include in their client files. These documents can then be utilized when completing various follow-up reports of client progress, treatment planning, or termination planning.

Chapter 5

Deciding Upon and Carrying Out a Positive-Psychology-Infused Treatment Plan

The process of deciding upon and carrying out a positive-psychology-infused treatment plan depends largely upon where a client falls within the Complete State Model of Mental Health as discussed in Chapter 2. For example, when working with clients who fall into the complete mental illness category (i.e., high symptoms of mental illness and low symptoms of well-being), using positive psychology activities to supplement "treatment as usual" is recommended. In contrast, the core of treatment should center on positive psychology exercises for those who fall in the incomplete mental health category (i.e., low symptoms of mental illness and low symptoms of well-being). Hence, appropriate treatment planning hinges upon the information gathered via the process of careful and complete, multiculturally appropriate, positive psychological assessment. In this chapter, a variety of sample treatment plans utilizing positive psychological interventions are provided, based upon the category of the Complete State Model of Mental Health (Keyes and Lopez, 2002) in which a client falls. Therapists are encouraged to use these sample treatment plans as *general guides* to developing their own treatment plans specific to the unique clients with whom they work.

5.1 GENERAL GUIDELINES FOR DEVELOPING POSITIVE PSYCHOLOGICAL TREATMENT PLANS

Before examining sample treatment plans for clients from various categories within the Complete State Model of Mental Health, it is important to reiterate the need to begin therapy by completing the process of positive psychological assessment as described fully in Chapter 2. Hence, in each of the case studies below, one can see that there are several staples utilized in the therapy process for all clients, including use of the four-front approach to client assessment (see Worksheet 2.1), the ADDRESSING model for evaluating client cultural identities (see Worksheet 2.7), and the OQ-45.2 (see Worksheet 2.4) and MHC-LF (see Worksheet 2.5) evaluations. These staples of therapy conducted from a positive psychological perspective are required in order to be able to fully complete the revised positive psychology seven-axis version of the current *DSM* assessment system (see Worksheet 2.2) and to plot where a client falls within the Complete State Model of Mental Health (see Worksheets 2.3 and 2.6). Once such information has been gathered, the next essential step in the therapy process is to share the findings of this thorough assessment process directly with clients and to collaboratively work toward developing treatment plans that will help them move toward experiencing complete mental health.

Several other important tips to consider whenever therapists strive to implement positive psychological concepts and exercises into their clinical work are as follows: (a) whenever possible, build in opportunities for clients to use their strengths in the process of overcoming their struggles; (b) provide rationales for all the activities and exercises in which clients are asked to partake; (c) always use people-first language; (d) be flexible by picking and choosing among those components of positive psychological approaches to therapy and related exercises that are most appropriate for each individual client at that particular point in time and considering his or her various cultural identities and current environmental context; (e) never invalidate the struggles or problems a client reports by jumping too quickly into exploration of the positives and resources; (f) help clients consider how to find meaning in their traumas or struggles without using clichéd expressions like "look on the bright side," "don't worry, things will be okay," or "everything happens for a reason"; (g) encourage clients to at least try various positive psychology activities and exercises, even if they are not convinced they will work; (h) set up realistic expectations about the utility of the exercises clients are being asked to do – some will likely be very powerful, while others may not be as useful; (i) do not force clients into activities they are not ready for, especially those that require free will, such as forgiveness exercises; and (j) when working primarily on symptom remediation, do not become overly focused on the problem; rather, remember to bring in the positives, strengths, and resources as well.

The following sections include brief case studies of and sample treatment plans for clients who meet criteria for one of each of the four categories of the Complete State Model of Mental Health.

5.2 COMPLETE MENTAL HEALTH OR FLOURISHING

Clients who fall within the complete mental health or flourishing category of the Complete State Model of Mental Health are individuals who experience very few, if any, symptoms of pathology and simultaneously experience an abundance of well-being. Chances are high that such clients may not seek out therapy, as they likely have a sense of purpose and meaning and find themselves satisfied with life. It is possible, however, that even those who are considered to be flourishing may have a specific area of concern that they would like assistance with or they may simply have a strong desire for continued personal growth, hence they may value the help of a professional who can guide them toward even greater levels of mental health and happiness. The case of Tracelyn is provided as an example of a client who falls into the flourishing category, yet desires assistance in terms of finding more satisfaction in one life domain.

5.2.1 The Case of Tracelyn

Tracelyn is a 35-year-old Jewish female who lives in a small city on the East Coast. She has obtained a master's degree in physical education and teaches at a local high school. She is also the coach of several sport teams there. She really enjoys her work, her colleagues, and her students. Tracelyn also reports that she owns a townhome in a nice neighborhood near the school that she works at and enjoys being able to bike to work when the weather allows.

Tracelyn has a very supportive family. Her parents are still married and reside about an hour away from her. She has two brothers and a sister who also live within driving distance from her home. She gets together often with her parents and siblings on weekends and school breaks. Tracelyn also has a number of good friends that she keeps in touch with regularly. She and two of her better friends from college make it a point to get together for a "girls' weekend" at least 4 times a year. When not at work or spending time with family or friends, Tracelyn reports that she goes to synagogue regularly and is also a volunteer for several organizations in her community.

Tracelyn feels as if her life has a lot purpose and meaning and she is satisfied in every important life domain, except one. She desires to get married and have a family of her own but to date, she has not found the "right guy." She states that she was in a serious relationship three years ago, but found out that her boyfriend had cheated on her several times with other women and had also lied to her about a number of other things throughout their two-year relationship. She comes to therapy hoping to get some assistance in this one area of her life with which she is dissatisfied.

5.2.2 Tracelyn's Treatment Plan and Results

1. Conduct an assessment using the four-front assessment approach, the ADDRESSING model, and administer the MHC-LF and the OQ-45.2. Using the results of these assessment tools, document where Tracelyn falls within the Complete State Model of Mental Health. Review the results directly with Tracelyn. See Figure 5.1 for a summary of Tracelyn's results.
2. Based on the results of Tracelyn's assessment, Hope Therapy may be the best option for helping Tracelyn to experience more satisfaction in terms of romantic relationships. Have Tracelyn complete the Adult Trait Hope Scale and the Domain Specific Hope Scale and discuss the results with her.
3. Assign Tracelyn to complete Worksheet 4.21 in which she will write short stories of her past goal pursuits. Have her complete stories related to areas

Four-Front Assessment Approach

1. Areas of client weakness (i.e., impaired social skills, low intelligence, emotion dysregulation, labile moods, personality problems)

 Tracelyn appears to have few areas of weakness. She reports being very busy, perhaps taking on too many commitments to keep the desired balance she would like in her life. She also reported having some difficulty overcoming a grudge against a previous romantic partner. No problems were observed in terms of social skills, moods or affect, or personality functioning.

2. Areas of client strength (i.e., hopeful, grateful, forgiving, courageous, resilient, high intelligence, mood stability, healthy personality)

 Tracelyn appears to have a number of personal strengths. She is highly intelligent, emotionally stable, and consistent in terms of mood functioning. She has good social skills and strengths of kindness, altruism, spirituality, resilience, and gratitude. She feels a sense of meaning and purpose in her life. Namely, she feels as if her purpose is to help her students to develop important life skills and to foster their physical health and development.

3. Deficits or destructive forces in the client's environment (i.e., unsafe living conditions/neighborhood, presence of abusive relationships or neglect, exposure to discrimination or victim of prejudice)

 Tracelyn reports that she has been exposed to prejudice throughout her life based on being a Jewish female. She also feels that she has been discriminated against within her chosen profession as a physical education teacher and coach of various sports, as the career she chose is male dominated. Although Tracelyn denies any history of abusive or neglectful relationships, she does report having been emotionally hurt by a previous boyfriend who was unfaithful.

4. Assets or resources in the client's environment (i.e., secure living conditions/neighborhood, supportive relationships, opportunities for success, stable employment)

 Tracelyn lives in a safe neighborhood, has a secure job, and owns her own home. She has very supportive family, social, and work relationships. She has a strong connection to her place of worship and is civically engaged in her community.

Definitions of ADDRESSING framework	Client Information
	Client name: Tracelyn
Age and generational influences	35 years old; third-generation US citizen, maternal and paternal grandparents were holocaust survivors, immigrated from Israel and earned US citizenship; first born of four children; first to move out of her home, but not first to marry; parental expectations that she will marry a Jewish man and raise a Jewish family.

FIGURE 5.1   Summary of Tracelyn's positive psychological assessment results.

Disability status (developmental disability)	None
Disability status (acquired disability)	None
Religion and spiritual orientation	Identifies strongly with Judaism; attends a Reform synagogue regularly; observes most Jewish holidays and eats a kosher diet.
Ethnicity	Jewish; mother and father and both sets of grandparents are of Jewish heritage.
Socioeconomic status	Currently middle-class with an undergraduate college degree and teaching certification; parents started off in lower middle-class when Tracelyn was born, now are considered upper-class. Both parents have post-high school educations.
Sexual orientation	Heterosexual; has never questioned her sexual orientation
Indigenous heritage	None
National origin	Born and raised in the USA; grandparents are US immigrants
Gender	Woman, as oldest of siblings, took on maternal role throughout later childhood and adolescence, never married but desires to get married and have children of her own.

SEVEN-AXIS SYSTEM OF POSITIVE PSYCHOLOGICAL ASSESSMENT

Axis I: V71.09 No diagnosis

Axis II: V71.09 No diagnosis

Axis III: None

Axis IV (broadened):

Environmental and psychosocial problems: Partner relational problems: difficulty with past romantic relationship currently affecting her ability to trust a new partner.

Environmental and psychosocial resources: Attachment/love/nurturance with primary support group; connectedness/empathic relationships; meaningful work/career satisfaction; safe housing with essential elements that foster healthy development; financial resources adequate to meet basic needs and beyond; access to high quality/reliable health care services; contributions made to society via donation of resources and time.

Axis V (broadened): Global Assessment of Functioning Scale score: 91

                            Global Assessment of *Positive* Functioning Scale score: 91

FIGURE 5.1 (Continued)

Axis VI: Client strengths: Kindness, altruism, spirituality, resilience, gratitude, sense of purpose and meaning in life

Axis VII: Client cultural background information: Tracelyn identifies as Jewish in terms of both her ethnicity and religious beliefs. Her family expects her and she desires to marry a Jewish man and to raise children in the Jewish faith. She has no developmental or acquired disabilities, nor do any of her family members. She is the first of her siblings to complete a college education, move out, and support herself. (SES = middle class) Two of her younger siblings are married.

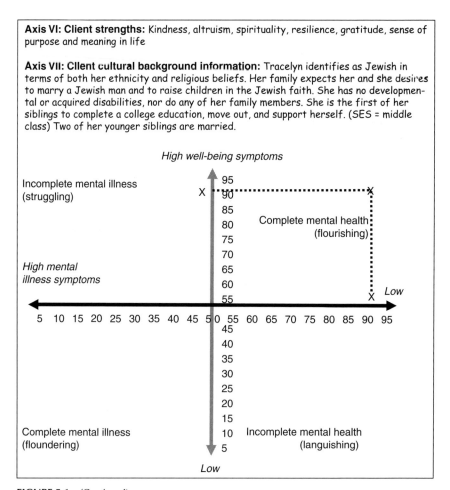

FIGURE 5.1   (Continued)

in which she has been successful, such as in the workplace and with family. Also have her tell a story or two related to past relationships with significant others. Review the elements of these stories related to hope at her next therapy session(s).

4. Have Tracelyn complete Worksheet 4.22 with an emphasis on romantic relationship goal pursuits.

5. Given the grudge that she is holding against her ex-boyfriend that is still affecting her attitude toward dating today, introduce the concept of forgiveness and provide her with options for forgiveness exercises as noted on Worksheets 4.9, 4.25, 4.26, and 4.27. Discuss her willingness/readiness to engage in these exercises. If she completes them, discuss her reactions to the experience.

6. Re-administer the Adult Trait Hope and Domain Specific Hope Scales. Discuss any changes on these measures from time one to time two.

7. Continue with the Hope Therapy process. Also, provide Tracelyn with Worksheet 4.14 on active–constructive responding and Worksheet 4.15 on strengths dates from Positive Psychotherapy, Worksheet 4.16 on Gottman's magic five hours, and Worksheet 4.28 on couples gratitude journaling. Discuss how these worksheets may become useful to her in her future romantic relationships.

8. Throughout the process of working on this one life domain, be sure to reinforce all the positives that exist in Tracelyn's life and possibly assign her Worksheet 4.7 on gratitude journaling to help keep her focus on the many positives that do exist in her life.

9. Re-administer the OQ-45.2 and MHC-LF scales to track changes/progress made from the start of therapy to the present. Also re-evaluate her GAF and GAPF scores.

10. Have Tracelyn complete Worksheet 4.23 on post-treatment goal planning and Worksheet 4.24 on hope letters just prior to therapy termination.

5.3 INCOMPLETE MENTAL HEALTH OR LANGUISHING

Clients who fall within the incomplete mental health or languishing category of the Complete State Model of Mental Health are individuals who experience very few, if any, symptoms of pathology, yet they do not experience many, if any, symptoms of well-being either. Clients who fall into this category are more likely to seek out therapy than those in the complete mental health category as previously described. The case of Thor is provided as an example of a person who falls into the languishing category.

5.3.1 The Case of Thor

Thor is a 21-year-old white male who resides with his mother in a small Midwestern town. He is currently unemployed, after dropping out of college in his senior year. Thor spends most of his time on the computer or playing video games. The majority of his friends are still in college and he has not kept in touch with them because he feels ashamed and embarrassed about dropping out. He does have a girlfriend whom he reports loving very much. In fact, once he is back on his feet, he plans to buy her a ring and to propose. He is not sure what he wants to do with his life or for a career, but he does know that living with his mom forever is definitely not what he wants and he knows he is capable of much more. He notes that he is extremely grateful to his mother for her willingness to support him now, as she has throughout his entire life, but he knows that he needs to get out on his own and be independent. He reports having an "okay" relationship with his mom currently, but the relationship is strained because he is at home all the time and she is a bit disappointed that he dropped out of college. He comes to therapy for some help figuring out his "next steps" at this difficult time in his life.

5.3.2 Thor's Treatment Plan and Results

1. Conduct an assessment using the four-front assessment approach, the ADDRESSING model, and administer the MHC-LF and the OQ-45.2. Using the results of these assessment tools, document where Thor falls within the Complete State Model of Mental Health. Review the results directly with Thor. See Figure 5.2 for a summary of Thor's results.

2. Based on the results of Thor's assessment, Strength-Centered Therapy (Wong, 2006) appears to be a good option for helping Thor to discover ways in which he can utilize his strengths to find a greater sense of purpose and meaning in life. In order to begin the Strengths-Centered Therapy process, have Thor complete the Values in Action Classification of Character Strengths on-line at www.authentichappiness.org or www.viacharacter.org and discuss the results together.

3. Proceed with the four phases of Strengths-Centered Therapy (see Chapter 3). During the various phases of this treatment approach, consider using Worksheets 4.5 (Putting Strengths Into Action Plan), 4.12 (One Door Closes, Another Door Opens), 4.19 (Giving the Gift of Time), 4.22 (Structuring Goals), 4.25 (Emotional Storytelling), 4.26 (Benefit Finding), 4.30 (Fun versus Philanthropy), 4.31 (Recalling Flow Experiences), and 3.32 (Top Ten Evaluation), as appropriate.

4. In order to address Thor's concerns about his career, review the principles of gainful employment (see Chapter 3) with him. Have Thor complete the Clifton StrengthsFinder 2.0 at www.strengthsfinder.com, and brainstorm careers that would allow him to capitalize upon his top five strengths from the VIA and CSF 2.0 inventories.

5. Re-administer the OQ-45.2 and MHC-LF scales to track changes throughout the therapy process. Also re-assess his GAF and GAPF scores.

6. Continue recycling through the process of Strengths-Based Therapy as needed.

(Note: the case of Thor could have also been treated following the principles of Well-Being Therapy or Hope Therapy as described in Chapter 4.)

5.4 INCOMPLETE MENTAL ILLNESS OR STRUGGLING

Clients who fall within the incomplete mental illness or struggling category of the Complete State Model of Mental Health are individuals who are experiencing enough symptoms of pathology to presently qualify for a *DSM* diagnosis, yet they are also experiencing a number of symptoms of well-being. Clients

---

Four-Front Assessment Approach

1. Areas of client weakness (i.e., impaired social skills, low intelligence, emotion dysregulation, labile moods, personality problems)

> Areas of weakness for Thor include a lack of self-efficacy related to academics and career, poor grades in college (due to lack of effort/interest, not lack of intellectual ability), lack of a sense of direction, purpose, and meaning in life.

2. Areas of client strength (i.e., hopeful, grateful, forgiving, courageous, resilient, high intelligence, mood stability, healthy personality)

> Thor's strengths include optimism and hope (although he is currently struggling in terms of working toward specific goal pursuits), stability of affect and mood, good social skills, a desire for personal growth, capacity to love and be loved, resilience, and gratitude.

3. Deficits or destructive forces in the client's environment (i.e., unsafe living conditions/neighborhood, presence of abusive relationships or neglect, exposure to discrimination or victim of prejudice)

> Thor reports that although the trailer home that he lives in with his mother is very small, it is comfortable and located within a safe neighborhood. Thor denies any history of abuse or neglect, though he does report that his father was abusive toward his mother when he was a young child. Thor has few memories of his father, who has not been in his life since the age of four when his parents' divorced. Thor used to be teased in school for living in a trailer home and for the out-of-style clothing that he wore due to a lack of steady income for his mom. Thor is currently unemployed and having academic difficulties. He seems to be lacking in terms of his community connections and civic engagement.

4. Assets or resources in the client's environment (i.e., secure living conditions/neighborhood, supportive relationships, opportunities for success, stable employment)

> Thor lives in a safe neighborhood, has a supportive mother, and a strong connection to a significant other. He reports having a lot of friends; however, he has chosen not to contact his friends at the present time due to embarrassment about dropping out of college. Thor has opportunities to further his education if he so chooses and would likely be a good candidate for several jobs if he were to apply for them.

Definitions of ADDRESSING framework	Client information Client Name: Thor
Age and generational influences	21 years old; only child; raised by a single mother (father has been absent since Thor was four years old); part of the Millennial generation – highly values technology, likes to multi-task, likes to be entertained (gets bored easily); concerned about global warming and wars in the Middle East; first-generation college student within his family of origin and extended families.

FIGURE 5.2   Summary of Thor's positive psychological assessment results.

Disability status (developmental disability)	None
Disability status (acquired disability)	None
Religion and spiritual orientation	Self-identifies as Lutheran, though is not currently active within the church. Does believe in God and spends some time in prayer. Mother is also Lutheran and does currently participate in worship activities on a regular basis.
Ethnicity	"White" – 3/4 German, 1/4 Irish; both parents were US born, not sure what generation of US American he is.
Socioeconomic status	Currently lower middle-class; grew up most of his life at or just above the poverty line. Mother has high school diploma; Thor has the opportunity to complete college if he so chooses. Primarily identifies with working-class people.
Sexual orientation	Heterosexual
Indigenous heritage	None
National origin	Born and raised in the USA
Gender	Male, never married but plans to propose soon to his girlfriend of 3 years. Desires to make his mom proud of him. As a child, strove to be the "man" of the family in his father's absence.

Seven-Axis System of Positive Psychological Assessment

Axis I: V62.3 Academic Problem

Axis II: V71.09 No Diagnosis

Axis III: None

Axis IV (broadened):

Environmental and psychosocial problems: Educational problems – client has intellectual capacity to do well in college, but has consistently underperformed; Occupational problems – currently unemployed and not seeking employment; Economic problem – savings account is running out and has no current income – dependent on his mother for shelter; Problems with access to health care services – no medical insurance.

Environmental and psychosocial resources: Attachment/love/nurturance with primary support group; connectedness/empathic relationships; safe housing; no criminal record; educational opportunity available.

FIGURE 5.2 (Continued)

Axis V (broadened):   Global Assessment of Functioning Scale score: 65
Global Assessment of *Positive* Functioning Scale score: 41

Axis VI: Client strengths: Optimism, hope, stability of affect and mood, good social skills, a desire for personal growth, capacity to love and be loved, resilience (has overcome obstacles related to poverty and being raised without his father in his life), and gratitude.

Axis VII: Client cultural background information: Thor identifies as a straight, white male of lower middle-class socioeconomic status. He has no developmental or acquired disabilities, nor do any of his family members. He is an only child who was raised by a single mother. If he returns to college and is able to graduate, he will be a first-generation college graduate within his family of origin as well as extended families. He is considered to be of the Millennial Generation, hence he has a strong interest in things like technology and finds himself easily bored in the classroom if the learning is not applied, active, and hands-on. He desires to help others, though he is unsure of how to do so and has not been civically engaged in his community to date.

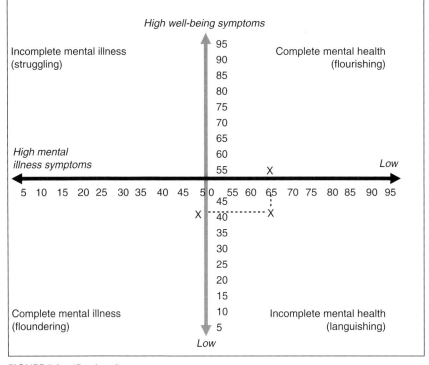

FIGURE 5.2   (Continued)

who fall into this category are likely to seek out therapy for their symptoms of pathology. If their symptoms of well-being are overlooked and therefore not utilized in the process of treatment planning, these clients are being done a disservice. Indeed, they may even backslide into the complete mental illness category if the focus in therapy becomes only upon their pathology. The case of Jim is provided as an example of a person who falls into the struggling category.

5.4.1 The Case of Jim

Jim is a 40-year-old African-American male who resides with his wife and children in an old rental home in a small city. He comes to therapy reporting that he is having problems with concentration. His concentration issues are most evident at work, but also affect his functioning at home. He notes that he has a really hard time staying focused when he reads, he always seems to lose or misplace his keys and other important items such as his checkbook, wallet, and cell phone, and his wife and others often complain that he does not listen or pay attention when they are talking to him. Jim reports that he has been functioning this way for years, but has found the problem to be worse after having recently been promoted at work to a position that requires much more reading and report writing than he was responsible for in the past. He feels as if he is taking too long to get the projects his manager asks him to do complete and is becoming worried that he may get terminated if he does not keep up with the pace of the rest of his colleagues. Indeed, Jim's boss has told him that he needs to step up his performance in his new role or disciplinary action will be taken. Jim's concerns about work have resulted in a number of anxiety symptoms, including almost constant worry, nausea, excessive perspiration, and difficulty sleeping.

Although these problems are negatively affecting his work and now starting to affect his functioning a bit at home as well, Jim reports that overall, he has a good life. He is *usually* very happy and energetic. He loves to spend time with his wife and children and finds a lot of meaning and purpose in being a good father to his kids. Although it is more of a challenge than usual, he does report spending quality time with his family and that doing so helps to relieve some of his worry. He notes that in comparison to many other people, his problems are not so bad. He is optimistic that with help, he will be able to figure out why he is struggling so much at work and find a way to work through these issues. Jim has a number of hobbies that he participates in regularly and he notes that these hobbies also help him to take his mind off the problems at work. He finds, however, that he is becoming less motivated to participate in his hobbies as his work concerns are consuming more and more of his time. Jim's hobbies include wood-working, training for a marathon, and participating in a recreation basketball league at his local gym.

5.4.2 Jim's Treatment Plan and Results

1. Conduct an assessment using the four-front assessment approach, the ADDRESSING model, and administer the MHC-LF and the OQ-45.2. Using the results of these assessment tools, document where Jim falls within the Complete State Model of Mental Health. Review the results directly with Jim. See Figure 5.3 for a summary of Jim's results.
2. Based on the results of Jim's assessment, it appears that more testing to evaluate whether or not he meets full criteria for attention-deficit disorder and possibly for an anxiety disorder is warranted.

Four-Front Assessment Approach

1. Areas of client weakness (i.e., impaired social skills, low intelligence, emotion dysregulation, labile moods, personality problems)

> Areas of weakness for Jim include attention and concentration problems, moderate to severe anxiety symptoms, and low self-efficacy in his new position at work.

2. Areas of client strength (i.e., hopeful, grateful, forgiving, courageous, resilient, high intelligence, mood stability, healthy personality)

> Jim's strengths include optimism (he believes that his work-related problems can/will be solved), perseverance, spirituality, capacity to love and be loved, gratitude, physically fit, and normally, achieves a good balance between his work, home, and social lives. He takes pride in his culture and passing on cultural traditions to his children. He also reports finding a sense of purpose and meaning in his life through his role as a father.

3. Deficits or destructive forces in the client's environment (i.e., unsafe living conditions/neighborhood, presence of abusive relationships or neglect, exposure to discrimination or victim of prejudice)

> Jim reports living in a rental home that has a number of problems. The roof is old and beginning to leak, the furnace and water heater go out on a semi-regular basis, and there is no air conditioning. He also notes that he and his family have been exposed to discrimination, especially related to housing. He notes that because they live in a small city that is primarily made up of white people, he and his family often get odd looks or stares from others when they are shopping at local stores, eating at local restaurants, and even sometimes at church.

4. Assets or resources in the client's environment (i.e., secure living conditions/neighborhood, supportive relationships, opportunities for success, stable employment)

> Jim lives in a safe neighborhood, has been employed at his current job for 5 years and recently was promoted (although the promotion has brought about many of his current struggles), gets along well with colleagues, has a loving wife and children, reports a good social network of supportive extended family members and friends.

Definitions of ADDRESSING framework	Client Information Client Name: Jim
Age and generational influences	40 years old; last born of 4 siblings; raised by parents who were active participants in the Civil Rights movement, older siblings attended segregated schools. Was raised to be proud of his heritage and accepting of all races/ethnic groups. Currently married to a white female - his family is supportive of his relationship; wife's family was not supportive initially, but now is.
Disability status (developmental disability)	None

FIGURE 5.3 Summary of Jim's positive psychological assessment results.

Disability status (acquired disability)	None for client himself, however, he has been taking care of his aging parents – mother had a stroke 2 years ago; father has start of dementia.
Religion and spiritual orientation	Was raised in a Baptist church, converted to Catholicism when married; attends mass with his family regularly. Finds great meaning in his spirituality/religious beliefs.
Ethnicity	African-American; married to a white woman, raising bi-racial children
Socioeconomic status	Currently middle-class; grew up most of his life in a middle-class home as well. Completed his degree at a technical school and has worked full time ever since. Wife also has an Associate's Degree and works full time outside the home.
Sexual orientation	Heterosexual
Indigenous heritage	None
National origin	Born and raised in the United States
Gender	Male, husband for 10 years, father of three children – two girls and one boy. Takes pride in role as father, enjoys sharing information about black culture with his children and passing on meaningful family stories and traditions.

Seven-Axis System of Positive Psychological Assessment

Axis I: 314.00 Attention-deficit/hyperactivity disorder, predominantly inattentive type 300.00 Anxiety disorder not otherwise specified

Axis II: V71.09 No diagnosis

Axis III: None

Axis IV (broadened):

Environmental and psychosocial problems: Problems with primary support group: responsibility for ill parents (mother had a stroke; father has dementia); Problems related to the social environment: exposure to discrimination; occupational problems; stress at work, fear of job loss; housing problems: old rental home with a number of problems.

Environmental and psychosocial resources: Attachment/love/nurturance with primary support group; connectedness/empathic relationships; safe neighborhood; no criminal record; good education, stable job for past 5 years with recent promotion (though the promotion has brought about many of his current problems)

FIGURE 5.3   (Continued)

Axis V (broadened):   Global Assessment of Functioning Scale score: 43
Global Assessment of *Positive* Functioning Scale score: 71

Axis VI: Client strengths: Optimism, perseverance, spirituality, capacity to love and be loved, gratitude, physically fit, typically has good work-life balance, cultural pride, sense of purpose and meaning in life.

Axis VII: Client cultural background information: Jim identifies as a straight, African-American male of middle-class socioeconomic status. He has no developmental or acquired disabilities, however, his parents are both currently living with disabilities. He provides assistance regularly to his aging parents. He is the youngest of four children who were raised by two African-American parents who were active in the Black Civil Rights movement. He has strong family values and takes much pride in his cultural heritage. He is in an interracial marriage and his children are bi-racial. He finds it important that his kids have a good sense of both sides of their cultural histories, hence, he spends much time passing on stories and traditions related to Black culture and history to his kids. He has been exposed to prejudice and discrimination throughout his life.

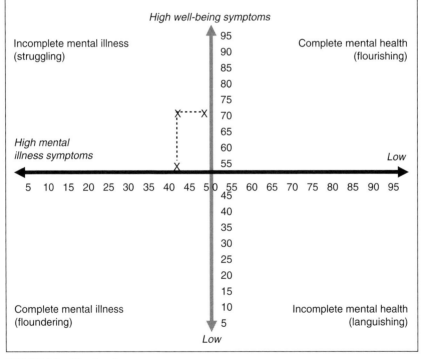

FIGURE 5.3   (Continued)

3. Provide treatment for Jim's symptoms of attention-deficit disorder and anxiety (i.e., education about ADHD, cognitive-behavioral treatments, medication options) utilizing the basic premises of Strengths-Based Counseling (Smith, 2006) as described in Chapter 4.

4. Examine and then capitalize upon Jim's ability to concentrate when engaging in his hobbies in order to discover potential ways in which he can become more focused in the workplace as well.

5. Have Jim complete Worksheet 4.33 on gainful employment to discover potential areas of dissatisfaction that may be contributing to his lack of focus on the job. Consider having Jim complete the VIA and CSF 2.0 inventories and then using Worksheets 4.34 and 4.35 as appropriate.

6. Re-administer the OQ-45.2 and MHC-LF scales to track his progress in therapy. Also, re-assess his GAF and GAPF scale scores.

7. Continue with treatment as needed, remembering to keep a balanced focus on Jim's areas of weakness as well as those areas of strength.

5.5 COMPLETE MENTAL ILLNESS OR FLOUNDERING

Clients who fall within the complete mental illness or floundering category of the Complete State Model of Mental Health are individuals who are experiencing enough symptoms of pathology to presently qualify for a *DSM* diagnosis and are not experiencing many, if any, symptoms of well-being. Clients who fall into this category are likely to seek out therapy for their symptoms of pathology and may initially scoff at the idea of working on well-being, because their lives are likely so wrapped up in their negative symptomology. They may see no point in working on well-being when in the midst of so much misery. The case of Karen is provided as an example of a person who falls into the floundering category.

5.5.1 The Case of Karen

Karen is a 55-year-old Latina female who lives alone in a small apartment in a suburb of Houston, Texas. Karen comes to therapy reporting that she is feeling suicidal. She states that she feels completely worthless since her last child moved out of the house one year ago. She no longer feels as if her children need her, since they are all successfully living on their own. She says that all she does is lay around the house and cry. She feels unmotivated to do anything. Indeed, she reports that even getting dressed is an overwhelming task for her. Karen has gained 40 pounds in the last year and has had lots of difficulty sleeping. About 4 months ago she was fired from her job and the unemployment checks that she has been receiving since then are about to run out. She is worried about how she will pay her bills and does not want to burden her children. Karen states that she hates everything about herself and her life and thinks that she and her adult children would all be better off if she were no longer around. Karen feels as if her life has no purpose anymore.

5.5.2 Karen's Treatment Plan and Results

1. Conduct an assessment using the four-front assessment approach, the ADDRESSING model, and administer the MHC-LF and the OQ-45.2. Using the results of these assessment tools, document where Karen falls within the Complete State Model of Mental Health. Review the results directly with Karen. See Figure 5.4 for a summary of Karen's results.

2. Based on the results of Karen's assessment, it appears that she meets criteria for a diagnosis of major depressive disorder, hence treatment for Karen's symptoms of depression are warranted (i.e., cognitive-behavioral therapy, interpersonal psychotherapy, medication options). In addition, Karen appears to be a prime candidate for various sessions of Positive Psychotherapy.

3. Implement cognitive-behavioral therapy or interpersonal psychotherapy and possibly the use of anti-depressant medications in conjunction with sessions 1, 2, 3, 6, 7, 9, 12, 13, and 14 of Positive Psychotherapy as appropriate.

4. Re-administer the OQ-45.2 and MHC-LF measures to track therapy progress. Also re-assess her GAF and GAPF scale scores.

5. As Karen's symptoms remit, consider other Positive Psychotherapy sessions that are applicable to her current level of functioning.

6. When Karen is ready to re-enter into the workforce, help her to find a meaningful job by reviewing information on gainful employment (see Chapter 3). Have Karen complete the Clifton StrengthsFinder 2.0 at www.strengthsfinder.com, and brainstorm careers that would allow her to capitalize upon her top five strengths from the VIA and CSF 2.0 inventories, as well as her cultural strengths. For example, consider helping Karen to find a career that capitalizes upon her bilingualism or her experiences as a member of a sexual minority group.

7. Given Karen's previous sense of purpose and meaning in life that came from parenting, help her discover ways in which to find this sense of purpose and meaning through mentorship activities with children in her community (either as a career or through volunteerism).

5.6 CHALLENGES ASSOCIATED WITH IMPLEMENTING POSITIVE PSYCHOLOGICAL INTERVENTIONS

There are a number of reasons why implementing positive psychological interventions may pose a challenge for therapists. Indeed, some of the challenges may come from clients, others from colleagues, or even from therapists themselves. In this section, some of the obstacles that therapists may face when working toward the implementation of positive psychological interventions in the workplace are discussed and possible ways to overcome such obstacles are presented.

Four-Front Assessment Approach

1. Areas of client weakness (i.e., impaired social skills, low intelligence, emotion dysregulation, labile moods, personality problems)

> Areas of weakness for Karen include mood and emotion dysregulation, loss of hope and sense of purpose and meaning in life, severe symptoms of depression.

2. Areas of client strength (i.e., hopeful, grateful, forgiving, courageous, resilient, high intelligence, mood stability, healthy personality)

> Although Karen reports being hopeless, she clearly has some hope that things can improve, as she sought out therapy voluntarily. She also appears to have had a sense of purpose and meaning in her life when her children still resided at home and "needed her". Hence, she likely has strengths of kindness, capacity to love and be loved, leadership, patience, and other strengths that are useful in good parenting. (Note: help Karen identify more strengths by taking the VIA and by having her ask her children about what strengths they see in her.) Karen is also bilingual, which is a cultural strength that she may be able to capitalize upon when she is ready to re-enter the world of work. She walks with a limp as a result of a car accident and she appears to have overcome this disability, which shows resilience. She left her husband because of his excessive drinking and abusive tendencies, which shows courage and bravery.

3. Deficits or destructive forces in the client's environment (i.e., unsafe living conditions/neighborhood, presence of abusive relationships or neglect, exposure to discrimination or victim of prejudice)

> Karen reports that although her apartment is small, it has plenty of room now that her five children no longer reside there. In the past, however, they were very short on living space. She reports that her neighborhood is fairly safe; however, in recent months several burglaries have occurred. Karen reports that her ex-husband had problems with alcohol and when he drank, he was prone to hitting her and once hit the children as well. She has been out of that relationship for 10 years and has very little contact with her ex-husband. She is currently unemployed after being fired for not going to work as a result of her symptoms of depression. She reports having experienced discrimination related to her bisexuality.

4. Assets or resources in the client's environment (i.e., secure living conditions/neighborhood, supportive relationships, opportunities for success, stable employment)

> Karen resides in a primarily Hispanic neighborhood so she feels as if she fits in well there. She enjoys being able to converse with her neighbors in Spanish, which is her primary language. She has a high school diploma and speaks English very well. Her bilingual abilities make her a prime candidate for many jobs as a translator in her community. Although she currently feels as if she is a "burden" to her children, Karen reports that her kids call her all the time to see how she is doing and how they can help. They also stop by or send her care packages; hence, they appear to be supportive.

FIGURE 5.4   Summary of Karen's positive psychological assessment results.

Definitions of ADDRESSING framework	Client Information
	Client Name: Karen
Age and generational influences	55 years old; middle born of 7 siblings in Venezuela; raised in Venezuela until the age of 5 when her family immigrated to the USA. Became a US citizen at age 23.
Disability status (developmental disability)	None
Disability status (acquired disability)	Client was in a severe car accident as a young adult. Walks with a limp; sometimes uses a cane.
Religion and spiritual orientation	Client reports that she was raised in a Catholic home and raised her children in this religion as well. However, at the current time she feels "out of touch" with her faith, as she questions her beliefs in God and her church's views on homosexuality.
Ethnicity	Born in Venezuela, refers to herself as a Latina; Spanish is her first language, though she is very fluent in English as well.
Socioeconomic status	Currently low middle-class, however, with loss of job, she is quickly heading toward poverty. Her adult children are willing to provide financial assistance, but she refuses their help at this time. Client has a high school diploma and a fairly consistent work history.
Sexual orientation	Bisexual; most recent relationship was with a woman after divorcing her husband. Currently not dating anyone.
Indigenous heritage	Venezuelan
National origin	Born in Venezuela and raised there until age 5. Then raised in the United States; officially earned US citizenship at age 23.
Gender	Female, divorced, mother of five adult children, has one grandchild and one on the way, used to find sense of purpose and meaning in raising her family/being a mother. No longer feels she is needed in these roles.

Seven-Axis System of Positive Psychological Assessment

Axis I: 296.33 Major depressive disorder, recurrent, severe without psychotic features

Axis II: V71.09 No diagnosis

Axis III: Client has an acquired disability: walks with a limp, reports constant, mild leg pain; constant back pain as a result of the limp as well.

FIGURE 5.4   (Continued)

Axis IV (broadened):

Environmental and psychosocial problems: Problems related to the social environment: difficulty adjusting to life cycle transition when last child moved out of the home; struggles to live alone; Occupational Problems: unemployed; Housing problems: safety of neighborhood is questionable; Economic problems: inadequate finances for long-term stability; Problems with access to health care services: no medical insurance.

Environmental and psychosocial resources: Attachment/love/nurturance with primary support group – children are supportive, although client is not accepting their support at this time; no criminal record; good education; relatively safe neighborhood where client "fits in" with her neighbors who share common cultural experiences.

Axis V (broadened): Global Assessment of Functioning Scale score: 31
Global Assessment of *Positive* Functioning Scale score: 30

Axis VI: Client strengths: Hope, kindness, capacity to love and be loved, leadership, patience, resilience, courage and bravery, and bilingual.

Axis VII: Client cultural background information: Karen identifies as a bisexual, Latina of low socioeconomic status. She has an acquired disability (limp) as a result of a car accident. She is the middle born of 7 siblings, born and raised in Venezuela for her first five years of life. Raised in the USA from age five on; became a US citizen at age 23. Was married and has five adult children. Is comfortable with her bisexuality, even though she experiences some discrimination related to this. Questioning her faith and religious beliefs. Enjoys living in her primarily Hispanic neighborhood and being able to speak in her native language (Spanish) with her neighbors regularly.

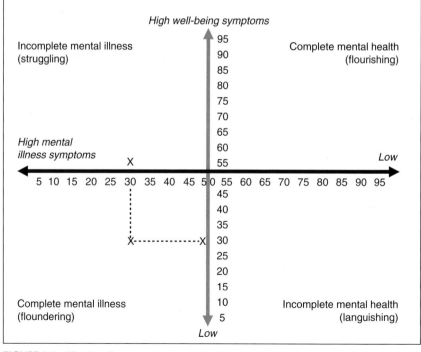

FIGURE 5.4   (Continued)

5.6.1 Client Challenges

As noted previously in Chapter 2, some clients may resist positive psychological interventions because they may not see the utility of such an approach to therapy. Indeed, most clients enter therapy because they have identified a problem or several areas of concern for which they are seeking assistance. They do not understand how or why attending to strengths and resources can actually help them to overcome or to better cope with their struggles. Typically, to overcome such resistance, clients simply need to be provided with a rationale for the utility of working from a positive psychological perspective in therapy.

Sometimes clients resist various positive psychological interventions and exercises, such as those provided throughout this text, because the exercises require them to complete activities outside the therapy room and they are simply not motivated or are feeling too overwhelmed to take on new tasks. This is similar to client resistance that occurs for many therapists who practice various forms of cognitive-behavioral or dialectical behavior therapy in which homework is assigned. In order to overcome this type of client resistance, it is helpful to address the resistance directly in order to find out why the client is not cooperating and to problem-solve what needs to happen in order to move the client into a place where he or she is ready, willing, and able to take on such assignments. For example, a client who is asked to complete a forgiveness letter may simply not be ready to forgive his or her transgressor. In this case, an alternative exercise, such as emotional storytelling, may be more appropriate. Other clients may resist exercises because they feel that the exercise is "silly" and not worth their time. In this case, providing a rationale for the activity and evidence of the utility of the exercise based on available research is recommended. For example, clients who scoff at the idea of keeping a gratitude journal can be provided with evidence from a variety of research studies that show a strong relationship between gratitude and a variety of physical and psychological health outcomes (see Chapter 4 for more details). In addition, Peterson (2006) notes that "if one approaches these [positive psychology] exercises with cynicism or half a heart, then of course they cannot work… [this happens for those] who are skeptical and seemingly afraid to try something that is not only new but also on the face of it corny" (p. 29). Discussing client fears or judgments related to the assignments may help them to overcome their fears or cynicism and find a willingness to at least try the exercises being assigned.

5.6.2 Colleague Challenges

Because positive psychology is a relatively new area of study in psychology, many mental health practitioners remain unfamiliar with what positive psychology has to offer within the context of counseling and therapy. Due to this lack of information, some colleagues may make light of such positive psychological interventions or refer to positive psychology as nothing more than "naiveté,"

"over-optimism," "happiology," or a "fluffy science." It may be difficult to practice positive psychology in the face of such unwarranted criticism from colleagues, especially if one values the relationship between oneself and his or her
colleagues. In order to circumvent this challenge, therapists are encouraged to
provide their colleagues with a variety of scholarly resources (e.g., the references
used to support the ideas proposed throughout this text) for learning more about
positive psychology beyond that which they may have come across in maga-
zines, newspapers, or on television that have been created for laypeople. Indeed,
in the popular media, positive psychology is often portrayed in rather non-
scientific terms and the scholarship behind the ideas presented is not reviewed.

Another way to overcome such challenges from colleagues is to listen to
what they have to say and if the literature does not support their concerns, to
proceed without consideration of their criticisms in order to see for oneself
how the positive psychological approach works. Although positive psychology
is not a panacea, the progress one typically observes in clients and the positive
feedback one often receives from clients when implementing positive psychological interventions can serve as motivation to continue such practices even if
colleagues continue with their criticisms.

5.6.3 Therapist Challenges

Perhaps the most difficult challenge therapists need to overcome in order to
practice from a positive psychological perspective is their own skepticism or
cynicism toward this new therapeutic approach. While critical thinking and
analysis of the literature is always encouraged for scientist-practitioners, cynicism without evidence is not. Striving to remain open-minded about this new
therapeutic process is recommended in order to overcome this obstacle.

Likewise, for those therapists who were trained prior to the development of
positive psychological research, changing one's way of practicing can be difficult, especially if one tries to implement the techniques described throughout
this text but is not initially successful at doing so. The tendency to revert back
to old methods is highly likely at that point. Therapists who find themselves
in such a situation are encouraged to realize that implementing any new skills
or procedures takes time and practice. Reverting back to a deficiency model of
therapy is not the answer. Rather, examining why the new skills did not work as
intended is encouraged. For example, was an exercise implemented without providing the client with a rationale for such an assignment? Was there a problem
with the timing of the activity or intervention? Were problems and destructive
forces in the environment ignored or minimized in favor of examining strengths
and resources? Was the exercise inappropriate based on the societal or cultural
factors influencing the client? These and other similar questions will likely allow
one to discover where things went wrong and to take reparative action. Indeed,
these are the same sort of questions that therapists must ask themselves when
interventions informed by other treatment perspectives (i.e., distress tolerance

skills in dialectical behavior therapy, exposure therapy techniques, or systematic desensitization training) do not work according to plan either.

Therapists may also face challenges with the implementation of positive psychological interventions when working with clients who experience extreme pathology. For example, implementing positive psychological exercises and homework assignments with clients who are actively psychotic is not possible. However, working from the four-front approach and utilizing the ADDRESSING model in order to conceptualize the client in a culturally relevant and balanced way is still possible. Once the clients' psychoses have subsided, many positive psychological interventions can then be implemented.

5.7 CRITICISMS OF POSITIVE PSYCHOLOGY AS NOTED IN THE LITERATURE

Perusal of the scholarly literature on the topic of positive psychology reveals several downfalls of positive psychology that need to be tended to in order for positive psychology to continue to flourish and to be applicable to the lives of *all* people. More specifically, these criticisms entail the largely individualistic nature of positive psychology. For example, Becker and Maracek (2008a) contend that individualism pervades positive psychology as evidenced by "the movement's endorsement of self-fulfillment as the ultimate life goal, its promotion of self-improvement via personal effort, and its narrow sense of the social" (p. 1751). They further argue that "the bounded, autonomous self that strides through a positive life is an illusion, as is the notion that human flourishing and happiness are readily available to all" (p. 1751). Similar criticisms of positive psychology as an ethnocentric, individualistic science are reported by Christopher and Hickinbottom (2008) as well. These scholars contend that one way to avoid such an ethnocentric approach is to remain open to multiple definitions of "the good life," and alternate interpretations of the meaning of values, strengths, and well-being. For example, self-reliance is valued by many individuals in the USA and Taiwan; however, what self-reliance means varies depending upon one's cultural context. More specifically, in the USA, self-reliance is synonymous with autonomy, maturity, and independence. In contrast, self-reliance in Taiwan represents that one is not a burden on others (Christopher, 1999). Becker and Maracek (2008b) further suggest that considering the individual within the context of his or her social environment and broadening the definitions of happiness and virtue will serve to make positive psychology more relevant to the many. (For a more thorough review of some of the criticisms of positive psychology and ideas for overcoming these areas of weakness within the field, see the 2008 special issue of *Theory and Practice* on "Thinking Through Positive Psychology" by Christopher et al., 2008.)

As noted throughout this text, positive psychological interventions *must* be designed around the various cultural identities and the environmental contexts that make up the backdrop for each client with whom one works. Consideration of the appropriateness, meaning, and utility of each of the measures and activities provided to clients must be done in a thoughtful and thorough fashion. When possible, adjusting the activities to better fit the needs of clients is recommended. For example, when engaging in Hope Therapy, practitioners may find that some clients from collectivistic cultures may struggle to create goals on their own, as their goals are that of the larger family or social group. In such instances, having clients develop their goals within the context of and with assistance from these family or social groups may serve to make the assignment more relevant to such clients. Likewise, capitalizing upon strengths that are identified through one's cultural experiences, rather than relying upon results of such strength measures as the VIA inventory may be more meaningful for some. Finally, allowing clients to choose what their goals are in terms of desired therapy outcome is also recommended. What complete mental health looks and feels like for some, will not be identical for others. Indeed, using a cookie-cutter type approach to incorporating positive psychology into clinical practice is not only likely to be futile, but could even serve to make clients worse.

5.8 CONCLUSION

Throughout this text, various scholarly information and practical resources have been provided for therapists who are interested in applying positive psychology in the therapy room. Additional resources for learning even more about positive psychology are available in the bibliography found in Appendix A. In addition, readers who are interested in learning more about the scholarly basis of many of the recommendations throughout this text are encouraged to seek out the original references for more of that information.

As research in positive psychology continues to proliferate, so too will the information relevant to the applications of positive psychology to counseling and therapy. Perhaps someday, positive psychology will become such an engrained part of the training and work of all therapists, that there will be no such thing as therapy that is not strengths-based, inclusive of client cultural and environmental factors, and based upon the Complete State Model of Mental Health.

References

Affleck G, Tennen H. Construing benefit from adversity: adaptational significance and dispositional underpinnings. *J Pers*. 1996;64:899–922.

American Psychiatric Association. *Diagnostic and Statistical Manual of Mental Disorders*. 4th ed., text revision. Washington, DC: American Psychiatric Association; 2000.

Arend R, Gove EL, Sroufe LA. Continuity of individual adaptation from infancy to kindergarten: a predictive study of ego-resiliency and curiosity in preschoolers. *Child Dev*. 1979;50:950–959.

Asplund J, Lopez SJ, Hodges T, Harter J. *Technical Report: Development and Validation of the Clifton StrengthsFinder 2.0*: The Gallup Organization; 2007.

Babyak MA, Snyder CR, Yoshinobu L. Psychometric properties of the hope scale: a confirmatory factor analysis. *J Res Pers*. 1993;27:154–169.

Bartlett M, DeSteno D. Gratitude and prosocial behavior: helping when it costs you. *Psychol Sci*. 2006;17:319–325.

Baskin TW, Enright RD. Intervention studies on forgiveness: a meta-analysis. *J Counsel Dev*. 2004;82:79–90.

Beck AT, Rush AJ, Shaw BL, Emery G. *Cognitive Therapy of Depression*. New York: Guilford Press; 1979.

Beck AT, Ward C, Mendelson M. Beck depression inventory (BDI). *Arch Gen Psychiatry*. 1961;4:561–571.

Becker D, Maracek J. Dreaming the American dream: individualism and positive psychology. *Social Pers Psychol Compass*. 2008a;2/5:1767–1780.

Becker D, Marecek J. Positive psychology: history in the remaking? *Theory Psychol* 2008b;18:591–604.

Bordin ES. The generalizability of the psychoanalytic concept of the working alliance. *Psychotherapy: Theory, Res Pract*. 1979;16:252–260.

Boulton MJ, Smith PK. The social nature of play fighting and play chasing: mechanisms and strategies underlying cooperation and compromise. In: Barkow JH, Cosmides L, Tooby J, eds. *The Adapted Mind: Evolutionary Psychology and the Generation of Culture*. New York: Oxford University Press; 1992:429–444.

Brim OG, Ryff CD, Kessler RC. *How Healthy Are We? A National Study of Well-Being at Midlife*. Chicago, IL: University of Chicago Press; 2004.

Brunstein JC. Personal goals and subjective well-being: a longitudinal study. *J Pers Soc Psychol*. 1993;65:1061–1070.

Bryan T, Bryan J. Positive mood and math performance. *J Learn Disabil*. 1991;24:490–494.

Bryan T, Mathur S, Sullivan K. The impact of positive mood on learning. *Learn Disabil Quarterly*. 1996;19:153–162.

Bryant FB, Veroff J. The structure of psychological well-being: a sociohistorical analysis. *J Pers Soc Psychol*. 1982;43:653–673.

Bryant FB, Veroff J. *A Process Model for Positive Psychology*. Unpublished manuscript; 2002.

Buckingham M, Clifton DO. *Now, Discover Your Strengths*. New York: Free Press; 2000.

Caro TM. Adaptive significance of play: Are we getting closer? *Tree*. 1988;3:50–54.

Chang EC. Cultural differences in optimism, pessimism and coping: predictors of subsequent adjustment in Asian American and Caucasian American college students. *J Counsel Psychol.* 1996;43:113–123.

Christopher JC. Situating psychological well-being: exploring the cultural roots of its theory and research. *J Counsel Dev.* 1999;77:141–152.

Christopher JC, Hickinbottom S. Positive psychology, enthnocentrism and the disguised ideology of individualism. *Theory Psychol.* 2008;18:563–589.

Christopher JC, Richardson FC, Slife BD. Thinking through positive psychology. *Theory Psychol.* 2008;18:551–561.

Clifton DO, Anderson EC. *StrengthsQuest: Discover and Develop your Strengths in Academics, Career and Beyond.* Washington, DC: The Gallup Organization; 2002.

Clifton DO, Nelson P. *Soar with your Strengths.* New York, NY: Dell Publishing; 1992.

Coffman S. Parents' struggles to rebuild family life after Hurricane Andrew. *Issues Ment Health Nurs.* 1996;17:353–367.

Constantine MG, Sue DW. Factors contributing to optimal human functioning in people of color in the United States. *Counsel Psychol.* 2006;34:228–244.

Costa Jr PT, McCrae RR. *The NEO Personality Inventory Manual.* Odessa, FL: Psychological Assessment Resources; 1985.

Csikszentmihalyi M. *Flow: The Psychology of Optimal Experience.* New York: Harper and Row; 1990.

Danner D, Snowdon D. Positive emotion in early life and longevity: findings from the nun study. *J Pers Soc Psychol.* 2001;80:804–813.

De Jong P, Berg IK. *Interviewing for Solutions.* 2nd ed. Belmont, CA: Thomson Brooks/Cole Publishing Co; 2002.

Della Fave A, Massimini F. The experience sampling method and the measurement of clinical change: a case of anxiety disorder. In: deVries M, ed. *The Experience of Psychopathology.* Cambridge, England: Cambridge University Press; 1992:280–289.

Diener E. Subjective well-being. *Psychol Bull.* 1984;95:542–575.

Diener E, Emmons RA, Larsen RJ, Griffin S. The satisfaction with life scale. *J Pers Assess.* 1985;49:71–75.

Duckworth AL, Steen TA, Seligman MEP. Positive psychology in clinical practice. *Annu Rev Clin Psychol.* 2005;1:629–651.

Dulin PL, Hill RD. Relationships between altruistic activity and positive and negative affect among low-income older adult service providers. *Aging Ment Health.* 2003;7:294–299.

Einon DF, Morgan MJ, Kibbler CC. Brief periods of socialization and later behavior in the rat. *Dev Psychobiol.* 1978;11:213–225.

Ellis A, Becker I. *A Guide to Personal Happiness.* Hollywood, CA: Melvin Powers Wilshire Book Company; 1982.

Emmons RA. Personal strivings: an approach to personality and subjective well-being. *J Pers Soc Psychol.* 1986;51:1058–1068.

Emmons RA. *Thanks! How the New Science of Gratitude can make You Happier.* New York, NY: Houghton Mifflin Company; 2007.

Emmons RA, McCullough ME. Counting blessings versus burdens: experimental studies of gratitude and subjective well-being. *J Pers Soc Psychol.* 2003;84:377–389.

Enright RD, Coyle CT. Researching the process model of forgiveness within psychological interventions. In: Worthington Jr EL, ed. *Dimensions of Forgiveness: Psychological Research and Theological Perspectives.* Philadelphia, PA: Templeton Foundation Press; 1998:139–161.

Fenell MJ, Teasdale JD. Cognitive therapy for depression: individual differences and the process of change. *Cognit Ther Res.* 1987;11:253–271.

Flores LY, Obasi EM. Positive psychological assessment in an increasingly diverse world. In: Lopez SJ, Snyder CR, eds. *Positive Psychological Assessment: A Handbook of Models and Measures*. Washington, DC: American Psychological Association; 2003:443–458.

Fordyce M. A review of research on the happiness measures: a sixty-second index of happiness and mental health. *Soc Indic Res*. 1988;20:355–381.

Fredrickson BL. What good are positive emotions? *Rev Gen Psychol* 1998;2:300–319.

Fredrickson BL. The role of positive emotions in positive psychology: the broaden-and-build theory of positive emotions. *Am Psychol*. 2001;56:218–226.

Fredrickson BL. The value of positive emotions. *Am Sci*. 2003;91:330–335.

Fredrickson BL, Branigan C. Positive emotions broaden the scope of attention and thought-action repertoires. *Cogn Emot*. 2005;19:313–332.

Fredrickson BL, Joiner T. Positive emotions trigger upward spirals toward emotional well-being. *Psychol Sci*. 2002;13:172–175.

Fredrickson BL, Losada MF. Positive affect and the complex dynamics of human flourishing. *Am Psychol*. 2005;60:678–686.

Fredrickson BL, Mancuso RA, Branigan C, Tugade MM. The undoing effect of positive emotions. *Motiv Emot*. 2000;24:237–258.

Fredrickson BL, Tugade MM, Waugh CE, Larkin G. What good are positive emotions in crises? A prospective study of resilience and emotions following the terrorist attacks on the United States on September 11th, 2001. *J Pers Soc Psychol*. 2003;84:365–376.

Freedman SR, Enright RD. Forgiveness as an intervention goal with incest survivors. *J Counsel Clin Psychol*. 1996;64:983–992.

Frijda NH. *The Emotions*. England: Cambridge University Press; 1986.

Frisch MB. *Manual and Treatment Guide for the Quality of Life Inventory or QOLI*. Minneapolis, MN: Pearson Assessments; 1994.

Frisch MB. *Quality of Life Therapy: Applying a Life Satisfaction Approach to Positive Psychology and Cognitive Therapy*. Hoboken, NJ: John Wiley and Sons, Inc; 2006.

Gable SL, Reis HT, Impett EA. What do you do when things go right? The intrapersonal and interpersonal benefits of sharing positive events. *J Pers Soc Psychol*. 2004;87:228–245.

Gelso CJ, Woodhouse S. Toward a positive psychotherapy: focus on human strength. In: Walsh WB, ed. *Counseling Psychology and Human Strengths*. New York, NY: Erlbaum; 2003:344–369.

Goldberg LR. Differential attribution to trait-descriptive terms to oneself as compared to well-liked, neutral and disliked others: a psychometric analysis. *J Pers Soc Psychol*. 1978;36:1012–1028.

Gottman J, Silver N. *The Seven Principles for Making Marriage Work*. New York, NY: Three Rivers; 1999.

Harter JK, Schmidt FL. Employee engagement and business-unit performance. *Psychol-Manager J*. 2002;4:215–224.

Hays PA. Addressing the complexities of culture and gender in counseling. *J Counsel Dev*. 1996;74:332–338.

Hays PA. *Addressing Cultural Complexities in Practice*. Washington, DC: American Psychological Association; 2001.

Howard KI, Leuger RJ, Maling MS, Martinovich Z. A phase model of psychotherapy outcome: causal mediation of change. *J Consult Clin Psychol*. 1993;61:678–685.

Hunter KI, Linn MW. Psychosocial differences between elderly volunteers and non-volunteers. *Int J Aging Hum Devel*. 1981;12:205–213.

Illardi SS, Craighead WE. The role of non-specific factors in cognitive-behavioral therapy for depression. *Clin Psychol: Sci Pract*. 1994;1:138–156.

Ivey AE, Ivey MB. *Intentional Interviewing and Counseling: Facilitating Client Development in a Multicultural Society*. 4th ed. Pacific Grove, CA: Brooks/Cole Publishing Company; 1999.

Jackson SA, Csikszentmihalyi M. *Flow in Sports: The Keys to Optimal Experiences and Performances*. Champaign, IL: Human Kinetics Books; 1999.

Janoff-Bulman R. *Shattered Assumptions: Toward a New Psychology of Trauma*. New York: Free Press; 1992.

Kanhouse DE, Hanson Jr LR. Negativity in evaluations. In: Jones EE, et al. ed. *Attribution: Perceiving the Causes of Behavior*. Morristown, NJ: General Learning Press; 1971:47–62.

Kendler KS, Liu X, Gardner CO, McCullough ME, Larson D, Prescott CA. Dimensions of religiosity and their relationship to lifetime psychiatric and substance use disorders. *Am J Psychiatry*. 2003;160:496–503.

Keyes CLM. Social well-being. *Soc Psychol Quarterly*. 1998;61:121–140.

Keyes CLM. The Mental Health Continuum: From Languishing to Flourishing in Life. *Journal of Health and Social Behaviour*. 2002;43:207–222.

Keyes CLM. Mental Health and/or Mental Illness? Investigating Axioms of the Complete State Model of Health. *Journal of Consulting and Clinical Psychology*. 2005;73:539–548.

Keyes CLM, Lopez SJ. Toward a science of mental health: positive directions in diagnosis and intervention. In: Snyder CR, Lopez SJ, eds. *Handbook of Positive Psychology*. New York: Oxford University Press; 2002:45–62.

Keyes CLM, Magyar-Moe JL. The measurement and utility of adult subjective well-being. In: Lopez SJ, Snyder CR, eds. *Positive Psychological Assessment: A Handbook of Models and Measures*. Washington, DC: American Psychological Association; 2003:411–425.

Keyes CLM, Ryff CD, Lee SJ. *Somatization and Mental Health: A Comparative Study of South Korean and U. S. Adults*. Unpublished manuscript. Emory University, Atlanta, GA; 2001.

King LA. *The Science of Psychology: An Appreciative View*. New York, NY: McGraw-Hill; 2008.

King LA, Miner KN. Writing about the perceived benefits of traumatic life events: implications for physical health. *Pers Soc Psychol Bull*. 2000;26:220–230.

Krause N, Ellison CG. Forgiveness by God, forgiveness of others and psychological well-being in late life. *J Sci Study Relig*. 2003;42:77–93.

Krause NM, Ingersoll-Dayton B, Liang J, Sugisawa H. Religion, social support and health among Japanese elderly. *J Health Soc Behav*. 1999;40:405–421.

Lambert MJ, Hansen NB, Umpress V, Lunnen K, Okiishi J, Burlingame GM, Reisinger CW. *Administration and Scoring Manual for the OQ–45.2 (Outcome Questionnaire)*. Salt Lake City, UT: American Professional Credentialing Services LLC; 1996.

Lawson D. Identifying pretreatment change. *J Counsel Dev*. 1994;72:244–248.

Lazarus RS. *Emotion and Adaptation*. New York: Oxford University Press; 1991.

Lee PC. Play as a means for developing relationships. In: Hinde RA, ed. *Primate Social Relationships*. Oxford: Blackwell; 1983:82–89.

Levenson RW. Human emotions: a functional view. In: Ekman P, Davidson R, eds. *The Nature of Emotions: Fundamental Questions*. New York: Oxford University Press; 1994:123–126.

Linley PA, Joseph S. *Positive Psychology in Practice*. Hoboken, NJ: John Wiley and Sons, Inc; 2004.

Little BR. Personal projects analysis: trivial pursuits, magnificent obsessions and the search for coherence. In: Buss DM, Cantor N, eds. *Personality Psychology: Recent Trends and Emerging Directions*. New York: Springer-Verlag; 1989:15–31.

Lopez SJ, Snyder CR. *Positive Psychological Assessment: A Handbook of Models and Measures*. Washington, DC: American Psychological Association; 2003.

Lopez SJ, Ciarlelli R, Coffman L, Stone M, Wyatt L. Diagnosing for strengths: on measuring hope building blocks. In: Snyder CR, ed. *Handbook of Hope*. New York: Academic Press; 2000a:57–88.

Lopez SJ, Floyd RK, Ulven JC, Snyder CR. Hope therapy: helping clients build a house of hope. In: Snyder CR, ed. *Handbook of Hope*. New York: Academic Press; 2000b:123–150.

Lopez SJ, Gariglietti KP, McDermott D, Sherwin ED, Floyd RK, Rand K, Snyder CR. Hope for the evolution of diversity: on leveling the field of dreams. In: Snyder CR, ed. *Handbook of Hope*. New York: Academic Press; 2000c:223–242.

Lopez SJ, Prosser EC, Edwards LM, Magyar-Moe JL, Neufeld JE, Rasmussen HN. Putting positive psychology in a multicultural context. In: Snyder CR, Lopez SJ, eds. *Handbook of Positive Psychology*. New York: Oxford University Press; 2002:700–714.

Lopez SJ, Snyder CR, Rasmussen HN. Striking a vital balance: developing a complementary focus on human weakness and strength through positive psychological assessment. In: Lopez SJ, Snyder CR, eds. *Positive Psychological Assessment: A Handbook of Models and Measures*. Washington, DC: American Psychological Association; 2003:3–20.

Lopez SJ, Snyder CR, Magyar-Moe JL, Edwards LM, Pedrotti JT, Janowski K, Turner JL, Pressgrove C. Strategies for accentuating hope. In: Linley PA, Joseph S, eds. *Positive Psychology in Practice*. Hoboken, NJ: John Wiley and Sons; 2004:388–404.

Lopez SJ, Magyar-Moe JL, Petersen SE, Ryder JA, Krieshok TS, O'Byrne KK, Lichtenberg JW, Fry N. Counseling psychology's focus on positive aspects of human functioning: a major contribution. *Counsel Psychol*. 2006;34:205–227.

Lucas RE, Diener E, Suh E. Discriminant validity of well-being measures. *J Pers Soc Psychol*. 1996;71:616–628.

Maddux JE. Stopping the madness: positive psychology and the deconstruction of the illness ideology and the *DSM*. In: Snyder CR, Lopez SJ, eds. *Handbook of Positive Psychology*. New York: Oxford University Press; 2002:13–25.

Magyar-Moe JL, Edwards LM, Lopez SJ. A new look at the working alliance: Is there a connection with hope? Paper presented at the *Division 17 National Counseling Psychology Conference*, Houston, Texas; 2001.

Maltby J, Macaskill A, Day L. Failure to forgive self and others: a replication and extension of the relationship between forgiveness, personality, social desirability and general health. *Pers Individ Dif*. 2001;30:881–885.

Martineau WH. A model of the social functions of humor. In: Goldstein JH, McGee PE, eds. *The Psychology of Humor: Theoretical Perspectives and Empirical Issues*. New York: Academic Press; 1972:101–128.

Maruta T, Colligan R, Malinchoc M, Offord K. Optimists vs. pessimists: survival rate among medical patients over a 30-year period. *Mayo Clin Proc*. 2000;75:140–143.

Matas L, Arend RA, Sroufe LA. Continuity of adaptation in the second year: the relationship between quality of attachment and later competence. *Child Dev*. 1978;49:547–556.

McCullough ME, Witvliet CVO. The psychology of forgiveness. In: Snyder CR, Lopez SJ, eds. *Handbook of Positive Psychology*. London: Oxford University Press; 2002:446–458.

Menninger K, Mayman M, Pruyser PW. *The Vital Balance*. New York: Viking Press; 1963.

Mikulincer M. Adult attachment style and information processing: individual differences in curiosity and cognitive closure. *J Pers Soc Psychol*. 1997;72:1217–1230.

Morrow-Howell N, Hinterloth J, Rozario PA, Tang F. Effects of volunteering on the well-being of older adults. *J Gerontol Series B: Psychol Sci Soc Sci*. 2003;58:S137–S145.

Mroczek DK, Kolarz CM. The effect of age on positive and negative affect: a developmental perspective on happiness. *J Pers Soc Psychol*. 1998;75:1333–1349.

Myers DG. *Digested from David G. Myers, The Pursuit of Happiness (Avon Books), Excerpted from Psychology*. 7th ed. New York: Worth Publishers; 2004.

Niederhoffer KG, Pennebaker JW. Sharing one's story: on the benefits of writing or talking about emotional experience. In: Snyder CR, Lopez SJ, eds. *Handbook of Positive Psychology.* London: Oxford University Press; 2002:573–583.

Norem JK, Cantor N. Defensive pessimism: "Harnessing" anxiety as motivation. *J Pers Soc Psychol.* 1986;52:1208–1217.

Norem JK, Illingworth KSS. Strategy-dependent effects on reflecting on self and tasks: some implications of optimism and defensive pessimism. *J Pers Soc Psychol.* 1993;65:822–835.

Ostir GV, Markides KS, Black SA, Goodwin JS. Emotional well-being predicts subsequent functional independence and survival. *J Am Geriatr Soc.* 2000;48:473–478.

Pennebaker JW. *Opening Up: The Healing Power of Expressing Emotions.* Rev ed. New York: Guilford Press; 1997.

Pennebaker JW. Confession, inhibition and disease. In: Berkowitz L, ed. *Advances in Experimental Social Psychology;* Vol. 22 New York: Academic Press; 1989:211–244. .

Pennebaker JW, Kiecolt-Glaser J, Glaser R. Disclosure of traumas and immune function: health implications for psychotherapy. *J Consult Clin Psychol.* 1988;56:239–245.

Peterson C. *A Primer in Positive Psychology.* New York: Oxford University Press; 2006.

Peterson C, Seligman MEP. *Character Strengths and Virtues: A Handbook and Classification.* New York: Oxford University Press; 2004.

Petrie KP, Booth RJ, Pennebaker JW. The immunological effects of thought suppression. *J Pers Soc Psychol.* 1998;75:1264–1272.

Radloff LS. The CES-D scale: a self-report depression scale for research in the general population. *Appl Psychol Meas.* 1977;1:385–401.

Rashid T. Positive psychotherapy. In: Lopez SJ, ed. *Positive Psychology: Exploring the Best in People;* Vol. 4. Westport, CT: Praeger Publishers; 2008:187–217.

Rashid T, Anjum A. Positive psychotherapy for children and adolescents. In: Abela JRZ, Hankin BL, eds. *Depression in Children and Adolescents: Causes, Treatment and Prevention.* New York: Guilford Press; 2007.

Rath T. *StrengthsFinder 2.0.* New York: Gallup Press; 2007.

Reivich K. *Letting Go of Grudges.* Assignment instructions for M. E. P. Seligman's *Authentic Happiness Coaching Program;* 2004.

Rich AR, Dahlheimer D. The power of negative thinking: a new perspective on 'irrational' cognitions. *J Cogn Psychother.* 1989;3:15–30.

Ripley JS, Worthington Jr EL. Hope-focused and forgiveness-based group interventions to promote marital enrichment. *J Counsel Dev.* 2002;80:452–472.

Robitschek C. Personal growth initiative: the construct and its measure. *Meas Eval Counsel Devel.* 1998;30:183–198.

Robitschek C. Personal growth initiative: an active ingredient for intentional positive change. Paper presented at the *4th National Conference of Division 17 of the American Psychological Association;* 2001.

Robitschek C, Kashubeck S. A structural model of family functioning and psychological health: the mediating effects of hardiness and personal growth orientation. *J Counsel Psychol.* 1999;46:159–172.

Rosenhan DL. On being sane in insane places. *Science.* 1973;179:250–258.

Ruini C, Fava GA. Clinical applications of well-being therapy. In: Linley PA, Joseph S, eds. *Positive Psychology in Practice.* Hoboken, NJ: John Wiley and Sons; 2004:371–387.

Ryff CD. Happiness is everything, or is it? Explorations on the meaning of psychological well-being. *J Pers Soc Psychol.* 1989;57:1069–1081.

Ryff CD, Keyes CLM. The structure of psychological well-being revisited. *J Pers Soc Psychol.* 1995;69:719–727.

Salovey P, Mayer JD, Rosenhan DL. Mood and helping: mood as a motivator of helping and help-ing as a regulator of mood. In: Clark MS, ed. *Prosocial Behavior*. Newbury Park, CA: Sage Publications; 1991:215–237.

Schreiner L. *A Technical Report of the Clifton StrengthsFinder with College Students*: The Gallup Organization; 2006.

Schwartz B, Monterosso J, Lyubomorsky S, White K, Lehman DR. Maximizing versus satisfying: happiness is a matter of choice. *J Pers Soc Psychol*. 2002;83:1178–1197.

Seligman MEP. *Learned Optimism*. New York: Knopf; 1991.

Seligman MEP. *Authentic Happiness: Using the New Positive Psychology to Realize your Potential for Lasting Fulfillment*. New York: Free Press; 2002.

Seligman MEP, Csikszentmihalyi M. Positive psychology: an introduction. *Am Psychol*. 2000;55:5–14.

Seligman MEP, Reivich KJ, Jaycox LH, Gillham J. *The Optimistic Child*. Boston, MA: Houghton, Mifflin and Company; 1995.

Seligman MEP, Steen TA, Park N, Peterson C. Positive psychology progress: empirical validation of interventions. *Am Psychol*. 2005;60:410–421.

Seligman MEP, Rashid T, Parks AC. Positive psychotherapy. *Am Psychol*. 2006;61:774–788.

Seybold KS, Hill PC, Neumann JK, Chi DS. Physiological and psychological correlates of forgiv-ingness. *J Psychol Christ*. 2001;20:250–259.

Sheier MF, Carver CS. Optimism, coping and health: assessment and implications of generalized outcome expectancies. *Health Psychol*. 1985;4:219–247.

Shmotkin D. Declarative and differential aspects of subjective well-being and implications for mental health in later life. In: Lomranz J, ed. *Handbook of Aging and Mental Health: An Integrative Approach*. New York: Plenum; 1998:15–43.

Smith E. The strengths-based counseling model. *Counsel Psychol*. 2006;34:13–79.

Snyder CR. *The Psychology of Hope: You Can Get There From Here*. New York: Free Press; 1994.

Snyder CR. Conceptualizing, measuring and nurturing hope. *J Counsel Dev*. 1995;73:355–360.

Snyder CR, Lopez SJ. *Handbook of Positive Psychology*. New York: Oxford University Press; 2002.

Snyder CR, Lopez SJ. *Positive Psychology: The Scientific and Practical Explorations of Human Strengths*. Thousand Oaks, CA: Sage; 2007.

Snyder CR, Harris C, Anderson JR, Holleran SA, Irving LM, Sigmon ST, Yoshinobu LR, Gibb J, Langelle C, Harney P. The will and the ways: development of an individual-differences meas-ure of hope. *J Pers Soc Psychol*. 1991;60:570–585.

Snyder CR, Sympson SC, Ybasco FC, Borders TF, Babyak MA, Higgins RL. Development and validation of the state hope scale. *J Pers Soc Psychol*. 1996;70:321–335.

Snyder CR, Ilardi S, Michael ST, Cheavens J. Hope theory: updating a common process for psy-chological change. In: Snyder CR, Ingram RE, eds. *Handbook of Psychological Change: Psychotherapy Processes and Practices for the 21st Century*. New York: John Wiley and Sons, Inc; 2000:128–153.

Snyder CR, Lopez SJ, Edwards LM, Pedrotti JT, Prosser EC, Walton SL, Spalitto SV, Ulven JC. Measuring and labeling the positive and the negative. In: Lopez SJ, Snyder CR, eds. *Positive Psychological Assessment: A Handbook of Models and Measures*. Washington, DC: American Psychological Association; 2003a:21–40.

Snyder CR, Lopez SJ, Rasmussen HM. Striking a vital balance: Developing a complementary focus on human weakness and strength through positive psychological assessment. In: Lopez SJ, Snyder CR, eds *Positive Psychological Assessment: A Handbook of Models and Measures*. Washington, DC: American Psychological Association; 2003b:3–20.

Sue DW. *Overcoming Our Racism: The Journey to Liberation*. San Francisco, CA: Jossey-Bass; 2003.

Sue DW, Arrendondo P, McDavis RJ. Multicultural counseling competencies and standards: a call to the profession. *J Counsel Dev.* 1992;70:477–486.

Sue DS, Sue DW, Sue S. *Understanding Abnormal Behavior.* 8th ed. Boston, MA: Houghton Mifflin Company; 2006.

Sympson S. *Validation of the Domain Specific Hope Scale: Exploring Hope in Life Domains.* Unpublished Doctoral Dissertation, University of Kansas, Lawrence; 1999.

Taylor SE. Adjustment to threatening events: a theory of cognitive adaptation. *Am Psychol.* 1983;38:1161–1173.

Tennen H, Affleck G, Mendola R. Casual explanations for infertility: their relation to control appraisals and psychological adjustment. In: Stanton A, Dunkel Shetter C, eds. *Infertility: Perspectives from Stress and Coping Research.* New York: Plenum; 1991a:109–132.

Tennen H, Affleck G, Mendola R. Coping with smell and taste disorders. In: Gechell T, Doty R, Bartoshuk L, Snow J, eds. *Smell and Taste in Health and Disease.* New York: Raven; 1991b:787–801.

Toobey J, Cosmides L. The past explains the present: emotional adaptations and the structure of ancestral environments. *Ethol Sociobiol.* 1990;11:375–424.

Touissant LL, Williams DR, Musick MA, Everson SA. Forgiveness and health: age differences in a U.S. population sample. *J Adult Devel.* 2001;8:249–257.

vanOyen Witvliet C, Ludwig T, Vander Laan K. Granting forgiveness or harboring grudges: implications for emotion, physiology and health. *Psychol Sci.* 2001;12:117–123.

Walsh F. *Strengthening Family Resilience.* New York: Guilford; 1998.

Walter JL, Pellar JE. *Becoming Solution-Focused in Brief Therapy.* New York: Brunner/Mazel; 1992.

Warr P. Well-being and the workplace. In: Kahneman D, Diener E, Schwartz N, eds. *Well-being: The Foundations of Hedonic Psychology.* New York: Russell Sage; 1999:393–412.

Watson D, Clark LA, Tellegan A. Development and validation of brief measures of positive and negative affect: the PANAS scales. *J Pers Soc Psychol.* 1988;54(6):1063–1070.

Weiner-Davis M, de Shazer S, Gingerich WJ. Building on pretreatment change to construct the therapeutic solution: an exploratory study. *J Marital Fam Ther.* 1987;13:359–363.

Witvliet CVO, Phipps KA, Feldman ME, Beckham JC. Posttraumatic mental and physical health correlates of forgiveness and religious coping in military veterans. *J Trauma Stress.* 2004;17:269–273.

Wong J. Strengths-centered therapy: a social constructionist, virtue-based psychotherapy. *Psychotherapy: Theory, Research, Practice and Training.* 2006;43:133–146.

Worthington Jr EL. An empathy-humility-commitment model of forgiveness applied within family dyads. *J Family Ther.* 1998;20:59–71.

Worthington EL. *Five Steps to Forgiveness: The Art and Science of Forgiving.* New York: Crown Publishers; 2001.

Worthington Jr EL, Drinkard DT. Promoting reconciliation through psycho-educational and therapeutic interventions. *J Marital Fam Ther.* 2000;26:93–101.

Wright BA. Attitudes and fundamental negative bias. In: Yuker HE, ed. *Attitudes Toward Persons with Disabilities.* New York: Springer; 1988:3–21.

Wright BA, Lopez SJ. Widening the diagnostic focus: a case for including human strengths and environmental resources. In: Snyder CR, Lopez SJ, eds. *The Handbook of Positive Psychology.* New York: Oxford University Press; 2002:26–44.

Zung WK. A self-rating depression scale. *Arch Gen Psychiatry.* 1965;12:63–70.

Bibliography of Useful Positive Psychology Resources

Overview Books

Aspinwall L, Staudinger U, eds. *The Psychology of Human Strengths: Fundamental Questions and Future Directions for a Positive Psychology*. Washington, DC: American Psychological Association; 2003.

Clifton DO, Nelson P. *Soar with Your Strengths*. New York: Dell Publishing; 1992.

Csikszentmihalyi M. *Flow: The Psychology of Optimal Experience*. New York: Harper and Row; 1990.

Huppert FA, Baylis N, Keverne B. *The Science of Well-Being*. Oxford: Oxford University Press; 2005.

Keyes CLM, Haidt J, eds. *Flourishing: Positive Psychology and the Life Well-Lived*. Washington, DC: American Psychological Association; 2002.

Linley PA, Joseph S. *Positive Psychology in Practice*. Hoboken, NJ: John Wiley and Sons, Inc; 2004.

Lopez SJ, Snyder CR. *Positive Psychological Assessment: A Handbook of Models and Measures*. Washington, DC: American Psychological Association; 2003.

Lopez SJ, *Positive psychology: Exploring the best in people,* Volumes 1–4. Westport, CT: Praeger Publishers; 2008.

Lopez SJ, *The encyclopedia of positive psychology,* Volumes 1 & 2. Hoboken, NJ: Wiley-Blackwell; 2009.

Peterson C. *A Primer in Positive Psychology*. New York: Oxford University Press; 2006.

Peterson C, Seligman MEP. *Character Strengths and Virtues: A Handbook and Classification*. New York: Oxford University Press; 2004.

Seligman MEP. *Learned Optimism*. New York: Knopf; 1991.

Seligman MEP. *Authentic Happiness: Using the New Positive Psychology to Realize Your Potential for Lasting Fulfillment*. New York: Free Press; 2002.

Snyder CR. *Handbook of Hope*. New York: Academic Press; 2000.

Snyder CR, Lopez SJ. *Handbook of Positive Psychology*. New York: Oxford University Press; 2002.

Snyder CR, Lopez SJ. *Positive Psychology: The Scientific and Practical Explorations of Human Strengths*. Thousand Oaks, CA: Sage; 2007.

Positive Psychology Websites

Authentic Happiness: http://www.authentichappiness.sas.upenn.edu/Default.aspx

Center for Applied Positive Psychology: http://www.enpp.org/

Center for Positive Organizational Scholarship: http://www.bus.umich.edu/Positive/

European Network for Positive Psychology: http://www.enpp.org/

Gallup Institute for Global Well-Being: http://www.gallup.com/consulting/wellbeing/107755/2008-Gallup-WellBeing-Forum.aspx

International Positive Psychology Association: http://www.ippanetwork.org/

National Wellness Institute: http://www.nationalwellness.org/

Positive Psychology Center: http://www.ppc.sas.upenn.edu/index.html

Positive Psychology Section of the American Psychological Association's Society of Counseling Psychology: http://div17pospsych.com/

StrengthsFinder: http://www.strengthsfinder.com

StrengthsExplorer: http://www.strengthsexplorer.com

StrengthsQuest: http://www.strengthsquest.com

Values in Action Institute on Character: http://www.viacharacter.org

Index

O